ECONOMICS OF EDUCATION AND HUMAN DEVELOPMENT IN INDIA

Economics of Education and Human Development in India

(Essays in Honour of Prof. K.S. Chalam)

Edited by

Prof. D. Pulla Rao

AKANSHA PUBLISHING HOUSE
NEW DELHI • GUWAHATI • VISAKHAPATNAM

AKANSHA PUBLISHING HOUSE
4649-B/21, Ansari Road
Daryaganj, New Delhi-110002
Phones: 23268193, 09435116718
Email: ektabooks@yahoo.com
visit us: www.akanshapublishinghouse.com

Economics of Education and Human Development in India

First Published 2010

ISBN 978-81-8370-229-4

PRINTED IN INDIA

Published by Akansha Publishing House, New Delhi-110002 and printed at Harmain Offset Press, Delhi.

Prof. K.S. Chalam

Member, U.P.S.C, New Delhi.

Prof. K.S. Chalam in whose honour the present book is edited is an alumni of Andhra University. Noted scholar and renowned Educationist, Political Economist and an innovator of Staff Development Programme in India, he entered the U P S C as a Member in 2005 after a brief stint as Vice- Chancellor at Dravidian University, A.P.

He served the Department of Economics, Andhra University as a Lecturer, Reader and Professor for more than three decades with dedication and distinction. He was trained as an Economic Planner at Central School of Planning and Statistics, Warsaw, Poland during 1981-1982. He has obtained first rank in the international diploma programme of the school. As a student of Prof. B. Sarveswara Rao, he has strengthened the teaching of Economics of Education and Human Development. He has delivered endowment lectures on Public Sector and on issues relating to educational development at several universities and institutes in the country. He has published so far 20 books in English and 6 in Telugu and about 90 research papers covering areas of Economics of Education, Political Economy, Public Economics, Dravidian Studies etc. Some of his articles published in the *Economic and Political Weekly* are still cited in several reference works. In his book on "Economic Reforms and Social Exclusion" he has made an attempt to bring interdisciplinary approach to study the impact of reforms on the socially excluded groups in India. His book on "Caste-based Reservations and Human Development in India" (2007) was reviewed in around 20 leading newspapers and journals including the *Hindu*, the *Tribune*, etc. appreciating the author for the innovative approach used to understand and solve the contentious issue of our times. The reviewers in Pakistan and DFID commended the book as "immense topical relevance, this book will be of interest to students and scholars of development studies....useful to policy makers and practitioners working in this area". The book is being translated into Tamil and Telugu. An honours diploma thesis was submitted by Natasha Azad to California University on this book.

Prof. K.S. Chalam is known in the country as the father of the famous Academic Staff Colleges Scheme as he was the one who initiated the concept in 1985. At a time when the professors of the university system were not given any structured training to improve the quality of higher education, Prof. Chalam initiated a training course with UGC support in 1985. The UGC has recognized his contribution and asked him to conduct the first national workshop to design the proposed Academic Staff Colleges in India. He himself founded the college in 1987 and organized the first orientation course. It became an important part of the system of higher education to improve the Quality of Higher Education. The UNESCO has appreciated the scheme as one of the largest schemes of Staff Development in the world. He was responsible in strengthening the scheme with his 3 important publications on staff development. The latest (2006) book on 'Modern Techniques of Teaching and Staff Development' is a reference volume for all teachers in higher education. He has delivered lectures on Staff Development and participated in deliberations of the Prof. Rastogi Committee. It has helped consolidate the scheme in the interest of Quality of University Education.

Chalam was the first student trained formally in a university system in Economics of Education in 1972 at Andhra University under Prof. B. Sarveswara Rao. Late J.P. Naik inaugurated the specialization. He has worked for his Ph.D. on 'Finances, costs and productivity of higher education'. The study published as a book was reviewed both in India and abroad. Late Dr. Malcolm Adiseshiah acclaimed it as 'an excellent analysis of the economics of education in Andhra Pradesh as such is an important addition to the limited literature in India'. Another reviewer Dijon Jean-Claude Eicher commended it as a "courageous and useful book". He was Professor of Economics in Andhra University and taught the specialization both in the Departments of Economics and Education for a generation of students. He has pioneered interdisciplinary research and published 'Education and Weaker Sections' in 1988. Prof. P.R. Panchamukhi in his review of the book mentioned that 'the interdisciplinary approach to the study of educational problems is a useful framework'. Some of his books are offered as Text books for P.G students. He is one of the very rare research guides who has trained a dozen research students on a variety of issues starting from Human Development in A.P (before HD Report, 1990), Child Labour, Primary Education, Dalit Poverty, Impact of Technology on Agriculture, Liberalization to name a few. He is a prolific writer in Telugu. Apart from 6 Books in Telugu, scores of edit page articles were published in all leading dailies. He has supervised 12 scholars successfully to obtain their Ph.Ds in Economics, conducted research studies funded by UGC, Govt. of A.P, UNICEF, etc.

The contributions of Prof. Chalam are cited by scholars and activists across the globe. He has kept a legacy of teaching at Andhra University. One of the citations of an award rightly remarked that he is a 'scholar with social consciousnesses'. A Volume of papers were contributed in his honour in the name of 'Development of Weaker Sections' in 1998. As the third Vice-Chancellor of Dravidian University for a brief period, he has produced a programme of action for the university. He is also known as the first Director of Swamy Ramanand Teertha Rural Institute, the first institute of NCRI, Govt. of India. His experiments with rural higher education for one year at Pochampally published later in a book are useful as a reference work. He is the founder Editor of 'South India Journal of Social Sciences'.

Prof. K.S. Chalam commands respect among the academicians and activists due to his committed service in public affairs over a period of three decades. He is not an armchair scholar. He has been actively involved in public affairs relating to education and social development. All his studies in economics are interdisciplinary in nature and contain social issues with economic analysis of development. Therefore one of his biographers Avinash Misra called him as Simon Kuznets of India.

He has single handedly projected the underdevelopment of North Andhra with his publications and lectures for the last three decades making the Govt. of Andhra Pradesh to appoint a separate development board for the region in 2007. He is not an idealist but a practical person who got himself married outside his caste and implemented the same principle for the entire family. He has performed more than hundred social marriages in A.P.

Prof. Chalam is not only a serious scholar and teacher, but also a social activist. He served as the National Secretary, Amnesty International during 1984-85, Secretary and Vice-President of Professional bodies like

A.P. Economic Association, Indian Political Economy Association etc. He has participated in international debates on caste and race at Durban, Cairo etc. He has presented papers on Education, Poverty, Political Economy at Cambridge, Wisconsin, Manchester, Colombo, Bangkok and at other international fora. He has been on several expert committees at center and State levels and has served on the World Bank teams. He is a builder of institutions. The Academic Staff College that he has nurtured at Andhra University became a model for the entire country. He has started Mahendra Degree College in his native place, Pathapatnam a decade ago to provide higher educational facilities in a remote tribal region. He got his Economics honours from S K C G College, Parlakhemundi, Orissa. He was the first Telugu person to receive honours degree from Utkal (Berhampur) University in 1968 at an age of 19. He became a Lecturer at a very young age that helped him develop passion for teaching and research. The passion for teaching made him to continue his advice to the UGC as Hon. Chairman of a 'High Power Committee on Academic Staff Colleges' even after joining the UPSC. He is on several committees including NCRI, ICPR on an advisory capacity. He has an impeccable character and sound knowledge in social sciences that helped him become Member, UPSC. It is said that his presence in the UPSC made people from lower socioeconomic background to get inspired to enter into civil services to serve the country and people. This is reflected in the results of recent Civil Services Examination.

CONTENTS

Foreword — *xiii*

Acknowledgements — *xv*

Introduction — 1

A. ECONOMICS OF EDUCATION

1. Economic Analysis and Education: Reasoned Issues in Application to Instructional Technology Evaluation — 11
   P.G. Raja Kumar & P.S.V.R. Babu
2. Emergence of India in Global Economics of Higher Education: Issues and Priorities — 21
   G. Satyanarayana & M.R. Geetha Bala
3. Economics of Higher Education - Fact and Direction — 31
   U.B. Kondewar & Smita Kondewar
4. Development of Higher Education in India: A Gender Perspective — 53
   D. Pulla Rao, P. Raj Kumar & A. Vamsi Krushna
5. The Intra-sectoral allocations of Education Expenditure in Andhra Pradesh — 66
   M.D. Bavaiah, K. Thulasi Naik & J. Narasimha Rao
6. Andhra Pradesh Human Development Report—A Critical Appraisal — 74
   G. Ramachandrudu & S. Prasada Rao
7. Education As Revenue Of Economic Growth — 79
   S.V. Lakshmana Rao & P. Easwara Rao
8. Cost Differential in Secondary Education of Rayalaseema Region in Andhra Pradesh — 86
   I. Narendra Kumar, V. Kodandarami Reddy & V. Balakrishnama Naidu
9. Financial Resources and Cost Effectiveness Analysis in Primary Education — 97
   G. Latchanna

10. Trends in the Growth of Higher Education in India: 1950-51 To 2005-06 105
A. Vamsi Krushna & D. Pulla Rao

B. HUMAN DEVELOPMENT

11. Dimensions of Economic Growth And Human Development in India: An Assessment 118
T. Nirmala Devi

12. Millennium Development Goals (MDGs) Indian Scenario 130
V. Krishna Murthy & R.V.L.N. Ratnakara Rao

13. Human Resource Development at National level 143
K.V.V. Devi Prasad & G. Syamala Rao

14. Human Resource Development Practices in University System 154
Jagannath, B. Kukkudi & Ramesh B. Agadi

15. Inter-State Variations of Human Development Index in India 168
M. Kumar Raju, C. Gangulappa & A. Reddappa

16. Globalization and Human Resource Development 178
A. Naga Raju & I.B. Raju

17. Climate Change: A Threat to Human Development 181
A. Ranga Reddy

18. Human Resource Development and Quality of Life 192
R. Ranganathan & M. Yogeswari

19. Importance of Human Resource Planning 199
P. Subba Rao

20. Human Development: Role of Anganwadi Worker for Child Development 207
P. Sujit Kumar & Swatilekha Sanyal

21. Health Education and Health Care in India 217
R.V.L.N. Ratnakara Rao & V.Krishna Murthy

22. Human Resource Development: A Special Focus on Indian Women 239
D. Sujatha

23. Continuing Education for Human Resource Development 258
E. Mahadeva Reddy, D. Uma Devi & P. Adinarayana Reddy

24. Human Resource Development in Voluntary Organization 267
V. Hari Babu & M. Mary

25. Trends in Human Development Spending in the States of India 274
K. Dasaratha Ramaiah & K.Thulasi Naik

26. Need of Knowledge Management Services for Human Development 292
M.Satyanarayana

27. Trickle Down Effect - A Key to Rural and Human Development 299
K. Mouurlin

28. Growth, Poverty And Human Resource Development in India 315
A.V. Naga Varma, Y.Rama Krishna & J. Chandra Prasad

29. Health Expenditure and Shifts in Human Development in Andhra Pradesh 323
(Mrs.) K. Rani Gopal & (Mrs.) B.Sailaja Kumari

30. Human Resources Development in India: An Overview 330
P.S.Ravindra & P.Rajya Lakshmi

31. Public Spending for Human Development in Andhra Pradesh 342
M. D. Bavaiah, K. Thulasi Naik & J. Narasimha Rao

32. Human Resources Development: Emerging Issues and Concerns in Education of the Weaker Sections 361
M.V.S.S.Prakasa Rao & P.Ch. Lakshminarayana

Index 377

FOREWORD

I am very happy to write a few words about the book edited by Prof. D. Pulla Rao in honour of his teacher who was a great teacher and scholar of our University.

The present volume "Economics of Education and Human Development" is the outcome of discussions and deliberations presented at a National Seminar on "Human Development and Social Exclusion" on the occasion of Shastiabdi Poorti Celebrations of Prof. K.S. Chalam, Member, UPSC, New Delhi in the Dept. of Economics, Andhra University on 6-7 October, 2008.

Economics of education and human development was offered as specialization at the Department of Economics, Andhra University for the first time in India and we take pride in this as the first student of the specialization, Prof. K.S. Chalam is now occupying an important constitutional post.

The subject of economics of education is being taught as an important branch of economics that discusses about the costs and benefits of education to the society and to individuals. The authors have analyzed several aspects of economic issues of education including the finances of education and have argued for more resources for education. I found that some writers have lamented that the recent trends in using our scarce human resources for BPO reflects our dependence on the west which reminds us of our slavery during the British India. There is an analysis of expenditure on higher education and I feel that the higher education is now in serious crisis as we are not able to meet our commitments from the existing resources. The analysis provides strong ground for more resources for higher education from the centre and state governments. There is no doubt that there is gender discrimination in the enrollment in higher education, but I feel this discrimination is neither due to the policies of the government nor due to the universities. It is the family that is largely responsible for girl's education and therefore all of us should educate the parents to encourage their daughters to send them to colleges and universities.

The millennium development goals of the UNO have targeted achievement of universalisation of elementary education in the world by 2015. This will provide a great motivation to governments to provide more resources and their effective utilization in retaining every child that enters the school. The book is really useful as a reference volume as it has discussed not only the theoretical aspects of economics of education and human development, but provided results from field studies and research output. This will definitely help not only policy makers but also scholars to think seriously about our education in general and higher education in particular.

I congratulate Prof. D. Pulla Rao for bringing out a useful and purposeful volume.

(B. SATYANARAYANA)

Vice-Chancellor Andhra University
Visakhapatnam

ACKNOWLEDGEMENTS

This book is an outcome of the Seminar on "Human Development and Social Exclusion" conducted in the Department of Economics, Andhra University, Visakhapatnam on the occasion of Shastiabdi Poorti Celebrations of my Guru and Director of my Ph. D work Prof. K.S. Chalam, Member, UPSC, New Delhi. About 350 delegates participated and more than 250 delegates presented papers and participated in the discussion and deliberations. I am highly thankful to the paper contributors for helping me in bringing out this book which will be of some help to the researchers and also policy makers in India. I am very much beholden to the Prof. K. Rama Krishna Rao, Chairman, Indian Council of Philosophical Research, New Delhi, for his financial assistance. My special thanks are due to our honourable Vice-Chancellor Prof. Beela Satyanarayana and Prof. V. Satyanarayana, Honorary Director, Indian Council of Social Science Research, Southern Regional Centre, Hyderabad for their financial assistance.

My sincere thanks to Prof. L.K. Mohana Rao, Principal, College of Arts & Commerce, Andhra University for inaugurating the seminar session. I express my grateful thanks to Prof. Beela Satyanarayana, Vice-Chancellor, Andhra University, for his inaugural address to the seminar. My sincere thanks are due to Prof. K. Rama Krishna Rao, Chairman, Indian Council of Philosophical Research, New Delhi for sparing his valuable time for preparing and delivering the keynote address. My special thanks to Sri D. Raja, M.P (Rajya Sabha) for attending as a guest of honour and released the Souvenir. My sincere thanks to Prof. Y. Satyanarayana, Vice-Chancellor, Andhra Pradesh University of Law for attending as a guest of honour and delivered valuable message.

I am very grateful to Prof Beela Satyanarayana, Vice-chancellor, Andhra University for having kindly written the foreword to this book sparing his precious time. I express my thanks to Sri S. Reghupathy, Hon. Minister for Environment and Forests,

Govt. of India for attending as the Chief Guest for Shastiabdi Poorti Celebrations of Prof. K.S. Chalam and valedictory function of the seminar session and released the book 'Dravida Udyamam Katha' written by Prof. K.S. Chalam.

I express my gratitude to Ms. Parveen Talha, Member, UPSC for attending the Shastiabdi Poorti Celebrations of Prof. K.S. Chalam and released the book 'Political Economy of Underdevelopment of Kalingandhra' written by Prof. K.S. Chalam.

My heartful thanks to Sri. P. Janardhana Rao, Mayor, Greater Visakhapatnam Municipal Corporation who presided over the function of the Shastiabdi Poorti Celebrations of Prof. K.S. Chalam.

I also thank to Prof. R. Sudarsana Rao, Head, Dept. of Economics and Prof. G. Ramachandrudu, Chairman, P.G. Board of Studies for their continuous support for the successful completion of the seminar.

Finally, my special thanks to the teaching and non-teaching staff, research scholars and students of the Dept. of Economics, Andhra University for their support for the successful completion of the seminar and Shastiabdi Poorti Celebrations of Prof. K.S. Chalam and also in bringing the book to the present shape. I place on record the excellent work done by publishers in the book on time.

Prof. D. Pulla Rao

INTRODUCTION

Economics of Education took its birth from the Presidential Address to the American Economic Association by Nobel laureate T.W. Schultz in 1960. Though economists from the time of William Petty, Adam Smith and others have examined the economic value of education, it was only after T.W. Schultz's address to the American Economic Association, the formal birth of the subject took place in 1960. Several scholars have enriched its methodology and content. The subject has influenced several other branches of knowledge and gave rise to the concept of human development. Originally, scholars were concerned with the contribution of education and health to economic development and later started more rigorous analysis of economic contributions of education. The concept of productivity and efficiency of education, economics of discrimination, economies of scale, rate of return studies etc were generated. One of the earliest departments that has started a structured course in Economics of Education and Planning in 1972 was the Department of Economics, Andhra University. Prof. K.S. Chalam was the first student of the subject in 1972. Later Prof. Chalam has continued to teach the subject in the department. He has guided research in the area of Economics of Education and published 6 books and scores of articles in reputed journals on the subject.

The present book consists of 32 papers which were presented at a national seminar on "Human Development and Social Exclusion" at the Department of Economics, Andhra University during 6-7 October, 2008. The seminar was organized in honour of Prof. K.S. Chalam on his 60th birthday on 7th October, 2008.

The volume is divided into two sections. In the first section of the book, **P.G. Raja Kumar and P.S.V.R. Babu** in their paper on the *"Economic Analysis and Education: Reasoned Issues in Application to Institutional Technology Evaluation"* discussed about the critical issues in application to institutional technology evaluation under three parts: role of economic analysis, outcome measures and relating inputs to outputs. They concluded that the difficulty with both cost-effectiveness and cost-benefit analysis practiced and the bias is towards those criteria that are mostly quantifiable, but undue emphasis is on cognitive outcome assessment. Economic analysis is most useful to the extent that it makes decision makers more aware and more explicit about alternatives and their various consequences.

G. Satyanarayana and M.R. Geetha Bala in their paper on *"Emergence of India in Global Economics of Higher Education: Issues and Priorities"* examined the major shortcomings in the Higher Education system and express a hope that with all the infrastructure keeping our fundamentals as laid in the Constitution and current requirements clear, we have to structure our education so that it enhances value of the human being than paving the way for another round of enslavement and new colonial rule where great resources – human and national are squandered in making only BPOs working for erstwhile rich western countries.

U.B Kondewar and Smitha Kondewar in their paper on *"Economics of Higher Education – Fact and Direction"* based on secondary data suggest that education policy should be employment oriented and that the government has to encourage research oriented education by providing more funds for research. It is also observed that there is inequality in regard to the availabilities of universities and colleges. One college for every taluka is essential.

D. Pulla Rao, P. Raj Kumar and A. Vamsi Krushna in their paper on *"Development of Higher Education in India: A Gender Perspective"* suggest alternatives for empowering women through professional studies, i.e. more women colleges including technical institutions be established, residential ladies hostel need to be opened in greater numbers, more scholarships need to be instituted and fellowship amount also be increased to attract female students and distance mode of education may be widened for women.

M.D. Bavaiah, K. Thulasi Naik and J. Narasimha Rao in their paper on *"The Intra-Sectoral Allocations of Education Expenditure* *in Andhra Pradesh"* found that the education sector share in social sector spending has declined to lower levels in 2000s from their higher levels in early 1990s. It was also observed that the share of education expenditure in total public expenditure is not only lower than 20 per cent, but also has been declining over a period or time. Similarly the share of education expenditure in Gross State Domestic Product (GSDP) is not been able to reach 3 per cent, the half of the target fixed by the New Educational Policy, 1986 in India.

G. Ramachandrudu and S. Prasada Rao in their paper on *"Andhra Pradesh Human Development Report - A Critical Appraisal"* find that the literacy rate of Andhra Pradesh is still lower (60.5) than the All-India literacy rate (65) but the overall literacy rate in Andhra Pradesh has gone up from 41 per cent in 1991 to 61 per cent in 2001. The value and rank of HDI, HPI and GDI of the district-wise in Andhra Pradesh revealed that 11 districts had lower levels of Human Development Index as compared to the Index value of the State (0.537).

S.V. Lakshmana Rao and P. Easwara Rao in their paper on *"Education As Revenue of Economic Growth"* consider that education is a strong means of human resource development. Economic development will follow the HRD which we can attain through education. Human Resource Development helps increase the economic growth by increasing the production of essential goods and services and also helps preserve and enhance the human dignity, freedom and worth of individuals. Human resources are developed through formal, informal, in-service, organized, self motivated education, health and nutrition programmes.

I. Narendra Kumar, V. Kodandarami Reddy and V. Balakrishnama Naidu in their paper on *"Cost Differential In Secondary Education of Rayalaseema Region in Andhra Pradesh"* observe that fifty years after Independence witness the slow progress of education, particularly secondary education in India. The study has revealed inconsistency in the behaviour of schools in managing their variable operations in terms of teacher-student ratio. Both number of students enrolled and fee per student were insufficient. Therefore, some positive and effective actions are needed in such direction.

Gara Latchanna in his paper on *"Financial Resources and Cost Effectiveness Analysis in Primary Education"* observes that the goals set to universalize primary education are at risk given the current trends. What can be done is that, lower costs to students and their families, improvement in the quality of school, increasing the efficiency of the school system and other options should be sought. Studies on input-output/cost-benefit, cost-effectiveness approaches in primary education might provide insights into the scope for increased efficiency of resource use.

A. Vamsi Krushna and D. Pulla Rao in their paper on *"Trends in the Growth of Higher Education in India: 1950-51 to 2005-06"* observe that the data shows that growth in enrollment of students has exceeded growth of the number of institutions and teachers. The student teacher ratio in higher education as it stood in 2005-06 was 26:1. Though there has been a massive expansion of institutional facilities during the last 55 years, the goal has moved farther with the number of students pursuing higher education increasing. Moreover there are glaring disparities based on caste, sex, religion, region etc. in what has been achieved.

In the second section of the book, **T. Nirmala Devi** in her paper on *"Dimensions of Economic Growth and Human Development in India: An Assessment"* observes that the human capabilities can clearly be enhanced by economic growth only when the nature of growth should be equitable and employment intensive. Better governance is the most essential thing to reap the benefits of social security nets like PDS and other related ones in the education and health sectors, which were limited earlier by the poor implementation. Care should also be taken in improving the social and physical structure, in order to at.ain the MDGs.

V. Krishna Murthy and R.V.L.N. Ratnakara Rao in their paper on *"Millennium Development Goals (MDGs) – Indian Scenario"* observe that UNMDGs are not easy to achieve because of dependency on welfare schemes, highest maternal deaths, diseases and nutrition deficiency, malnutrition among women and children, need for inputs from UN agencies, need to ensure a healthy and happy future, sanitation and need for well planned actions.

Areas of slowdown include secondary education, maternal and infant mortality rates, non-enrolment in primary schools, gender parity, poverty, measle deaths, drinking water, medicines, child birth and pregnancy, and undernourished children, along with a record of progress among different countries.

K.V.V. Devi Prasad and G. Syamala Rao in their paper on "*Human Resource Development at National Level*" present the need for HRD at national level and the role of UNDP in NHRD along with HRD facilitators and proposed HRD policies at national level. Also, suggestions to HRD facilitators while implementing NHRD are presented including the role of NGOs, alternative financial schemes, professionalism, cost- effectiveness, strengthening agriculture, and HRD interventions.

Jagannath B. Kukkudi and Ramesh B. Agadi in their paper on "*Human Resource Development Practices in University System*" discuss about Training and Resources in University, HS Employee Assistance Programme, Mediation Services, Health System, Information Resources, Habit of Writing by Faculty Members, Publication and Research Papers.

M. Kumar Raju, C. Gangulappa and A. Reddappa in their paper on "*Interstate Variations of Human Development Index in India*" discussed the position of Human Development in Indian States, and in Andhra Pradesh. It is concluded that there has been notable improvement in Human Development of Andhra Pradesh, but the relative performance of the state remained stagnant as shown by its ranking across states. There seems to be some convergence across districts in Human Development in Andhra Pradesh indicating that the backward districts are catching up with the developed districts.

A. Naga Raju and I.B. Raju in their paper on "*Globalisation and Human Resource Development*" observe that the progress in Human Development in India is marked by unevenness and stagnation. They suggest that the public policy both at the State and at the Central level has to be designed to meet different kinds of challenges in different parts of the country.

A. Ranga Reddy in his paper on "*Climate Change: A Threat to Human Development*" highlights the impact of climate change on human development, especially on India. The more emissions of gases led to warming up of globe, which creates disasters like droughts, famines, cyclones, forest fires, unseasonal rains, and spread of diseases. The girl and women are the worst sufferers in this development. These can be controlled by using multi-lateral and multi-dimensional measures like afforestation, reducing carbon use in transport, etc. taxes on carbon producers, using wind and solar power, riding on cycles, eating vegetarianism. Government of India had approved 526 projects to bring relief and rehabilitation from climate change.

R. Ranganathan and M. Yogeswari in their paper on *"Human Resource Development and Quality of Life"* observe that under the Constitution, persons with disabilities have been guaranteed the fundamental rights as available to other citizens of the country viz. equality of opportunity, non-discrimination, no untouchability, freedom of religion, right to the language, script or culture, right to franchise, right to property, right to enforce fundamental rights, access to education in any educational institution and right to work. The concern has been concretized in the Constitution of the Ministry of Human Resource Development (MHRD) from birth through childhood to adulthood by way of providing education and care along with professional input which have been integrated into this ministry. Family childhood care and education, general and technical education, sports and youth services, cultural development etc have been brought within its fold. Education of the disabled has yet to be fully integrated into this Ministry of Human Resource Development.

P. Subba Rao in his paper on *"Importance of Human Resource Planning"* observes that human resource planning is a vital sub-activity of employment function. In fact, employment process begins with human resource planning. It pervades through a number of activities after the process of human resource planning. These activities include teaching for prospective human resources, attracting them to the work and/or organization, finding out their suitability to the job, and organizational requirements and finally taking steps to absorb those human resources as organs of the company.

P. Sujit Kumar and Swatilekha Sanyal in their paper on "*Human Development: Role of Anganwadi Worker for Child Development*" observe that children are the pillars of the nation. So child development is essential for human development. The Integrated Child Development Services is one of the instruments and the Anganwadi Worker is the key person for the mental and physical development of the child. They concluded that the Anganwadi workers who have already attained the job training and refresher training course successfully implemented the programme in their field.

R.V.L.N. Ratnakara Rao and V. Krishna Murthy in their paper on "*Health Education and Health Care in India*" observed that India needs to do a lot more for education, especially secondary education (classes 5 to 10), health and undertake poverty eradication measures on a large scale so that life expectancy, literacy and standard of living will be improved to the possible extent, leading to over all improvement of human development.

D. Sujatha in her paper "*Human Resource Development – A Special Focus on Indian Women*" observes that the UNDP Sixth Human Development Report (1998) contains two gender aware measurements. One is the Gender related Development Index and the second is the Gender Empowerment Measure. It becomes necessary to have a framework and evolve development strategies that large and strengthen the link between the economic attainment and quality of life and encourage the most effective use of available resources for promoting the well-being of the people.

E. Madhava Reddy, D. Uma Devi and P. Adinarayana Reddy in their paper on "*Continuing Education for Human Resource Development*" observe that there are four types of Continuing Education Programmes called Equivalency Programmes (EPs), Income Generating Programmes (IGPs), Quality of Life Improvement Programmes (QLIPS) and Individual Interest Promotion Programmes (IIPPs). They conclude that the Continuing Education Programmes are organized at the grass root level involving all sections of the population and empowering them with required skills and competencies to promote their productivity and converting them as the assets of the society through the process of human resource development.

V. Hari Babu and M. Mary in their paper on "*Human Resource Development In Voluntary Organization*" opined that to develop rural areas NGOs are to be encouraged to take up certain activities with the required managerial and financial support. The officials of the Government organizations are to be posted compulsorily to work with the Voluntary organizations for some period so that they can serve better. The involvement of NGOs should be encouraged for the development of social sectors for cost effective implementation of various programmes and also higher level of people participation in various programmes.

K. Dasaratha Ramaiah and K. Thulasi Naik in their paper on "*Trends in human development spending in the States of India*" highlights that there is considerable catching up to do in order to meet the targets set for the Tenth Plan. Among the non-special category States, the richer States tend to allocate less resources as a percentage of GSDP to human development and they are content to ensure that the per capita expenditures in them are higher. In other words, they allocate proportionately more to other sectors. In contrast, the special category States tend to allocate more to social sectors even as a ratio of GSDP as their per capita GSDP increases. This indicates that they assign high priority to human development expenditures.

M. Satyanarayana in his paper on "*Need of Knowledge Management Services for Human Development*" opined that the Knowledge Management Services enhance the ability and capacity of persons for their development in all spheres. The entry of Information and Communication Technologies paved the way in the Information Management Services to create digital collections for improving the services in order to satisfy the changing information needs. The existing Information Management Services are to be redesigned for the availability of information which enhances human development.

K. Mouurlin in his paper on "*Trickle down effect - A key to Rural and Human Development*" explained how rural development strategies and programmes could promote sustainable livelihood for rural people by reducing poverty and unemployment and increase their income status. Finally rural development is one the pillars on which the future of economy stands. Most of the rural development programmes undertaken thus far have lacked focus and seem to be misdirected, though some of the programmes have yielded exceptionally high economic and social return. However it is his firm belief that, focused infrastructure development and people's participation combined with gainful, sustained employment, industrialization and effective fiscal decentralization can pave way to a much resilient economy and lead to achievement of our lofty targets in future.

A.V. Naga Varma, Y. Rama Krishna and J. Chandra Prasad in their paper on *"Growth, Poverty and Human Resource Development in India"* confined to the concept of Human Development (HD) from the vantage point of policy makers and planners who believe in intervention of the state and civil society for better social order for development of all. With the present rate of growth and other things remain constant; India would require at least next sixty years to attain high position in HD index. Assumption is that growth and HD are not only related but they have linear direction. As they have seen in the case of India the economic growth has not generated employment. It is a jobless growth. The present development of high technology reduces a requirement for human-labour.

K. Rani Gopal and B. Sailaja Kumari in their paper on *"Health Expenditure and Shifts in Human Development in Andhra Pradesh"* stated that besides raising the public expenditure on health, there is a great need for the introduction of a comprehensive scheme of health insurance, where the contribution of the Government decreases as we go up to the higher levels of income and it will be maximum at the lowest level. Significant improvement in HDI will enable us to achieve the goal of development with a human face.

P.S. Ravindra and P. Rajya Lakshmi in their paper on *"Human Resources Development In India: An Overview"* observed that HRD plays a significant and crucial role in market economics under dynamic environments. HRD to be effective should essentially have a strong base of human resources planning. Recruitment and selection based on effective HRD requirements.

Right man should be placed at a right time and right place / job. The success of the organization depends upon the quality and potentiality of its human resources. Thus, HRD plays a significant role in any organization to achieve the organizational goals and objectives.

M. D. Bavaiah, K. Thulasi Naik and J. Narasimha Rao in their paper on *"Public Spending for Human Development in Andhra Pradesh"* examined the trends and patterns of public spending on Social Sectors that are important for human development in Andhra Pradesh. There is necessity to substantially raise the allocations to Social Priority Sectors in order to raise the present low level of Human Priority Ratio to the level of UNDP norm of 5 percent. There is an urgent need for stepping up Expenditure on Social Sectors, particularly on Rural Health Services and Rural Water Supply Programmes, because the present levels of expenditure on these services are very low and they are very effective in improving the health conditions of people.

M.V.S.S. Prakas Rao and P.Ch. Lakshminarayana in their paper on *"Human Resources Development: Emerging Issues and Concerns in Education of the Weaker Sections"* suggested measures to improve weaker sections educational status. Abolition of tuition fee in all states in government schools at least up to the upper primary level. Incentives like free textbook, uniforms, stationery, school bags etc., for these students. The Constitutional (86th Amendment Bill, notified on December 13, 2002), provides for free and compulsory elementary education as a fundamental right for all children in the age group 6-14 years. SSA is a historic stride towards achieving the long cherished goal of Universalition of Elementary Education (UEE) through a time integrated approach, in partnership with states SSA, which promises to change the face of elementary education sector of the country.

Prof. D. Pulla Rao

SUB-THEME: A.
ECONOMICS OF EDUCATION

1

ECONOMIC ANALYSIS AND EDUCATION: REASONED ISSUES IN APPLICATION TO INSTRUCTIONAL TECHNOLOGY EVALUATION

P. George Raja Kumar & Pechetty S.V.R. Babu***

The economic analysis of a project helps select and design projects that contribute to the welfare of a country. Various tools of economic analysis help determine the economic and fiscal impact of the project, including the impact on society and the major stakeholders involved, as well as the project's risks and sustainability.

The importance of economic analysis is, nowadays all countries face the problem of allocating limited resources such as capital, skilled and unskilled labour, land and other natural resources to a variety of different uses such as production of consumer goods, investment in industry, infrastructure, education, health etc. with an aim to reach a more fundamental goal of reducing poverty, accelerating economic growth and reducing income inequalities. Limited resources, choices have to be made between alternative uses of these resources such that the benefit to the economy and society is as large as possible.

In this paper, we discussed about critical issues in applications to instructional technology evaluation of economic analysis and

* Principal, S.S.R College of Education, Kothapeta, East Godavari Dist., Andhra Pradesh.

** Research Scholar, Dept of Education, Andhra University, Visakhapatnam.

education under three parts. They are the role of economic analysis, outcome measures, and relating inputs to outputs.

The Role of Economic Analysis

Over the last few decades, developing countries have confronted a growing set of interrelated problems relative to the utilization of their education systems to meet the perceived needs of national development. On the one hand, there has been rapidly rising social demand for the provision of educational services, while at the same time the cost of providing such services has increased rapidly. In many instances, resource scarcities such as a shortage of teachers preclude immediate satisfaction of this demand at what is considered an affordable price. The inertia and inefficiencies inherent in most existing education systems create difficulties in responding to the problems mentioned above.

Faced by these significant problems, many nations have attempted to experiment with variation from traditional educational practices, with the advent of technological advances in communications media. Many countries have turned to these innovations as a basic element in the design of new instructional systems. In a broad sense, it is hoped that new technological approaches can contribute to advances in efficiency and productivity for the education sector. It has been hope that innovations in instructional technology can aid the education sector in increasing its productivity along with the more progressive sectors of the economy.

Economics, more than the other social sciences, has been looked to provide more rigorous analytical approaches to practical problem solving. In particular, economists have brought a rather broad framework to systems evaluation of alternative educational strategies under the rubric of cost, cost-effectiveness and cost-benefit analysis. A basic problem is that research has not been directed at uncovering the specific circumstances, type of learning, or characteristics of learners, which would lead to more consistent findings. Faced with the potential for different strategies yielding different educational outcomes, economists turn to both cost-effectiveness and cost-benefit analysis to aid in the choice of an alternative.

The distinction between these two types of analysis is sometimes blurred, although this distinction is clear in a technical sense and centers on the difference between effects and benefits. Economists use "effects" to refer to the various dimensions of system outcomes with which one might be interested. In educational system, educationists use "effects" to refer to the student cognitive development, student affective development, student psychomotor development, the number of students, the system enrolls, the number of graduates, etc. The term "benefits", on the other hand, refers to evaluation of these multidimensional outcomes so that all may be summarized in a single index such that the outcome index is directly comparable with the cost index used. This usually means measuring benefits in rupee terms and these we have been a number of studies looking at rates of return to educational investments in which the costs of the investments are compared with the future income benefits that may be received by programme participants and by society in general.

In this paper, we discuss what we consider to be some of the more critical facets of the present state-of-the-art of the application of cost-effectiveness and cost-benefit analyses the evolution of educational system alternatives. Cost analysis for instructional technology system is an essential ingredient to the above two approaches. At this juncture we should recognize that cost analysis alone can never yield criteria to serve as the sole basis for a rational decision; decisions require either information or assumptions about system outcomes as well. A reasonable substantial body of economic literature dealing with education from these perspectives has been developed, especially over the last a decade and half.

Many educators have rejected the work of these economists in education as too narrow, as focusing on only quantitatively measurable benefits and often only on those that can be measured in rupee terms. Their point of view is quite understandable in that, there is an excess of "one dimensional" economics and the limitations of this type of analysis for policy decisions are apt not to be sufficiently stressed. Nonetheless, we do believe that the overall frame works that different economists bring is useful to educational evaluation. Most educational research focuses on short term effects, often to the complete neglect of examining both system costs and long run individual and social benefits. The economist's framework, on the other hand, stresses the analysis of costs, effects, and benefits in an integrated fashion in order to compare alternative system strategies and perhaps to discover which is most cost-effective or most cost-beneficial.

Again we want to stress that what we consider most beneficial about economic analysis is that it can provide useful alternative conceptual framewor s for thinking about various aspects of the social system within which we live. It is important to remember that economics, like all other social science disciplines, is an artificial partition of a simplified model of the world. Although Anthropology, Economics, Psychology and Sociology may sometimes be of description of the geographical divisions within many university buildings, they should be employed as reality partition only to the extant that they are useful for thinking and doing. We briefly survey the approaches that economic analysis takes to educational evaluation and their limitations, with a focus on the application to instructional technology alternatives.

Instead of dividing this paper into separate treatments of cost-effectiveness and cost-benefit analysis, we have integrated them to some extent and divided the paper into what we consider to be the two major focal points for discussion in this field: the choice and treatment of the outcomes of alternative educational strategies that will be studied and the theory and methodology of relating system inputs to outputs. The points below are generally applicable to the relation between economic analysis and educational evaluation.

Outcome Measures

Much attention has been centered upon cognitive achievement, as measured on standardized tests, as the sole criterion of educational effectiveness. While this is an important process –

outcome, it is by no means the only one of interest. Other effectiveness measures considered important include changes in the distribution of test scores to determine potential reductions in educational outcome inequality; dropout rates; repetition rate; analytic capabilities; creativity; inquisitiveness; and wide range of social and economic behaviour. To a developing country like India, expanding its educational systems differences among systems in terms of the rapidity with which the school population can be reached are also of importance.

For non-formal education programmes such as those in community development or agriculture, one is also interested in imparting knowledge. However, there should be an even greater interest in affecting the likelihood of fostering an ability to convert knowledge gained into action.

To make decision about educational alternatives one must evaluate educational outcomes. Economic analysis contributes to this evaluation by providing frameworks and methods to approach the question of assigning value to these different outcomes of interest so their relative "worth" may be compared. A primary conceptual stress of conventional economic thought applied to education is to aggregate outcomes of interest by assigning monetary value to certain educational system outcomes and thus compare educational alternatives by weighing their monetary benefits against their costs. An alternative approach to this question of aggregating outcome measures to a single index is also provided by economics, through the methods conventional economics uses is to study individual choice. Below we discuss essential features of each of these two contributions to educational evaluation.

a) Outcomes from Effects to Benefits

The key problem of cost-benefit analysis is in translating the alternative educational system outcomes under consideration into measures that can be compared directly with costs, so that the question, "Is this activity worth devoting these resources to it?" can be answered. The connections necessary to answer this question have been derived over the past two centuries (dating primarily from Adam Smith's, *The Wealth of Nations*, in 1776) by economists concerned with the operation of a capitalist economy, or the operation of a socialist economy according to competitive market principles. If market prices truly represent social value (Jamison, Klee's and Well's 1976, discussion of shadow prices), profits in this theoretical system represent a signal to the producer that the output they produce is more valuable to society than the societal resources that are utilized in the production process.

Cost-benefit analysis involves the valuation of the outcomes of public sector investment in monetary terms and the comparison of these benefits with the costs of the investment. As with profits as a guide for the private sector, cost-benefit analysis provides a criterion of social worth for investment decisions, again given that prices truly reflect social value. If the monetary benefits exceed monetary costs, the investment is deemed worth while. The trick, of course, is to translate public sector investment outcomes, which are not directly marketed, into some monetary value equivalent.

In educational system evolution, most economists have taken the approach that although educational outcomes of interest are not measured in monetary terms, they can be translated, at least in part, into monetary outcomes since the main "products" of educational services, the students, enter the labour market. The hypothesis made is that formal and non-formal educational experiences result in the embodiment of additional skills and traits in the individual, yielding "human capital" that makes the educated individual more economically productive, and, thus, increase the general productive capacity of the economy and thereby contributes to economic growth. If this additional productivity due to schooling can be measured, then one can compare a measure of the societal benefit in monetary terms with that of societal costs in monetary terms for a particular educational endeavour. Unfortunately, economic productivity is not easily measurable and the alternative most economists choose to measure is income. The connection between the two is again based on competitive market theory; in a perfectly competitive economic system the wage an individual receives is equal to the productivity that the person or the individual he/she adds to the firm. If this connection holds well, then the additional income due to schooling is also a measure of the additional productivity due to schooling.

Empirically, economists have approach this cost / benefit evaluation of educational systems in four ways; through rate of return, production function, labour force planning and social demand studies. Rate of return analysis yields measurers of the individual and social return on investment in education through examining the relation of schooling to earnings. Production function analysis attempts to establish more direct connections between education and productivity. Labour force planning efforts use assumed relations between education and sectoral growth to yield guidelines for educational expansion. Social demand evaluation places reliance on the implicit value which the educational consumers place on educational services. All four approaches differ to some extent, and each has its relative limitations and strengths.

b) Outcomes from Alternative Aggregations

Apart from an extensively developed framework that looks at questions of social efficiency, economists also bring a set of technical approaches of combining multiple educational outcomes or outcomes that occur over a period longer than one year. As most commonly utilized, cost-effectiveness analysis does not go beyond the stage of determining the impact of alternative strategies on the criteria of interest. It is left to the decision-maker to implicitly evaluate the overall worth of each alternative, presuming that one does not automatically dominate, and then make her/ his decision. However, from the point of view of instigating the decision-maker to think through the effectiveness tradeoff more carefully and to allow these tradeoffs to be scrutinized by other decision-makers and public interest groups, it can be useful to employ techniques which bring out these tradeoffs explicitly.

Economists would examine outcomes over time from the perspective that positively valued outcomes that occur in the present are valued more by the individual and the society than if the same outcomes were to accrue sometime in the future. To the extent that this is true, if different educational strategies have a different incidence of effects over time, they may be valued quite differently, even if they have similar effects. There are alternative methodological means of aggregating several outcome measures. Generally, such methods involve having the decision-maker convert all outcome measures to common numerical scale with interval properties and then assigning relative weights to each equally scaled outcome measure. Two of the more serious limitations of this technique for treating multiple effectiveness criteria are: the reliance on the subjective value judgments of the decision-makers and the potential effect of ignored criteria on the decision. The second limitation in some way is even more serious. As the analytic difficulty increases with the number of criteria chosen for analysis, decision-maker utilizing the technique described will eliminate many criteria from consideration. It is important that this elimination be of the criteria which are considered less valued, rather than those criteria which are difficult to analyze.

Relating Inputs to Outputs

In the discussion of how an economist looks at educational outcome measures have, we have ignored the critical question of translating system inputs to system outputs. In this part of the paper, we look at whether, even assuming the efficiency framework of most economists is a reasonable one, the empirical investigation techniques currently available to social science are capable of shedding light on casual input –output relationships. The economists' approaches to both cost-effectiveness and cost-benefit analysis require answering such questions as,

- How do educational resources affect educational outcomes of interest, such as cognitive achievement of various types?
- How much of income differences between individuals are actually caused by differences in education?
- How much of the productivity differences between workers or farmers with different educational levels are

actually caused by those educational differences?

- What specifically does education do that can yield any income or productivity differences that do exist?
- How does consumer demand for education react to changes in the price of that education?

The classic scientific response of questions of impact, the experiment is often politically or practically difficult to accomplish with much rigor and the assignment of cause to some broad 'black box' treatment labeled "education" or "new educational strategy" is usually somewhat ambiguous. This is due, impart to a growing concern for practical significance which brings even the proper form of the experiment open to question.

The lack of possibilities for structuring what science considers rigorous experimental tests to examine the impact of education, or of alternative forms of education, has led many social scientists to embrace recently developed statistical methods to analyze non-experimental information collected in the 'field'. The growing literature on educational production functions, educational demand functions, earning functions, and agricultural and manufacturing production functions, attest to the dominance of regression analysis as the principal method for such empirical investigations.

For regression analysis (or its related methods-e.g., analysis of variance, partial correlation analysis or path analysis) to generate accurate answers to these questions, at least three principal conditions must be met. There must be a theory that specifies a complete casual model, one that includes all the relevant casual variables. The concepts one is trying to relate must be quantified and, moreover, quantified in a fairly rigorous manner, such that differences between variable values are meaningful. Finally, this theory must indicate exactly in what manner these variables are related to each other (e.g., linearly, exponentially, logarithmically, etc.).

In conclusion, there are a few important points that should be mentioned and a few tentative conclusions that should be drawn out of the total analysis. First, an obvious difficulty with both cost-effectiveness and cost-benefit analysis as usually practiced is the bias towards those criteria that are most easily quantifiable. Second, even given the penchant toward quantification, there appears to be an undue emphasis on cognitive outcome assessment. Third, throughout this paper we have emphasized the analysis and effectively ignored the analysis.

Finally, we should recognize that there exist competing descriptions of the social reality we live in, and that what we have discussed indicates that the analysis of system costs, effects, and benefits depend in part on the description of the world we choose. The distinction between decisions made for 'political' reasons and that for reason of 'economic rationality' may be less a distinction on the basis of rational decision-making (for both may or may not be rational), but more a distinction along the lines of what specific goals are being sought after, how one evaluates benefits divided among competing interest groups and, in general, who has what degree of control of the relevant decision-making power. Economic analysis is most useful to the extent that it makes decision-makers more aware and more explicit about alternatives and their various consequences. But, again, such analysis should not be taken as definitive, but as informative, to be interpreted with caution and common sense, based on the knowledge of both its strengths and weaknesses.

2

EMERGENCE OF INDIA IN GLOBAL ECONOMICS OF HIGHER EDUCATION: ISSUES AND PRIORITIES

*G. Satyanarayana** & *M.R. Geetha Bala***

Economic experts and various studies conducted across the globe envisage India and China to rule the World in 21st Century. This is truer with the case of India than with China as we have a well qualified work force and an excellent education and research oriented institutional infrastructure than China which neglected Higher Education all through Chairman Mao times until Deng era which started in late seventies. There is a direct relationship between a country's economic growth and its qualified well educated workforce. Though China Deng era was and is investing heavily in higher education, research and IT, to catch up on world scenario with western or Indian standards in terms of quality will definitely take two more decades.

For over five decades since World War II, United States with her qualified highly technical workforce has been the largest economy in the world. Major developments like dismantling of Soviet Empire, emergence of European Union (former Western Europe) and the vanishing multipolar economic model in to a unipolar economic model have taken place in the world geo-political scenario since nineties which paved the way for the concepts of globalization and liberalization. This led the shift

* Professor, Department of Economics, Sri Krishnadevaraya University, Anantapur Dist., Andhra Pradesh.

** Sri Satya Sai University, Anantapur Campus, Andhra Pradesh.

of focus from the US, EU and Japan to the two Asian giants - India and China. The rapid and astonishing growth that India and China achieved in mere 20 years outpaced the five decade growth of many industrial nations combined by a factor of 5.

During eighties ASEAN Countries and during nineties Korean Peninsula, China and India contributed to the rising economic share of Asia in World GDP. The super rich countries of Europe have seen the greatest decline in their share of global GDP by 4.9% followed by the US and Japan with each declining about 1% each. By contrast the rising share of China and India GDP in the world scenario more than compensated for the decline of rich countries GDP decline. According to experts, the share of US in World GDP is expected to fall from 21% to 18% and that of India to rise from 6% to 11% by 2025. This positions India as third largest economy in the world after the US and China.

By 2025 the Indian economy is projected to be about 60% the size of the US economy. The transformation of world markets in to tri-polar economic spheres of influence will be complete by 2035, with the Indian economy only a little smaller than the US economy but larger than that of Western Europe and Japan. By 2035, India will be larger economic growth driver than the six largest countries in Western Europe. India, which is now the fourth largest economy in terms of purchasing power parity (PPP) will overtake Japan and become third major economic power within next 10 years.

The advent of the IT revolution in digital age coupled with large number of young and educated population fluent in English is gradually transforming India as an important 'back office' destination for global companies for outsourcing of their BPO, customer services and technical support operations. India is a major exporter of highly- skilled workers in Software and financial services all across the world. The reasons for this massive upward vertical airlift of the Indian economy is possible because of huge untapped natural resources and vast numbers of human resources both skilled and unskilled yet willing to be trained to cultivate new pastures of economic growth.

Having said the above, however two thirds of the Indian workforce still earns their livelihood directly or indirectly through agriculture. Services are a growing sector and are playing increasingly important role in contributing towards Indian economic growth. Yet these two sectors, IT and services, contribute only a small part in the panorama of the Indian workforce scenario. Given the dependencies on agriculture, India faces a burgeoning population and the resulting challenges of economic and social inequality and abject poverty. Poverty although seems to have declined in percentage-wise since Independence, in terms of real numbers there are more number of people who are below poverty line than any time in Indian history.

Priorities for India

Given the opportunities envisaged above to achieve the global dominance in next two decades the following are laid out as priorities. No country can ever think of becoming an economic sphere of influence if the underlying economic fundamentals are strong enough. The tri-pillar French model of economic sphere laid in late sixties 1) self-sufficiency in agriculture- self reliance of food 2) self-sufficiency in industrial development - self-reliance in industry which leads to self-reliance in defense and 3) the development of educated qualified citizen force to achieve the above objectives will hold good in the Indian context also. To achieve the three above said fundamentals the following action priorities are essential:

- Boosting agricultural growth through diversification and development of agro processing.
- Redrawing priorities and parameters to discourage anti-agriculture practices like donating agricultural lands to SEZs.
- Sustaining the growth momentum and achieving an annual average growth of 8% in the next five years, (already our growth rate is 9%).
- Diversification of Industrial base at a faster rate by at least 10% per yr to integrate not only the surplus labour

in agriculture but also the unprecedented number of women and teenagers joining the labour force every year.

- Developing world-class infrastructure for sustaining growth in all the sectors of the economy.
- Checking the growth of Population. GNI per capita remain very poor. It was only US$ 2880 in 2003 according to World Bank reports.
- Empowering the population through Universal education and health care.
- All the above through domestic capitalization rather than letting the exploitative foreign capital to enslave us.

To achieve all above in an integrated manner one of the chief priorities of today's economic and social needs of the nation is Education. To quote Sulbha Nataraj "Education is essentially a process, rather than a product and where knowledge is not an end itself but a means to promote general welfare. The objective of the educational system is to create a healthy and holistic human progress." In order to achieve the said goals our education should build the following capacities:

- **The ability to think**: this includes the ability to explore, analyze, reason out logically and to criticize as well as appreciate and to keep an open mind.
- **The ability to earn a decent living**: equip people with occupational skill that will enhance their employability.
- **The ability to achieve self-actualization**: the need for self-actualization is the highest level of human needs according to Abraham Maslow's theory of Motivation. Education should enable the utilization of one's full potential for development in physical, moral, ethical, emotional, intellectual and creative terms.
- **The ability to be sensitive** towards emerging issues, like concern for the environment, equality, prevention

of violence and corruption, need for tolerance, cooperation and cohesion.

Needless to say, this is easier said than done. In the 21st century education has become an 'internationally traded good' ITG. The current student in India, who is the "nucleus" of the education system is gradually looking for education that is 'Quantitative and in turn with the requirements of the times with sole focus on earning potential'.

According to V.S. Prasad (2004) "Education should focus on the whole development of the individual apart from his occupational training. Learning to earn is one of the four key skills to be developed among learners."

As a medium for the flowering of the human personality it is important to support learners with the 7 P's – Passion, Persistence, Pro-activeness, Personable ness (adaptation), Positivity, Preparation and Professionalism which will make learning a truly fulfilling process.

Education is an effective instrument of social change. It is an index of growth. In the Indian context, quantitative growth is desirable, however and important facet of growth is the qualitative one. Without education being provided to the citizens of this country, the objectives set forth in the preamble to the constitution cannot be achieved. The fact that right to education occurs in as many as 3 Articles in Part IV viz., Articles 41, 45 and 46 shows the importance attached to it by the founding fathers.

Higher Education

Current Scenario

Higher Education is the education beyond 10+2 stage. It is a powerful tool in an information-based society. In the five decades since Independence India's Higher Education system has undergone remarkable transformation from an elite system, having deep colonial roots, to an egalitarian system striving to meet the aspirations of a vibrant democracy. The growth of the Indian Higher Education system is a result of the Nation's Policy adopted after Independence to promote education among the masses. The National Policy on Education (1986) visualizes education to be for development and for quality.

Today, India is the third largest Higher Education system in the world (after China and USA) in terms of enrolment which in 2005-2006 was over one crore five lacs. However, in terms of the number of institutions, India has the largest Higher Education system in the World with 17,973 institutions (371 Universities, and 18000 colleges). Of these there are 63 unaided deemed Universities with enrolment of 60,000 students, and 7,650 unaided private colleges with enrolment of 31, 50,000 students. Thus nearly one third of total students are studying in unaided private institutions. Unaided institutions are 'growing rapidly' and others are 'not growing'.

Even with a huge system in place, Higher Education in India is in a miserable condition. Student enrolment grew at an estimated rate of 7% between 1987 and 1993 but has now declined to 5.5% compound rate of growth. Even then, after nearly six decades of independence, Higher Education is not accessible to the poorest groups of the population. Hardly 7 to 8 % of the population in the age group of 17 to 23 yrs is enrolled in the institutions of Higher Education. Enrolment in India has been below the average for the Asian countries the latter; South East Asian countries show much higher enrolment. Philippines 31%, Thailand 19%, Malaysia 27% and China 13% as compared to 7 to 8% in India. The enrolment figure for the USA is 81%, in UK 54% and in the Japan 49%.

Some of the major Short comings in the Higher Education system:

- Inadequate access to Higher Education – the worst sufferers is persons from the weaker sections of the society.
- Variable quality of Higher Education in different institutions. There co-exist internationally recognized institutions and institutions which are substandard and sub-viable.

- The system of affiliation of colleges followed by most Universities, with centralized decisions, which discourages accountability.
- Inflexibility in academic structure that inhibits innovation and promotes mediocrity (unevenness).
- Inadequate and diminishing financial support for Higher Education from the Government.

Quality Manpower

According to Mckinsy (2020), only 25% of Indian engineers, 15% of its finance and accountancy professional and 10% of Indian professionals with general degrees are suitable to work for multinational companies. To stay in the lead, India needs to improve the quality and skills of its workforce.

The Financial Situation

India is one of the lowest Public expenditure on Higher Education per student at US$460, which compares unfavorable with China US$2728, Brazil US$3986, Indonesia US$ 666, Malaysia US$625. The expenditure in the USA is 9,629 dollars, in the UK 8,502 dollars and in Japan 4,830 dollars. India's public spending on Higher education and gross enrolment ratio levels are quite low, even when compared with several other developing countries.

Export of Education Services

The emerging demographics have ensured that the demand for Higher Education is greater in 'younger' countries as compared to graying countries. Similarly the supply of education services is greater in graying countries since there are fewer young students to enroll in Universities. The USA is the largest exporter of education services in the world. The other large exporters are UK, Australia and New Zealand. Developing countries such as India and China are the largest importers of education in the World.

A study by the New York based International Institute of Education (IIE) that the Asian countries had 3,25,000 students in US colleges and Universities in 2004-05, including 80,466 from India, 63,000 from China, 53,000 from South-Korea and 42,000 from Japan. Further, 15,000 Indian students were enrolled in the UK, 22,279 in Australia and 2,567 in New Zealand in 2004, nearly 14% of all international student in the US were from India. Education itself generated as much as 13.4 billion dollars in export revenues for the US in 2003.

The following table shows the number of Indian students abroad in the last 2 yrs.

Indian Students Abroad

Name of the Country	*2003 – 04*	*2004 - 05*
USA	79736	80466
UK	11000	15000
Australia	17853	22279
New Zealand	2405	2567

Source : WENR (World Education News and Reviews) IDP Australia, IIE.

The Universities in the exporting countries see a huge opportunity and are going all out to attract students from developing countries such as India and China. The US is the World's number one educational destination and attracts about half a million students every year. It is therefore quite clear that there is a huge excess demand in India for Quality Higher Education, which is being met by foreign campuses. Most students from India pay their way through these education programmes thereby keeping the foreign universities going and even subsidizing foreign students. The services negotiations could be used as an opportunity to invite foreign universities to set up campuses in India, thereby saving billions of dollars for the students traveling abroad. In fact this would be win-win situation for both sides since foreign universities would get a chance to expand their markets and Indian students would get World class higher education at a fraction of the cost in foreign universities located abroad. A balance would however have to be struck between domestic regulation and providing adequate flexibility to such universities in setting syllabus, hiring teachers, screening students and setting fee levels.

Internationalising Higher Education

The educational services in India are one of the important subject areas of negotiations under General Agreement on Trade in Services (GATS) primarily because such services have participation of private entrepreneurs and higher education is not considered as an area which is entirely provided for by one government. Under such circumstances, it is inevitable that the pressures from foreign educational providers would be intense, competition fierce and with far reaching consequences.

Keeping this in mind India should gear for utilizing the infrastructure it has toward of western interest oriented education practices to reintroduce those that are needed for the overall development of human being which is the purpose of education in the first place any way.

- Strong University Net work - with over 371 universities and 18,000 colleges offering the widest spectrum of courses, India has the second largest education system in the World.
- Global Recognition - Professionals trained in Indian Institutions are recognized globally. Over the 200 of Fortune 500 Companies recruit from Indian campuses regularly.
- English Medium - India has the third largest English speaking population in the world after USA and England. Medium of Instruction in Higher education is primarily in English.
- Moderate Fee and Cost of Living - India offers quality Education at a fraction of cost compared to other educational destination.
- Quality - Quality of Education is assured through National bodies of Accreditation such as NBA and NAAC.

Welcoming Environment - India extends an unbiased welcome to students of all nationalities, cultures and religions. Further cultural and religious diversity on Indian campuses contributes towards all round development of an individual.

With all the infrastructure keeping our fundamentals as laid in the constitution and current requirements clear we have to indigenize our education so that it enhances value of the human being than paving the way for another round of enslavement and neo colonial rule where great resources – human and natural, are squandered in making only BPO s working for erstwhile rich western countries.

3

ECONOMICS OF HIGHER EDUCATION: FACT AND DIRECTION

U.B. Kondewar & Smita Kondewar***

Introduction

Education plays an important role in shaping human development. Specially, higher education is essential to make life better and to make future of Nation bright. It is very essential at this juncture to understand the Economics of Higher education. The topic is very vast and can be explained through different angles. Few important objectives are considered to understand facts of Economics of higher education. The growth of colleges and universities since 1950-51 is considered in the paper, The Economics of education can be understood properly, if we consider the final number of graduates, post graduates, research students and Diploma holders. This is in a regard to the evaluation of higher education. In democratic country, like India, We have given equal right to every citizen. It is necessary to consider the level of higher education on the basis of demographic variables like S.C/ S.T. enrolment etc.

Mere enrolment is not sufficient to assess the work but it is also necessary to study the percentage of pass-out students. It is necessary to study enrolment of students from point of

* Principal, Sharda College, Near Government Hospital, Subhash Road, Parbhani - 431 401. Maharashtra.

** Shankarrao Chavan Arts and Commerce College, Adhapur, Dist Nanded, Maharashtra.

view of faculty. Finance is important factor to spread education with faster speed. It is necessary to study the financial arrangements made for higher education. Equal educational facilities are essential to all states and spread of education among states is vital points. It is also necessary to assess educational progress from the point view of spread of higher education on state level.

All the points discussed above are considered in this paper. All these points are very important to study the progress of higher education in India. The paper is divided into three parts. In first part, Introduction, objectives, Methodology review of literature and causes are studied. Second parts are devoted to cover important conclusions and suggestions. Part three contain the list of references.

Causes of the Study

1. Higher education is an important factor to grow economy with higher speed.
2. Human capital is the key for economy growth and development, higher education is essential for it.
3. There is direct relationship between development of higher education and economic development
4. Knowledge and skills can be acquired through education.
5. Financial assistance to higher education.
6. Link of higher education with research and employment guarantee.

Objectives

1. To study the status of higher education and stage wise enrolment of students.
2. The distribution of enrolment of students on basis of demographic variables.
3. Examination result, pass out rates.
4. To study Government expenditure on education
5. State wise date on higher education.
6. Students enrolment faculty-wise.

Data Collection and Methodology

The entire paper depends upon secondary data. Data is collected through standard periodicals. Percentage and index are used to arrive at concrete results.

Review of Literature

Education plays important role in shaping human development. Every citizen has to take education to acquire skill by which it is possible for him to fulfill his and his family's requirement. Specially, higher education is essential to make life better and to make future of nation bright several steps are necessary to get up date higher education.

In the world of today, competition in any field is competition in knowledge. That is why we need to build institution of excellence.[1] It is becoming imperative for higher education institutions the country to become quality conscious. They have to become more professional and committed in their thought and action.[2]

Higher education is now being considered as a commercial product to brought and sold in the market like other commodity. Internationalization of higher education is the pressing need of the time because we are one of the members of the world trade organization.[3] In the emerging scenario, universities and colleges have to play important role. They have to respond to the public needs.[4]

It is necessary to assess the role of CHB Teachers. Findings of the overall perception indicate that CHB/ contractual appointment is perceived negatively by all teachers of the degree college.[5] Use of latest information and communication technology requires sound financial base and also competent manpower. Unfortunately, in most of the universities either required financial resources are lacking or the teachers and staff who in many cases have been selected on the basis of considerations other than merit, are incompetent.[6]

Profit higher education appears to be inevitable. One, the sharp increase in the higher education age group population and increased enrollment ratio of this age co-hort propelled by the first economic development of the country and second, obvious failure of the traditional higher education system in India, which is now dragging amidst the otherwise rapidly growing sectors of the Indian economy and society.[7]

Universities must become the hub of research activities once again to capture synergies between teaching and research that enrich each other.[8] Linkages should always remain established with trade and industry and support services in designing curriculum and on the job training facilities.[9] Imparting of education is a process of skill development through learning.[10]

Need based approach can be achieved with the positive response from the student community. Planned and continuous efforts of the teaching faculty and active support and cooperation of the college department.[11] Development of higher education in India has not been systematic. The level of development also varies from state to state.[12]

In non-grantable college, there is no security either of employment or salary. Most of basic facilities are also lacking. Many college do not have full fledged principal nor is their students, teacher ratio is satisfactory.[13] these is cause of failure of standard of higher education. The quality of knowledge, generated within higher education institutions, is increasingly determining the nation's global competitive; Higher education must be able to respond to rising student expectations and the demands of global competition.[14]

Higher education, if meaningfully and sincerely implemented can assist in removing disparities, promote development of our regions and provide social and economic security, so as to ensure a better quality of life that is essential for sustaining the social capital and human resource of the region.[15]

Conclusions and Suggestions

Universities and college are important factors to assess overall educational development. Total universities increased from 27 to 355 during 1950-51 to 2005-2006. The growth of universities is 13 times more compared to the number of universities during

1950 -51, the growth of teachers during same period is twenty times, growth of colleges is 31 times while growth in enrolment of students is 41 times. India made rapid progress in the field of higher education if situation is compared with situation of education facilities available during 1950-51. In reality, India has to take more rapid steps for overall educational improvement in the country.

In order to understand economics of higher education in India, one has to consider the graduate, post graduate, Research and Diploma / Certificate holders. During 2005-2006 the total students under enrolment of Graduate, post-graduate, Research and Diploma/ certificate was only 1,10,28,020 (approximately 1 crore and 10 lac) The figure is very small if we compare it with total population of youths in the age of 18 to 23 years. The percentage of research student in total enrolment is only 0.64. The percentage of enrolment of students of post graduation in total enrolment is only 9.42%. The figures are not encouraging. More hard efforts are essential to enhance the percentage of youths.

Attempt is made to study the enrolment of students on the basis of demographic variables. The percentage of S.C. student enrolment was only 0.53 during 1986-87; it has gone to 11.66 during 2001-2002. The percentage of S.T. student enrolment enhanced from 0.49 to 4.10 during period 1986-87 to 2002-2003. The percentage of female student enrolment increased from 6.42% to 30% during 1986-87 to 2002-2003. The percentage of rural student enrolment is grown up from 23% to 25.42% during period 1990-91 to 2002-2003.

It clearly shows the progress pertaining to enrolment of students belonging to SC, ST, female and rural class concerned is not satisfactory; more efforts are essential to enhance the enrolment of students of the categories mentioned above.

More enrolment of students is not important factor to determine the progress of education, the percentage of pass out student during 1991 was only 13.1% of total enrolment of students, it is improved to 34% of total enrolment of students during year

2006. There is lot of improvement in regard to percentage of pass out students in total enrolment of students. However 66% percentage of total enrolment of students failed. This is sorry state of affair.

Attempt is made to consider the percentage of pass out students in total enrolment of student faculty wise. The students registered for exam during 2002-2003 and total pass out students are studied. It is shocking to note that the percentage of students pass out in B.A. was 11.9%, in B. Com. 17.6% and in B.Sc. it was 16.6%. The result is dismal.

Finance is important factor for rapid educational development during 1950-51, 7.92% of the total expenditure was allotted to education by government of India while it rose to 14.42 up to 2001-2002.

In terms of G.D.P., the percentage share of education is not satisfactory. It was only 0.64 during 2000-2001. The amount is not sufficient as per the requirement of educational sector concerned.

It is necessary to consider three stages of education. The percentage of primary sector in regard to share in G.D.P. was only 1.09 during 1981-82 and it is raised to 1.66% during 2001-2002. The share is slowly increased during 1981-82 to 2001-2002. In regard to share of secondary education in total G.D.P. during 1981-82 was 0.81 percent while it had gone to 1.66 percent during 2001-2002. The percentage of share of secondary education in total G.D.P. remains near about constant. The percentage of higher education in total G.D.P. remain constant during period 1981-82 to 2001-2002 in the range of 0.3 to 0.4%.

It is worth while to consider expenditure of other selected countries at this juncture. U.S.A. spending 6.5% of the total G.D.P. on education while Germany is spending 4.6% of its G.D.P. on education.

In India, Government was spending 1% of its G.D.P. on higher education during 1971, the amount gradually declined and during 2001, Indian Government spent only 0.4% of its

G.D.P. on higher education. The financial assistance to universities and colleges are substantially reduced.

Attempt is made to study number of universities and enrolment of student state wise. The Education growth rate is not same for all states. The persons of 17-23 age group are considered for higher education. The enrolment of persons of 17-23 age group for higher education is very discouraging. 22.40% of the persons of Chandigarh enrolled for higher education while only 3.22% of the total persons of in the age group of 17-23 are enrolled for higher education. It clearly shows inequality pertaining to enrolment of students on state level in regard to higher education.

The student teacher ratio in higher education in regard to Rajasthan state was very high, it was about 90 while the student's teacher ratio in higher education in regard to Andaman and Nicobar is only 6.

Study is made to assess enrolment of student's faculty wise. 38% of total enrolment of students was in science faculty while the 5% of the total enrolment of students was in Commerce/ Management faculty. The enrolment of students in agriculture faculty was only 2% of the total enrolment. It is quite clear that 76% of the total enrolment of students is in arts, science and Commerce faculties.

Suggestions

1. India crossed population over 100 crores and there are about 6000 districts in India. It is necessary to provide more access for higher education. There should be one university for four districts or one university for population of 4 lakh which ever less is. Roughly total number of universities in the country should be 1500. We had only 355 universities during 2005-2006. There is need of for more enrolment of students for higher education. Roughly there should be one college for each taluka. Lot up work we have to do to achieve the target.

2. The percentage of post graduate student in total enrolment is only 9.42% while percentage of research students in total

enrolment of higher education is only 0.64% percent. It is necessary to encourage students for post graduation and research work. Infrastructure facilities should be enhanced, at least all universities should be well equipped to satisfy need of research work. Internet facilities, books, periodicals should be available at every university. All reputed periodicals should be available at every university. All the abstract of the thesis should be available in every university. This will useful to avoid same type of research work. Students will get guideline to select topic for their research work.

3. In order to provide equality, it is essential to provide equal access to all students in the age group of 17 to 23. The percentage of S.C. students in total enrolment of higher education is only 11.66%, the percentage of S.T. was 4.10 percent during 2002-2003* was only 30% Urgent steps are essential to raise the percentage of the categories mentioned above.

Scholar students of all castes should be provided with hostel facilities and standard meal at subsidised rates. The cost of education should be low, so that it is possible for students to enroll their names for higher education. At the same time the students who availed facilities, should pay 10% of their salary to government exchequer in order to reduce the finical burden of the government, for four years only.

4. The percentage of students in age group of 17 to 23 is low in regard to higher education. The story does not end here. The students take admission but not appearing for examination during 1991, 71.3% of the total students who enrolled their name appeared for examination. The pass out percentage of these students is 13.1% during 1991, while the percentage of students appeared for examination during 2006 was 76.3% of the total enrolment for higher education. The percentage of pass out students during 2006 was 34%. All above facts show the critical position of higher education in India. Examination reform is essential. It is necessary to improve the situation. Appointment of eligible staff is urgent and need to improve the situation.

The percentage of female student enrolment during 2002-2003.

It is very necessary to take proper steps to provide books

before implementation of syllabus. The examination method should be explained properly, by teachers to the students. Teacher should arrange examination at the end of each chapter. This is effective step to reduce the fear of examination among the minds of students.

Teacher should conduct seminars and group discussion in relation to the subject allotted to them. These steps are useful to improve the result. Model answer paper should be provided to persons who have to do the work of assessment.

5. The drop out rate is high. It is observed that, the enrolment of students at the start of the programme and registered in final year exam is a matter of grave concern. In Art faculty only 30.7% of the total students enrolment reaches for final examination. This is matter of grave concern and the pass out result of these students is only 11.9%. In regard to commerce faculty, only 17.9% of the total enrolment at the beginning appeared for final examination and result is 17.9% only. The same story is repeated in science faculty, only 14.6% of the total enrolment at beginning reached to examination of final year and pass out rate is only 16.6%.

6. Adequate finance is essential to run education system properly. Government of India was spending 7.92% of the total expenditure on education in 19950-51, the percentage of expenditure on education in total expenditure has been gradually on increasing scale, however amount allotted for education is not satisfactory.

In terms of G.D.P., Government of India was spending 0.64 percent of its G.D.P. on education while this share rose to 4.3% up to 2000-2001. The expenditure on higher education is meager. Even poor African countries spend about 6% of their G.D.P. on education.

7. The share of higher education in terms of G.D.P. was 1% of the total G.D.P. during 1971 it has been gradually declined to 0.4 percent during 2001. The picture is not satisfactory. Share of G.D.P. on higher education should be enhanced. This is in fact long term investment. It is necessary to improve the infrastructure of education system.

8. On state level, there is inequality in regard to the availabilities of universities and colleges. One college for every taluka is essential. There must be one university at least for four districts or one university for the population of four lakh persons.

9. The percentage of students in Arts, Science and Commerce/ Management in total enrolment is 76%. This is time to think over this issue. The graduates and post graduates are not getting jobs. They are in frustration after getting their degree. This discourages the enthusiasm among our youths. The person has power to satisfy the needs of family but due to unemployment, he has to depend on his family. He has to adjust with employer. He has to accept all conditions lay down by employer. This is nothing but failure of our education system.

The education must have power to satisfy the need of degree holder. In our higher education system such power is not there in degree. In order to avoid this situation at least Arts, Science and Commerce student should be trained in one skill which can surely provided gainful employment. Government has to provide adequate funds to colleges and universities to provide skill formation in education to all the students of Arts, Science and Commerce faculties.

10. It is very essential to adopt Manpower planning in order to avoid disappointment among our youths. One higher power committee should be constituted at Taluka level to consider the available sources, required goods by people, and skilled manpower to provide essential goods to the needy persons. Committee should consider require number of services at taluka level.

The decision should be taken on district level in consultation with college management all college principals. Required education should be given to the students. On National level high power committee will take survey of foreign countries. The foreign goods and services should be provided to these countries, by students who acquired higher education.

Table 1
Status of Higher Education in India

Institution / Year	*1950-51*	*1990-91*	*2005-2006*
Universities	27(100)	184 (6.81)	355 (1314)
Colleges	578 (100)	6627 (1146)	18064 (3125)
Enrolment	2,63,00(100)	49,25,000 (1872)	1,1028,000(4193)
Teachers	24,000(100)	2,72700 (1136)	48800(203)

Source: - U.G.C. Annual report, MHRD and Report of CABE - 2005-2006.
* Figures in brackets show the index and are derived.

Table 2
Stage wise Student's Enrolment (2005-2006)

Stage wise Enrolment	*Universities*	*Affiliated College*	*Total (%to total)*	*% in Affiliated College*
Graduate	950892	8854085	9804977 (88.91%)	90.30
Post graduate	347096	691714	1038810 (9.42%)	66.58%
Research	64161	6555	70716(0.64%)	9.27%
Diploma / Certificate	646144	48873	113517 (1.03%)	43.05%
Total	1426793	9001227	11028020 (100%)	87.06%

Source: U.G.C. Report, 2005-2006 (Excluding open distance learning)

Education policy should be employment oriented.

It is not to make unemployed technicians, Engineers, Doctors and graduates and post Graduates of other faculties. It is necessary to accept such education policy which assures sure job to the degree holders.

11. Government is not in position to provide more funds. It is not among to allow private persons to invest in education and provide adequate education to the needy person. Norms and fees structure, infrastructure facilities should be as per rule laid down for this purpose.

Table 3
Distribution of Year-wise Enrolment on the basis of Demographic Variable (in %)

Year	*SC*	*ST*	*General and OBC*	*Male*	*Female*	*Rural*	*Urban*
1986-87	0.53	0.49	98.98	93.58	6.42		
1987-88	7.53	1.72	90.75	87.72	12.28		
1988-89	8.63	3.01	88.36	76.92	23.08		
1989-90	7.51	3.03	89.46	77.34	22.66		
1990-91	6.78	2.73	90.49	80.28	19.72	23.0	77
1991-92	0.00	0.00	0.00	75.09	24.91	38.40	61.50
1992-93	5.20	3.10	91.00	73.70	26.30	20.90	79.10
1993-94	4.72	2.34	92.94	77.54	22.46	22.90	77
1994-95	4.16	2.14	93.73	77.75	22.25	18.80	77
1995-96	3.88	1.57	94.65	78.00	22.00	8.68	91.32
1996-97	5.32	1.69	92.99	77.18	22.82	16.48	83.52
1997-98	4.18	3.03	92.79	71.52	28.48	17.90	82.10
1998-99	8.22	2.21	89.51	73.56	26.44	17.83	79.82
1999-2000	4.43	4.46	93.11	73.10	26.90	21.30	78.70
2000-01	4.66	2.52	92.82	71.76	28.24	22.69	77.31
2001-02	11.66	4.13	84.24	70.24	29.76	25.88	74.12
2002-03	10.88	4.10	85.02	70	30.00	25.42	74.58

Source: *University News*, 46 (03), January 21-27, 2008.

12. Government has to encourage research oriented education by providing more funds for research work.

13. India has potentials to develop with high speed, people are brilliant and ready to take hard efforts for development of the Nation. Lack of proper guidance is main problem in our education system.

Table 4
Government Expenditure on Education

Year	*% of expenditure to total expenditure*	*% expenditure on education to G.D.P.*
1950-51	7.92	0.64
1955-56	10.65	1.15
1960-61	11.19	1.48
1965-66	9.28	1.69
1970-71	10.16	2.11
1975-76	10.30	2.44
1980-81	10.67	2.18
1985-86	12.99	3.49
1990-91	13.37	3.48
1995-96	13.34	3.58
2000-01	14.42	4.30
2001-02	13.17	4.02

20* *University News*, 46 (03), January 21-27, 2008.

14. We have to compete on global level, our syllabus must be of international standard. The degree holder should get access to earn money in the economy. This will enhance the confidence among students. India will become super power financially, the need is of suitable education policy.

15. Hard efforts are essential to avoid unemployment among, persons with higher education. The unemployment means, loss of wealth of our nation.

Government has to take all necessary steps to avoid unemployment among educated youth. Youths are assets of the country, there talent must be utilized to enhance growth rate of the economy.

Table 5
Number of Students Enrolled, Appeared and pass out in terms of End Examinations

(Year wise)

Year	*Students enrolled in numbers*	*Students appeared in exam in numbers*	*Students appeared in Exam in %*	*Pass out students in Nos.*	*Pass out students in %*
1991	52376	37342	71.3	4907	13.1
1992	62375	69189	110.9	4444	6.4
1993	75666	70953	93.8	7580	10.7
1994	84180	81808	97.2	9246	11.3
1995	91398	99258	108.6	12301	12.4
1996	130228	156845	120.4	16150	10.3
1997	162540	221091	136.0	25196	11.4
1998	163394	261078	159.8	33119	12.7
1999	172550	319004	184.9	53298	16.7
2000	196650	370187	188.2	62369	16.8
2001	291360	507395	174.1	77846	1534
2002	288734	508541	176.1	81931	16.1
2003	316547	527283	166.6	76603	14.1
2004	334315	510804	152.8	71298	14.1
2005	366167	522133	153.6	74174	13.2
2006	429542	327640	76.3	111679	34.1

Source: *University News*, 46, (03), January 21-17, 2008.

Table 6
Level-wise Share of Education Expenditure in G.D.P

Year	*% of G.D.P. for Primary*	*Secondary*	*Higher*
1981-82	1.09	0.81	0.38
1985-86	1.39	0.92	0.42
1990-91	1.58	1.10	0.36
1995-96	1.44	0.98	0.37
1999-2000	1.58	0.94	0.47
2001-2002	**1.66**	**0.98**	**0.43**

Source: Gaeta Rani.

Table 7
Funding the Higher Education in terms of G.D.P. in Some Selected Countries

S. No.	*Country*	*% of G.D.P.*
1	U.S.A.	6.5
2	France	5.8
3	Germany	4.6
4	Thailand	5.0
5	Kenya	6.2

Source: University News, Vol. 44 No 33, August. 14-20, 2006.

Table 8
Financial Support for Indian Higher Education in terms of G.D.P.

S. No.	*Year*	*Percentage*
1	1971	1.00
2	1981	0.8
3	1991	0.6
4	2001	0.4

Source: Raj Shekhar Pillai, Statement in *The Hindu*, Delhi, March 21, 2006.

Table 9

State-wise Data on Higher Education

States	*Population*	*No. of Colleges' 1999-2000*	*No. of Universities + Deemed Universities#*	*Population (17-23) 1991*	*Population (17-23) 2001 Projected*	*Higher Education Enrolment*	*% age of 17-23 age group*
Andhra Pradesh	75727541	1353	20+4	8620073	9913083	580301	5.85
Arunachal Pradesh	1091117	8	1 -	104450	120117	4374	3.64
Assam	26638407	340	6	2931334	3371034	200346	5.94
Bihar	82878796	823	17+1	9734023	11194126	688095	6.15
Delhi	13782976	110	11+8	1345249	1547036	267798	17.31
Goa	1343998	43	1	184505	212180	16226	7.65
Gujarat	50596992	530	11+2	5702670	6558070	398671	6.08
Haryana	21082989	222	5+2	2193826	2522899	166750	6.61
Himachal Pradesh	6077248	82	3	695830	800204	75268	9.41
Jammu & Kashmir	10069917	72	3	--	--	48226	--
Karnataka	52733958	1354	16+4	5972584	6868471	929617	13.53
Kerala	31838619	342	8	4351646	5004392	263568	5.27

Madhya Pradesh	60385118	827	17+2	8162869	9387299	302274	3.22
Maharashtra	96752247	1731	27+11	10263316	11802813	944114	8.00
Manipur	2388634	65	2	259306	298201	27641	9.27
Meghalaya	2306069	47	1	218750	251562	14862	5.91
Mizoram	891058	30	0	95662	110011	8132	7.39
Nagaland	1988636	35	1	175079	201340	7502	3.73
Orissa	36706920	645	5	3777370	4343975	160707	3.70
Punjab	24289296	285	6+1	2785514	3203341	185672	5.80
Rajasthan	56473122	363	10+4	4359503	5013428	225873	4.51
Sikkim	540493	6	1	57170	65745	2212	3.36
Tamil Nadu	62110839	713	22+8	7823340	8995691	414176	4.60
Tripura	3191168	21	1	348749	401061	19273	4.81
Uttar Pradesh	166052859	1291	28+6	12471225	14341908	1170710	8.16
West Bengal	80221171	436	14+1	7713789	8870835	569666	6.42
Andaman & Nicobar	356265	4	0	39248	45135	1869	4.14
Chandigarh	20795956	28	2	94543	108724	24354	22.40

(contd.)

Table 9 *(Contd.)*
State-wise Data on Higher Education

States	*Population*	*No. of Colleges* 1999-2000*	*No. of Universities + Deemed Universities#*	*Population (17-23) 1991*	*Population (17-23) 2001 Projected*	*Higher Education Enrolment*	*% age of 17-23 age group*
Dadra & Nagar	220451	–	0	18610	21401	0	0.00
Daman & Diu	158059	2	0	15386	17693	670	3.79
Lakshadweep	60595	–	0	6937	7977	0	0.00
Pondicherry	973829	23	1	108014	124216	11853	9.54
Chhattisgarh	20795956	–	–	–	–	–	–
Jharkhand	26909428	–	–	–	–	–	–
Uttaranchal	8479562	–	–	–	–	–	–

Source: UGC Annual Report 1999-2000, #WWW.Education.nic.in. * Ministry of Education, Annual Report 2000-2001

Table 10
State / Sex-wise Number of Teachers, Enrolment and Student Teacher Ratio.

States / UTS	Number of Teacher	Enrolment			Student Teachers Ratio	In higher education institute % of boys in total % & girls in total %		
		Boys	Girls	Total	19	Boys	Girls	Total
Andhra Pradesh	39551	480780	288897	(100) 769677	24	(62.47)	(37.53)	100
Arunachal Pradesh	274	4556	2099	(100) 6655	18	(68.46)	(31.54)	100
Assam	13357	145803	96948	(100) 245751	20	(59.33)	(40.67)	100
Bihar	27537	375856	184493	(100) 560349	32	(67.08)	(32.92)	100
Chhattisgarh	4676	96503	54092	(100) 150595	12	(64.08)	(35.92)	100
Goa	1549	8056	11021	(100) 19077	36	(42.23)	(57.77)	100
Gujarat	15025	298270	239463	(100) 537733	26	(55.47)	(44.53)	100
Haryana	9391	146758	100508	(100) 247266	27	(59.35)	(40.65)	100
Himachal Pradesh	3281	()51422	38292	(100) 89714	15	(54.04)	(42.68)	100
Jammu & Kashmir	3958	31472	26769	(100) 58241	26	(63.40)	(45.96)	100
Jharkhand	8217	137240	79236	(100) 216476	11	(60.36)	(36.60)	100

(contd.)

Table 10 *(contd.)*

State / Sex-wise Number of Teachers, Enrolment and Student Teacher Ratio.

States / UTS	*Number of Teacher*	*Enrolment*			*Student Teachers Ratio*	*In higher education institute % of boys in total % & girls in total %*		
		Boys	*Girls*	*Total*	*19*	*Boys*	*Girls*	*Total*
Karnataka	48073	328556	215799	(100) 544355	13	(41.33)	(49.64)	100
Kerala	19305	101226	143720	(100) 244946	30	(62.94)	(58.67)	100
Madhya Pradesh	15663	297166	175007	(100) 472173	23	(59.48)	(67.06)	100
Maharashtra	53654	738905	503366	(100)1242271	9	(56.70)	(40.52)	100
Manipur	3973	20161	15399	(100) 35560	9	(53.76)	(42.30)	100
Meghalaya	3003	15075	12966	(100) 28041	22	(56.64)	(46.24)	100
Mizoram	467	5928	4538	(100) 10466	12	(61.80)	(43.36)	100
Nagaland	1000	7515	4645	(100) 12160	17	(65.03)	(38.20)	100
Orissa	19534	221608	119188	(100) 340796	22	(48.19)	(34.97)	100
Punjab	10750	115031	123694	(100) 238725	40	(62.50)	(51.81)	100
Rajasthan	12706	320489	192315	(100) 512804	90	(57.89)	(37.50)	100

Sikkim	47	2457	1787	(100)	4244	14	(56.21)	(42.11)	100
Tamil Nadu	47833	389532	303420	(100)	692952	24	(59.00)	(43.79)	100
Tripura	859	12014	8349	(100)	20363	41	(61.34)	(41.00)	100
Uttar Pradesh	28801	724335	446093	(100)	1170428	38	(61.34)	(38.66)	100
Uttaranchal	3206	73903	46575	(100)	120478	30	(62.93)	(38.66)	100
West Bengal	23191	436757	257304	(100)	694061	8	(51.00)	(37.07)	100
Andaman & Nicobar	285	1222	1174	(100)	2396	6	(43.32)	(49.00)	100
Chandigarh	5394	14049	18383	(100)	32432	14	(53.25)	(46.75)	100
Daman & Diu	43	311	273	(100)	584	17	(51.74)	(48.26)	100
Delhi	10724	92658	86422	(100)	179080	20	(51.21)	(48.79)	100
Pondicherry	925	9691	9233	(100)	18924	22	(59.95)	(40.05)	100
India	436243	5705305	3811468	(100)	9516773			3811468	100

Source: Department of Secondary and Higher Education, Ministry of Human Resource Development Govt. of India.

Notes: Percentage to the total students is shown in parentheses

REFERENCES

1. Council to Prime Minister Convocation Address, The twenty fourth annual convocation of Mangalore University. *University News*, 44(20) May 15-21, 2006, p. 22.

2. In house monitoring for Academic Audit in College. Yoginder Verma. *University News* 44(20), May 15-21, 2006, p. 8.

3. Higher Education in India and emerging tends Mukeshkumar, *University News* 42 (15), April 12-18, 2004, p. 10.

4. Challenges Ahead, University News, 42 (16), April 19, 25 2004, p. 3.

5. Impact of Globalisation on UGC regulated CHB Teacher appointment in higher Education Institutions. A perception study. Snehal S. Donde, *University News*, 46 (1) March 17-23, 2008.

6. Management of Universities in India, Major Challenges and required Responses. Surendra Singh, *University News* 43 (33), August 15-21, 2005 p. 3.

7. For profit provision of Higher education. Mohandra Sodha, *University News*, 46 (01 January 7-13, 2008 p. 12.

8. Reforming and Restrucring India Higher education, *University News*, 46 (19), May 12-18, 2008 p. 20.

9. Vocational Education and training prepares for the job of Tomorrow, Gitika S. Johry, *University News*, 46 (20) May 19-25, 2008, p. 18.

10. Moderation of Evaluation in higher education, Baldev Singh, *University News*, 44, (03), Jan 16-22, 2006.

11. Commerce curriculum in higher education. A need based Approach, M.R. Patil, *University News*, 41 (49), December 8-14, 2003.

12. Qualitative improvement in higher education, Sunil Behari Mohanty, *University News*, 41 (48), December 1-7, 2003, p. 7.

13. College education, Teachers, students and NAAC, P.B. Patil, *University News*, 41 (20) May 19-25, 2003, p. 6.

14. Quality Imperatives in Higher education, M. Aruchami, *University News* 42 (05), February, 2-8, 2004, p. 1.

15. Higher education for ensuring empowerment, By S.C. Jamir, *University News*, 44(01), January 9-15, 2006.

4

DEVELOPMENT OF HIGHER EDUCATION IN INDIA: A GENDER PERSPECTIVE

D. Pulla Rao, P. Raj Kumar** & A. Vamsi Krushna****

Introduction

Higher education is the pinnacle of educational system in any country at any period of time. In India, higher education has been an integral part of educational system. The importance of higher education has been pointed out by the International Commission on Education for 21st Century: "Higher education is at one and the same time one of the driving forces of economic development and the focal point of learning in a society. It is both repository and creator of knowledge. Moreover, it is the principal instrument for passing on the accumulated experience, cultural and scientific, of humanity". In developing societies, higher education is considered a speedy vehicle for upward social mobility, especially by the socially and economically deprived and underprivileged sectors.

Education of girls has been high on both national and state agendas. Special commissions and committees were set up from time to time to assess the progress of girls' education and to

---

* Professor, Department of Economics, Andhra University, Visakhapatnam, A.P.

** & *** Research Scholars, Department of Economics, Andhra University, Visakhapatnam, A.P.

propose suitable interventions to promote their educational participation. Several strategies were adopted to promote education of girls as an integral part of the planned socio-economic development of the country. The removal of women's illiteracy and obstacles inhibiting their access to, and retention in primary education will receive overriding priority, through provision of special support services, setting of time targets, and effective monitoring.

In ancient India women enjoyed a high status in the society. They were provided educational opportunities comparable to men. The social evils like purdah, sati, enforced widowhood and child-marriage crept into the society much later and resulted in the degradation of their status. There were no institutions for education of girls during Muslim period, but girls did receive religious education in the recitation of the Quran in their homes.

Under the British rule, the East India Company was reluctant to take up the responsibility of girl's education for a long time, due to the doctrine of religious neutrality, which was adopted by the Government so as not to offend the natives even on social customs that had nothing to do with religion. The Indian Education Commission (1882) took a serious note of the status and education of women and rated it to be extremely backward and recommended measures for improvement. But, because of certain socio-political reasons, no noticeable progress could be made.

After Independence, the government of India had set up the University Education Commission in 1948-49. It had laid special emphasis on the education of women and recommended that in view of the similar fields of activity for men and women, and also due to specific requirements of women, greater facilities should be given for women in Home Economics and Home Management studies.

During the post-independence period, the main strategy adopted to achieve equalization of educational opportunities has been to make school accessible to every child. It was thought that expansion of educational facilities, as a part of providing universal elementary education for all would make education available to the weaker sections of the society including women.

Gender inequality has become one of the major areas of concern for educationists and policy makers in the developing countries in the 21st century. Gender inequality in India stems from two important sources of differences between men and women i.e. (1) earning capacity that make women utterly dependent upon men and (2) cultural taboos and traditions that greatly restrict the autonomy of women. Biological differentiation has perpetuated a structure, which has deprived women of normalcy of life chances as available to men.

As long as Indian society remains male dominated, the constitutional provisions for legal equality of women with men matters very little. Perhaps, in no area are the laws so openly and widely violated as in the case of women, whether it is a question of education, health, and securing employment or equal wages for equal work. The prevailing mindset of the people of the society is primarily responsible for the gender inequalities, which force women to be submissive. This calls for special empowerment of women in the field of higher education.

Objectives

This paper addresses itself to assess the present status of women in higher education in India and to examine the alternatives for their higher participation particularly in professional studies.

The specific objectives are:

1. To estimate the growth of educational institutions in India from 1950-51 to 2001-02.
2. To estimate the growth of enrollment of females in primary, upper primary, secondary and higher education in India for the last five decades.
3. To estimate the growth of institution in higher education during the period of the study.
4. To estimate the state-wise percentage of female enrollment in higher education in India during the year 2001-02, and
5. To analyze the faculty-wise enrollment of females in higher education during the year 2001-02.

The Data

The secondary data relating to the growth of educational institutions, female enrollment in higher education, growth of universities and colleges, state-wise enrollment of women and faculty-wise female enrollment in India are obtained from the UGC Annual reports, Universities Hand Books, Selected educational statistics ana Ministry of HRD, Government of India, Annual reports.

Growth of Educational Institutions

After Independence, the government took serious steps to establish a large number of primary, upper primary, higher secondary, colleges for general education, colleges for professional education and universities in the country. Table - 1 provides data on the number of recognized educational institutions in the country between 1950-51 to 2001-02.

Table 1: Growth of Recognized Educational Institutions from 1950-51 to 2001-02

Year	*Primary*	*Upper Primary*	*High/Hr. Sec/Inter Pre.Jr. Colleges*	*Colleges for General Education*	*Colleges for Professional Education (Engg., Tech., Arch., Medical & Education Colleges)*	*Universities/ Deemed Univ./ Instt. of National Importance*
1	*2*	*3*	*4*	*5*	*6*	*7*
1950-51	209671	13596	7416	370	208	27
2001-02	664041	219626	133492	8737	2409	272
Growth	316.7	1615.4	1800.1	2361.4	1158.2	1007.0

Source: (www.education.nic.in)

During the last five decades the establishment of educational institutions increased in primary, upper primary, higher /high secondary, colleges for general education, colleges for professional education and universities/deemed universities from 209671 to 664041, from 13596 to 219626, from 7416 to 133492, from 370 to 8737, from 208 to 2409 and from 27 to 272 respectively. The growth rates are calculated for the periods 1950-51 to 2001-02. The rates are 316.7 for primary, 1615.4 for upper primary, 1800.1 for high / high secondary, 2361.4 for colleges for general education, 1158.2 for colleges for professional education and 1007 for universities/deemed universities.

Percentage Share of Female Enrolment of Total

After Independence, the government of India has designed several strategies for promotion of girls/women education. Separate institutions for girls/women education were opened. Special incentives to attract the girls/women into the academic institutions were introduced. As a result, the female literacy rate has gone up from 7.93 per cent in 1951 to 54.16 per cent by 2001. In the field of higher education also the share of female's enrollment into various faculties has increased very substantially. The increase in women enrollment in the educational institutions has its impact on the women employment in educational institutions.

Let us now examine the progress of females' enrollment in primary, upper primary, secondary/high secondary and higher education stages. As shown in Table – 2 in 1950-51, the enrollment of girls was 28.1 per cent at primary school stage, 16.1 per cent at the upper primary stage, 13.3 per cent at secondary/higher secondary level and 10.0 per cent in higher education level compared with the corresponding percentage of 71.9, 83.9, 86.7 and 90.0 per cent among boys/men.

By 2000-01, the situation has considerably improved at all levels, in favour of females to 43.7 per cent at primary level, 40.9 per cent at upper primary level, 38.6 per cent in at secondary/ higher secondary level and 36.9 per cent in higher education as against 56.3 per cent in primary stage, 59.1 per cent in upper primary stage, 61.4 per cent in secondary/higher secondary level and 63.1 per cent in higher education stage among boys/ men.

Career counseling is being actively promoted to ensure that the skills acquired by girls and they appropriately utilize women. These positive initiatives have helped in improving the participation of girls/women at all levels of education especially in higher education since the post-independent period. It is evident that the enrollment of girls/ women has increased at a faster rate than that of boys at primary, upper primary, secondary / higher secondary and higher education stage. The foregoing analysis shows that during the whole period of five decades after implementation of our constitution, the growth rate of enrollment of girls/women in all stages of education has been higher than that of boys/men.

Table 2: Percentage of Girls' Enrolment of the Total Enrolment by Stages

Year	*Primary I-V*	*Upper Primary VI-VIII 10+2/ Intermediate*	*Secondary Sr. Secondary Education*	*Higher Education (Degree and above)*
1	2	3	4	5
1950-51	28.1	16.1	13.3	10.0
1955-56	30.5	20.8	15.4	14.6
1960-61	32.6	23.9	20.5	16.0
1965-66	36.2	26.7	22.0	20.4
1970-71	37.4	29.3	25.0	20.0
1975-76	38.1	31.3	26.9	23.2
1980-81	38.6	32.9	29.6	26.7
1985-86	40.3	35.6	30.3	33.0
1990-91	41.5	36.7	32.9	33.3
1995-96	43.1	39.5	36.1	37.2
2000-2001	43.7	40.9	38.6	36.9

Source: Selected Educational Statistics 2000-2001.

Growth of Universities and Colleges

After independence, the growth of higher education was rapid. Central and state governments had taken intensive measures and established many universities and colleges. As a result, various kinds of institutions of higher education came into existence. Institutions of higher learning in Technology, Medicine, Agriculture, Electronics and Engineering were established. During a period of three years from 1947 to 1950, 7 new universities were created raising the total number to 27. By 2002 the number of universities increased to 272. By looking at the table - 3, one would agree that there has been a commendable progress in the expansion of higher education. Taking the whole system of higher education, the Indian higher educational system is the second largest in the world, next only to the United States. The government policies and the opportunities that are created by the government for higher education have made the system very huge.

Table 3: Growth in Universities and Colleges in India

Year	*No. of Universities*	*Index*	*No. of Colleges*	*Index*
1	2	3	4	5
1950-51	27	100	695	100
1955-56	33	122	1,025	147
1960-61	47	174	1,542	222
1965-66	75	278	2,572	370
1970-71	100	370	3,604	518
1975-76	120	444	4,395	632
1980-81	144	533	4,722	679
1985-86	164	607	5,816	837
1990-91	180	667	7,346	1057
1995-96	226	837	9,252	1331
2001-02	272	1007	11146'	1604
Annual Compound Growth Rate		4.54		5.48

Sources:1. UGC Annual Reports, 1993-94, 1995-96, 1998-99, 1999-2000.
2. Ministry of Human Resource Development, Govt. of India, Annual Report, 1996-97, 2000-2001.
3. Universities Hand Book 2003.

The affiliated colleges have a very important role in higher education in India with most of the undergraduate and postgraduate teaching being done in them. The number of colleges increased from 695 in 1950-51 to 11,146 by 2001-02. The enrolment in the colleges increased from 1,74,000 to 88,21,095 between 1950-51 and 2001-02. The index of growth of universities and colleges taking 1950-51 as the base shows that the increase is not substantial as compared to the enrolment of students in universities and colleges. The index of growth of colleges is much higher than that of the index of growth of universities. The annual compound growth rate of universities and colleges during 1950-51 and 2001-02 was 4.54 per cent and 5.48 per cent respectively. As may be seen the annual compound growth rate of colleges is higher than that of universities. Table - 3 below shows the growth of higher education.

State-wise Enrolment of Women in India during 2001-2002

There is a wide variation from one state to another regarding the enrollment of women in higher education. Distribution of women enrollment shows that there has been a marginal increase of 2.19 per cent in the enrollment of women as a percentage of enrollments in all states during 2001-2002. Table - 4 shows the state-wise enrollment of women to total enrollment in higher education. There are states like Kerala with 60 per cent, Goa with 58.6 per cent and Chandigarh with 55.5 per cent women's enrollment in higher education, but there are in some states like Arunachal Pradesh with 29.7 per cent, Jharkhand with 30.5 per cent and Bihar with only 23 per cent enrollment of women in higher education. There were 18 states, which had higher enrollment of women than the national percentage of 39.84. In the remaining states, the percentage of women enrollment was less than national average. There has been a substantial increase in number of women colleges during the last decade. In 1991 number of women's colleges was 994 while it increased to 1600 in 2001. But the women enrollment was not increased in this ratio.

Table 4: State-wise Women's Enrolment in Higher Education (2001-2002)

Sl. No.	*State*	*Total Enrolment*	*Enrolment Women*	*Women Percentage*
1	2	3	4	5
1.	Andhra Pradesh	704075	275276	39.1
2.	Arunachal Pradesh	5832	1732	29.7
3.	Assam	194245	78602	40.5
4.	Bihar	479035	110178	23.0
5.	Chhattisgarh	143906	52526	36.5
6.	Delhi	166039	76046	45.8
7.	Goa	19245	11278	58.6
8.	Gujarat /Daman & Diu	488129	216241	44.3
9.	Haryana	239217	96882	40.5
10.	Himachal Pradesh	86319	36858	42.7
11.	Jammu & Kashmir	55603	26133	47.0
12.	Jharkhand	191413	58381	30.5
13.	Karnataka	537025	214272	39.9
14.	Kerala	240038	144023	60.0
15.	Madhya Pradesh	450745	166776	37.0
16.	Maharashtra	1220167	499048	40.9
17.	Manipur	35424	15705	44.3
18.	Meghalaya	27271	13063	47.9
19.	Mizoram	10345	4836	46.7
20.	Nagaland	11460	4431	38.7
21.	Orissa	341761	118249	34.6
22.	Punjab	233745	123651	52.9
23.	Rajasthan	341198	111230	32.6
24.	Sikkim	3808	1534	40.3
25.	Tamil Nadu	697343	313107	44.9
26.	Tripura	19215	7840	40.8
27.	Uttar Pradesh	1100887	422758	35.4
28.	Uttaranchal	108594	43437	40.0
29.	West Bengal	620372	243806	39.3
30.	A & N Islands	1943	1123	57.8

(contd.)

Table 4 *(contd.)*

1	2	3	4	5
31.	Chandigarh	30882	17140	55.5
32.	Daman & Diu	536	252	47.0
33.	Pondicherry	15278	8036	52.6
	TOTAL	8821095	3514450	39.84

Source: UGC Annual Report: 2001 02.

Faculty-wise Enrolment of Women

In India higher education programme is classified in terms of faculty. The enrollment of females in various faculties though increased substantially during the last five decades, it continued to be lopsided with greater enrollment in Arts (44.72%), followed by Science (39.87%), Commerce / Management (36.93%), Education (51.79%), Engineering / Technology (21.76%), Agriculture (17.29%), Veterinary Science (22.16%) and Law (20.30%). (Table – 5). The distribution of female students in various faculties reveals the fact that more than half (52 per cent) of the total enrollment was into Arts and only about 28 per cent was in the professional faculties during the year 2001-02. It is also revealed that approximately 90 per cent women were enrolled in general education consisting of Arts, Science and Commerce and only 10 per cent were enrolled in technical disciplines. This clearly shows that there is a need of an effective policy, which can balance this type of variation in women's enrollment, particularly into technical and professional fields.

Conclusions and Suggestions

Women constitute about 50 per cent in the total population in India. But, they are not given equal opportunities either in education or in employment and hence they are left far behind their male counterparts in all most all the fields of life. They are deprived in the social, economic, political and educational sectors. Lack of equal access to education deprived them equal access to the legislatives both at state level and at the central level.

Table 5: Faculty-wise Enrolment of Women in Higher Education (2001-02)

S. No	*Faculty*	*Total No. of Students*	*No. of Women students*	*Faculty wise percentage share of col. (4)*	*Col. (4) as a per cent of Col. (3)*
1	2	3	4	5	6
1	Arts	4069632	1820134	51.79	44.72
2	Science	1754110	699376	19.90	39.87
3	Commerce/Management	1575940	581993	16.56	36.93
4	Education	114678	59394	1.69	51.79
5	Engineering/Technology	605597	131792	3.75	21.76
6	Medicine	275943	123006	3.50	44.58
7	Agriculture	52833	9137	0.26	17.29
8	Veterinary Science	14270	3163	0.09	22.16
9	Law	280449	56934	1.62	20.30
10	Others	77643	29521	0.84	38.02
	Total	8821095	3514450	100.00	39.84

Source: UGC Annual Report: 2001-02,

After Independence, the government of India has designed several strategies for promotion of girls/women education. Special incentives to attract the girls/women in to the academic institutions were introduced. During the last five decades the establishment of all types of educational institutions increased in the country. The growth rate of colleges for general education during our study period (1950-51 to 2001-02) was 2361.4, the rate of growth of colleges for professional education was 1158.2 and the growth of universities and deemed universities was recorded 1007.0.

It is evident that the enrolment of girls/women has increased at a faster rate than that of boys in all the stages of education. In the field of higher education also the share of female's enrolment in to various faculties has increased very substantially. However, it is less than 40 per cent in the year 2001-02. The positive initiatives by the government have helped in improving the participation of girls/women at all levels of education especially higher education since the post-independent period. The analysis shows that the period of the study, the growth rate of enrolment of girls / women in all stages of education has been higher than that of boys / men. Central and state governments took intensive measures and established many universities and colleges. The number of universities increased from 27 to 272 and colleges from 695 to 11146 during period 1950-51 to 2001-02. The annual compound growth rate of colleges is higher than the growth rate of universities.

There is a wide variation from one state to another regarding the enrolment of women in higher education. The highest enrolment of women in higher education was recorded with 60 per cent in the state of Kerala and in the lowest was recorded with 23 per cent in the state of Bihar during the academic year 2001-02 in the country. The enrolment of females in various faculties has increased very substantially during the last five decades. The distribution of female students in various faculties' reveals that about 52 per cent of the total enrolment was in Arts, and only 28 per cent was in the professional faculties during the year 2001-02. It indicates that nearly 90 per cent women were enrolled in general education consisting of Arts, Science and Commerce. Only 10 per cent were enrolled in technical disciplines.

In the above context there is a need of rethinking about the higher education for women. There is a general agreement that the enrolment of women to higher education must be raised at least to cover their share in the total population, which is around 50 per cent. Efforts must be directed to retain the girls in primary and secondary educational levels and enable them to pursue higher studies. And again, in the field of higher education, enrolment into technical, medicine, veterinary sciences and law should be increased through special measures in favour of women.

Alternatives for Empowering Women through Professional Studies

1. More women colleges including technical institutions to be established.
2. Residential ladies hostels need to be opened in greater numbers.
3. More scholarships need to be instituted and fellowship amounts also be increased to attract the female students, and
4. Distance mode education may be widened for women.

REFERENCES

1. Chalam, K.S. (1988): *Education and weaker sections*, Inter-India Publications, New Delhi.
2. Chauhan, C.P.S. (2000): 'Contemporary issues in Higher Education', *University News*, AIU, New Delhi, December 2004.
3. Chauhan, C.P.S., (1990) *Higher Education in India: Achievements, Failures and strategies*, Ashish Publishing House, New Delhi.
4. Government of India. *National Policy on Education* (NPE), 1986 and its revised version 1992, MHRD, New Delhi, 1986 and 1992.
5. Mira Seth (2001): *Women and Development – The Indian experience*, Sage Publications, New Delhi.
6. Nurullah, S and Naik, J.P. (1943): *History of Education in India during the British period*, Macmillan & Co. Ltd., Bombay.
7. Power, K.B. (2000): 'Higher Education in the Twenty-First century', *University News*, AIU, New Delhi, December 4.
8. Sakuntala Narasimhan (1999): *Empowering women – an alternative strategy from rural India*, Sage Publications, New Delhi.
9. Sangeetha Purushothaman (1998): *The empowerment of women in India – grassroots women's networks and the state*, Sage Publications, New Delhi.
10. University Grants Commission. *Annual Reports*, 1959-60, 1993-94, 1995-96, 1998-99 and 2001-02, UGC, New Delhi.

5

THE INTRA-SECTORAL ALLOCATIONS OF EDUCATION EXPENDITURE IN ANDHRA PRADESH

M.D. Bavaiah K. Thulasi Naik** & J. Narasimha Rao****

Education is an important social sector. It plays catalytic role in socio-economic development. It is essential for the economic modernization of the societies and the potential instrument for bringing about social transformation and for making democracy a success. It is an integral part, an inescapable and an essential part of the development process itself. Education plays an important role in the physical, intellectual, scientific, moral, and spiritual development of an individual. It has become an important Lever for higher incomes, prestigious positions and access to power and position.

Education is investment in mankind. It has the highest productivity in the human capital. Investment in education is a nation's wealth in its people. It is essential to invest heavily in human resource development (education) to get a country started on the road to self-sustained growth. There is no doubt that expenditure on education is viewed as social investment in

* Professor, Department of Economics and Applied Economics, S.K. University, Anantapur, Andhra Pradesh.

** Associate Professor, Department of Economics and Applied Economics, S.K. University, Anantapur

*** Associate Professor, Department of Economics Osmania University, Hyderabad.

man that ultimately enhances the productivity of labour force. Investment in education increased the quality of people and plays a crucial and overwhelming role in the economic development of a country. Education is integrally linked with the development process. It is a long cherished belief that education is a powerful engine of economic stability[1].

The importance of education in economic and social development is well known and can hardly be overemphasized. Education plays a key role in both economic and social development. Education develops basic skills and abilities, and thereby boosts productivity. It also fosters a value-system conducive to the national development goals and preserves and promotes the cultural ethos of the State. Schultz[2] measured the contribution of education to the development of the economy of the United States of America and according to his estimate education was found to be 3.5 times more attractive than investment in physical capital. The studies by Williamson[3] and Selowsky[4] indicated a significant contribution of education to economic growth in contrast to nearly all economic studies until the first half of this century, which emphasized the importance of physical capital in acceleration the rate of economic growth.

In the fast developing technological and electronic revolution, education today has become an economic necessity more than anything else. In a developing economy too, education is the most vital resource for socio-economic development of the State.

Studies have shown exceedingly high rates of return on education investment in developing count ies as well, thus pointing out the particular importance of this form of capital formation[5].

In India, the development of human resources constitutes a central objective of all development efforts from the beginning of the planning era. The basic importance of education in promoting economic and social development has been explicitly recognized.

The significance of education was realized even during the national movement and stress was laid on the need to provide a quality of education, which was commensurate with the economic aspiration as well as social and cultural milieu of India. The resolution of National Policy of Education adopted in 1968, therefore, emphasized the need for a radical reconstruction of education system in India. The resolution stressed the need

(i) to transform the educational system so as to relate it more closely to the life of people,

(ii) to make continuous effort for expanding educational opportunities,

(iii) to make sustained efforts for raising the quality of education at all levels;

(iv) to-give a special emphasise to the development of science and technology and

(v) to promote and cultivate moral and social values[6].

As per the constitutional division of powers in India, education mainly comes under the purview of State governments.

Education is critical for economic and social development. Evidence in India and elsewhere show that women with higher levels of schooling have smaller, healthier families, and that both women and men with higher levels of education have higher levels of labour productivity. Differences in educational development between States are a major cause of variations in poverty as well as economic growth[7]. However, there is evidence that returns to schooling are constrained until some minimum level of educational coverage is reached across the population[8].

This is being the importance of education, the present paper tries to analyse the Public Expenditure on Education in Andhra Pradesh, in general, and the Intra-Sectoral Allocations of Education Expenditure in Andhra Pradesh, in particular. The data on Education Expenditure and its share in Expenditure on Social Sectors, Total Public Expenditure and Gross State Domestic Product is provided in Table - 1.

It is obvious from the Table - 1 that Education Sector has the major share in the expenditure on Social Services and it has been contributing more than 40 percent to the social services during the period of study, with some exceptions in some years.

However, its share in Social Sector Spending has declined to lower levels in 2000s from their higher levels in the early 1990s.

Table - 1: Education Expenditure as Per Cent of Expenditure on Social Services, Total Public Expenditure and Gross State Domestic Product in Andhra Pradesh

(Rupees in Crores)

Year	*Education*	*Social Services*	*Education as Per cent of Social Services*	*Total Expen-diture*	*Education as per cent of Total Expen-diture*	*Gross State Demestic Product (GSDP)*	*Education as per cent of GSDP*
1990-91	1015	2158	47.04	5967	17.01	37194	2.73
1991-92	1156	2416	47.83	6871	16.82	45225	2.56
1992-93	1358	2790	48.67	7993	16.99	49157	2.76
1993-94	1468	2999	48.95	9384	15.64	60033	2.45
1994-95	1699	3483	48.78	11436	14.86	71410	2.38
1995-96	1724	4717	36.54	13036	13.22	82674	2.08
1996-97	1999	5290	37.78	14524	13.76	93333	2.14
1997-98	2251	5551	40.56	15630	14.40	99214	2.27
1998-99	2846	7179	39.63	18329	15.52	119021	2.39
1999-2000	3317	7531	44.04	20030	16.56	129403	2.56
2000-01	3740	8317	44.97	25794	14.50	145090	2.58
2001-02	3871	8699	44.50	27817	13.92	157150	2.46
2002-03	4027	9422	42.74	29853	13.49	168143	2.40
2003-04	4668	10859	42.99	34081	13.70	190880	2.45
2004-05	4599	11257	40.85	36722	12.52	210449	2.19
2005-06	5370	12313	43.61	42577	12.61	236034	2.28
2006-07	6114	15533	39.36	51342	11.91	269173	2.27
2007-08 (RE)	8745	21589	40.51	68588	12.75	311752	2.81

Source: Government of Andhra Pradesh: Budget Documents

Further, it is evident from the table that the share of Education Expenditure in Total Public Expenditure is not only lower than 20 percent, but also it has been declining over a period of time.

Similarly, it is observed from the table that the share of Education Expenditure in Gross State Domestic Product (GSDP) is not even able to reach 3 percent, i.e., the half of the target fixed by the New Educational Policy, 1986 of India.

Intra-sectoral changes in Education Sector

The expenditure on education in this section refers to Revenue Expenditure under the budgetary head "General Education" and Revenue Expenditure under the budgetary head "Technical Education". The General Education is sub-divided into Elementary Education, Secondary Education, University and Higher Education, Adult Education, Language Development and other general education. The data relating to these sub-heads within the Education Sector is given in Table - 2 and their percentage contribution to education expenditure is shown in Table - 3.

An examination of the trends of revenue expenditure on different components of General and Technical education in Andhra Pradesh State as provided in Tables 2 and 3 inferred that between 1990-91 and 2008-09, Expenditure on Elementary Education has the lion's share followed by Expenditure on Secondary Education, Expenditure on University and Higher Education and Technical Education in that order.

Expenditure on Elementary education constitutes the bulk of expenditure on education in Andhra Pradesh and it contributed more than 40 percent throughout the period of study.

Expenditure on Secondary education constitutes the second largest component of expenditure on education in Andhra Pradesh and its contribution has been increased from 28 percent in 1990-91 to 35 percent in 2008-09.

Expenditure on University and Higher Education constitutes the third largest component of expenditure on education in Andhra Pradesh, but its contribution has been declined from 21.25 percent in 1990-91 to 14.76 percent in 2008-09. This indicates

Table-2: Composition of Revenue Expenditure on General and Technical Education in Andhra Pradesh

Year	Elementary Education	Secondary Education	University and Higher Education	Adult Education	Language Development	Technical Education	General	Total
1990-91	457.49	279.87	211.71	7.27	3.71	30.47	5.88	996.40
1991-92	501.25	331.99	244.63	7.49	4.41	32.24	6.66	1128.67
1992-93	607.95	394.28	299.98	12.35	5.00	43.64	7.73	1370.94
1993-94	655.64	418.48	313.35	12.57	5.31	50.22	220.09	1675.66
1994-95	724.07	517.71	349.29	9.96	6.51	49.72	10.01	1667.27
1995-96	724.80	538.01	351.91	3.68	6.41	66.61	11.51	1702.93
1996-97	852.65	608.13	392.35	4.30	8.72	64.40	12.99	1943.54
1997-98	943.10	657.04	457.28	22.09	7.58	63.02	12.95	2163.06
1998-99	1284.79	760.10	508.98	13.64	2.22	82.13	19.28	2671.14
1999-2000	1486.62	913.17	690.35	-1.13	10.51	85.94	18.31	3203.77
2000-01	1569.77	1103.51	855.01	11.38	13.26	86.31	21.87	3661.11
2001-02	1659.43	1110.58	765.02	23.20	14.07	87.68	21.03	3681.01
2002-03	1728.69	1219.09	784.35	11.97	13.64	122.91	33.18	3913.83
2003-04	2010.32	1350.01	870.20	11.93	13.56	103.63	33.54	4393.19
2004-05	2102.53	1313.78	848.66	11.75	13.87	142.65	37.30	4470.54
2005-06	2412.57	1540.56	928.41	12.57	14.81	160.66	50.33	5119.91
2006-07	2705.26	1808.04	1062.61	12.22	18.32	202.28	43.10	5851.83
2007-08 RE	4441.27	2281.39	1336.29	13.04	20.02	226.86	69.08	8387.95
2008-09 BE	4748.55	3682.51	1516.91	15.38	21.68	224.29	68.01	10277.33

Source: Government of Andhra Pradesh: Budget Documents

Table – 3: Percentage Composition of Revenue Expenditure on General and Technical Education in Andhra Pradesh

Year	*Elementary*	*Education Secondary*	*Education University and Higher Education*	*Adult Education*	*Language Development*	*Technical Education*	*General*	*Total*
1990-91	45.91	28.09	21.25	0.73	0.37	3.06	0.59	100.00
1991-92	44.41	29.41	21.67	0.66	0.39	2.86	0.59	100.00
1992-93	44.35	28.76	21.88	0.90	0.36	3.18	0.56	100.00
1993-94	39.13	24.97	18.70	0.75	0.32	3.00	13.13	100.00
1994-95	43.43	31.05	20.95	0.60	0.39	2.98	0.60	100.00
1995-96	42.56	31.59	20.66	0.22	0.38	3.91	0.68	100.00.
1996-97	43.87	31.29	20.19	0.22	0.45	3.31	0.67	100.00
1997-98	43.60	30.38	21.14	1.02	0.35	2.91	0.60	100.00
1998-99	48.10	28.46	19.05	0.51	0.08	3.07	0.72	100.00
1999-2000	46.40	28.50	21.55	-0.04	0.33	2.68	0.57	100.00
2000-01	42.88	30.14	23.35	0.31	0.36	2.36	0.60	100.00
2001-02	45.08	30.17	20.78	0.63	0.38	2.38	0.57	100.00
2002-03	44.17	31.15	20.04	0.31	0.35	3.14	0.85	100.00
2003-04	45.76	30.73	19.81	0.27	0.31	2.36	0.76	100.00
2004-05	47.03	29.39	18.98	0.26	0.31	3.19	0.83	100.00
2005-06	47.12	30.09	18.13	0.25	0.29	3.14	0.98	100.00
2006-07	46.23	30.90	18.16	0.21	0.31	3.46	0.74	100.00
2007-08 RE	52.95	27.20	15.93	0.16	0.24	2.70	0.82	100.00
2008-09 BE	46.20	35.83	14.76	0.15	0.21	2.18	0.66	100.00

Source: Government of Andhra Pradesh: Budget Documents

that the Government of Andhra Pradesh has been reducing its financial support to the Universities and demanding them to search for alternative sources of finance.

REFERENCES

1. Narendra Prasad (1996): "Social Sector Development", IEA, 79th Conference Volume, Gwalier, p. 277/
2. Schultz, T.W. (1961): "Investment in Human Capital", *American Economic Review*, March.
3. Williamson, J.G. (1969): "Education in Post-War Philippine Economic Progress", *Quarterly Journal of Economics*, February.
4. Solowsky, M. (1969): "On Measurement of Educational contribution to growth", *Quarterly Journal of Economics*, August, 1969.
5. Musgrave R.A. and Musgrave, P.B. (1976): *Public Finance in Theory and Practice*, Second Edition, McGraw Hill, p. 673.
6. Jamal Khan, M. (1993): *Patterns of Public Expenditure and Financing in India*, Pragathi Publications, Delhi, p. 58.
7. Datt, G and Ravallian, M. (1994): *Why have some Indian States done better than others at raising rural standards?* Policy Research Department, World Bank.
8. World Bank (1996): *India – Primary Education – Achievements and Challenges*, South Asia Department, p. 2.

6

ANDHRA PRADESH HUMAN DEVELOPMENT REPORT – A CRITICAL APPRAISAL

G. Ramachandrudu & S. Prasada Rao***

There has been a paradigm shift in the concept of measurement of socioeconomic progress of any society ever since Adam Smith proposed that the size and growth of National Income (Wealth of Nation) is the best measure. Later economists proposed a number of concepts like economic growth, economic development, human resource development, sustainable development, human development, social development and so on. The UNDP initiated a scientific analysis by calculating and ranking the countries by the concept called "Human Development Index" consisting of four critical variables, viz., literacy rate, school enrolment rate, life expectancy and per capita GNP.

According to United Nations Development Programme (UNDP), Human Development is defined as the process of enlarging people's range of choice, the most critical of these wide ranging choices are to live a long and healthy life, to be educated and to have access to resources needed for a decent standard of living. Additional choices include political freedom, guaranteed human rights and personal self-respect. The HDR focus on indicators of longevity, literacy and per capita income.

* Professor of Economics, Andhra University, Visakhapatnam.

** Research Scholar, Department of Economics, Andhra University, Visakhapatnam.

The World Bank has provided funding for preparing the state level human development reports in India. The task was entrusted to the Center for Economic and Social Studies (CESS) to prepare Andhra Pradesh Human Development Report. The most important contribution of the report is that it gives HDI, HPI, GDI and GEMI for the districts of Andhra Pradesh. The HDI does not reflect any new dimensions except that it reflects economic situation. The components of HDI show that there is no correlation between income and health/education for some of the districts. The rank in terms of per capita income is much higher than the rank for education and health for three districts viz, Visakhapatnam, Medak and Khammam. On the other hand, the rank for education is higher than for per capita income in West Godavari, Krishna, Nellore, Chittoor, Kadapa and Nalgonda. Similarly, the rank for health is higher than the rank for income in Krishna, Guntur, Kadapa, Nizamabad and Karimnagar, it is clear that apart from looking at aggregate HDI the components of the index have to be examined in order to have more effective policies. Social scientists have now realized that economic growth or development has no significance where majority of the poor and socially disadvantaged sections are excluded from its process and produce. The Eleventh Five - Year Plan rightly stressed the need for policies for inclusive growth. Therefore, there is a need for developing Inclusive Growth Index (IGI) consisting of the participation of socially disadvantaged groups in various political, social and economic activities for each district or mandal, so that the plans grants are allocated to those District or mandals with lower Inclusive Growth Index.

A Brief Note on A.P. Human Development Report

- This report throws light on the Human Development Indicators and it encompasses Human Development Indices, computed both for State and Districts as well.
- The purpose of the Report is to provide an independent and objective assessment of the status of human development.
- The State Government had entrusted this massive academic

exercise to the Centre for Economic and Social Studies (CESS). The CESS has brought out a good report with valuable information, which will be helpful in Development.

- It focuses on the levels of achievement, the areas of concern and the possible ways of progress with reference to crucial socio-economic indicators.
- It helps in identifying strengths and gaps and making suggestion for relevant policy measures to address the emerging areas of concern.

Important Features of the Report

- Human Development Index (HDI), Gender Development Index (GDI) and Gender Empowerment Indices (GEM) across districts are constructed.
- The report notices that there has been a significant improvement in the state in terms of human development over time and inter-district disparities in GDI are reducing gradually.
- For sustaining these trends, the report suggests that the state needs to invest in infrastructure and improve the quantity and quality of the social sector.
- The performance of the state in terms of improvements in education (both literacy and schooling) is one of the best among the Indian states. The trends indicate that the state is nearing the universal school attendance very soon.
- Women in Andhra Pradesh are better placed when compared to All India situation in terms of gender disparity. The participation of women in public sphere has improved the functioning of the public institutions delivering the child services and reduced the discriminatory practices against women and children.
- On the whole, the progress of the state in human development is impressive over a period of time. There

are strong social, economic and political reasons for raising human development following inclusive growth approach.

Uniqueness of Andhra Pradesh

- Host of several social movements
- Forerunner of Green Revolution
- Uniqueness in participatory institutions (water user, JFM, Self Help Groups etc)
- Achievements in higher education (technical: engineering and medicine, IT)
- Known for innovative poverty alleviation programmes ('Two Rupees a kilo scheme, women's empowerment through SHGs, Indira Kranti Padham)
- Initiatives of the present government INDIRAMMA, pensions, housing, land distribution, irrigation
- Distinctiveness in demographic changes - AP is one of the states with lowest growth rate of population and TFR - Total Fertility Rate
- Emergence of good NGOs
- Forefront in economic reforms.

Social Indicators District-wise in Andhra Pradesh

1. The literacy rate of Andhra Pradesh is still lower (60.5) than all India literacy rate (65), while the overall literacy rate in Andhra Pradesh has gone up from 44 per cent in 1991 to 61 per cent in 2001. The male literacy rate has increased from 55 to 70 per cent whereas the female literacy rate has increased from 33 to 51 per cent.

2. Across the districts in Andhra Pradesh the higher literacy rate is registered in Hyderabad (78.8) and it is very low in Mahaboobnagar district (44.4). However the same trend is revealed among the Social Disadvantaged groups in Andhra Pradesh. The SC and ST literacy rate is very high in Hyderabad

(69.4% and 55.4) and they are very low in Mahaboobnagar (32.6% and 25.8%).

3. The fertility rate is registered as high as in Medak (2.9) and it is very low in Krishna, Guntur,
4. The Ranking of Income, Education, and health, the three dimensions of human development across the districts of Andhra Pradesh revealed that, Visakhapatnam district has registered 1st rank in Income and Vizianagaram district has recorded Very least rank in income (23) and also health (23). Similarly the rank of education and health was first place in Hyderabad district, whereas the last place got Mahabubnagar district (23) in Education.
5. As per the National Human Development Report 2001 Andhra Pradesh has improved position that is 10 in across the states in India. The Value and rank of HDI, HPI and GDI of the district wise in Andhra Pradesh revealed that 11 districts had lower levels of Human Development Index (HDI) as compared to the state index value of the state (0.537). Out of these, 5 districts in Telangana region (Warangal, Nizamabad, Adilabad, Nalgonda, and Mahabubnagar. Three from Rayalaseema (Kadapa. Kurnool, Anantapur) and three in Kosta Andhra region (Srikakulam, Vizianagaram, and Prakasam).
6. Among the districts in Andhra Pradesh, the Hyderabad district has first rank in HDI (0.717) and it is very low in Mahabubnagar district (0.397).
7. On the basis of HPI, there are three districts most backward districts in Andhra Pradesh namely Mahabubnagar (0.592), Vizianagaram (0.597) and Srikakulam (0.566).
8. The gender development index (GDI) is the third important index in the series used the by the UNDP; it takes into account the inequalities in achievement between women and men. The GDI Rank is in first place in Krishna District and it is very low in Mahabubnagar district.

7

EDUCATION AS REVENUE OF ECONOMIC GROWTH

S.V. Lakshmana Rao & P. Easwara Rao***

Introduction

In any society its educational system should be geared to changing goals. It should serve as an instrument for social welfare as well as a tool for the economic development of the nation as a whole. In all countries of the world the education system has come to be closely related to the economic order. Education helps in training in an economic change. In China and Malaysia and other countries it was the student's power established as a result of the education which through the political change followed by the change in economic order. In 1776, Adam Smith, in his book Wealth of nations, referred education as an investment in human resource.

In 1960, education be defined as "consumption" or "investment" was debated by Schultz in presidential address to the American Economic Association. As a result of it four different components have emerged in accordance with which the benefits of education can be sub divided i.e. Education for current consumption, education for long period future consumption, education as an intermediate good and capital in education. The economists have different opinions regarding relative importance of each one of these categories.

* &**Research Scholars, Department of Education, Andhra University, Visakhapatnam, Andhra Pradesh.

Education is a strong means of human resource development. In actual practice development is a multi dimensional concept. Economic development will follow the HRD which we can attain through education. The basic assumption in relation to education and economic growth is the potentiality of education to contribute to the national economy.

Economics of Education

The birth of Economics of Education took place in 1960 from the presidential address of T.W. Schultz to the annual meeting of the American Economic Association. Adam Smith has recognized the importance of education and the labour power in the creation of wealth in his opening sentence of the wealth of nations.

Education Economists analyze both what determines or creates education and what impact education has on individuals and the society and economics in which they live. Historically at the World Bank a great deal of emphasis has been placed on determining outcomes to educational investment and the creation of human capital. The primary mission of the economics of education group is to identify opportunities for improved efficiency, equity and quality of education and promote effective education reform processes; to help improve among both World Bank staff and clients. Knowledge of what drives education outcomes and results; to better understanding how to strengthen the links of education systems with the labour market, and to build and support a network of education economists and build bridges to all those who are interested in their work.

In this concern we can say that there is a strong relation between Education and Socio-Economic Development. This paper discusses about how the education acts as a powerful means of Economic Growth.

The size of the educational economy in the total economy of the country becomes large and large as the country moves from the underdeveloped to the advances status through developing and partially advanced status. Education indeed is a 'Growth industry' an industry that promotes and acts as a condition and an agent for change, growth and development.

Education as a part of the total economy of a country has higher importance than any other sector of economy. It provides employment and produces services (non-material goods) required for the total economy. It contributes to the gross national product of a country also increases. It has been provide that investment in (allocation of more resources to) education as vital effect on the economic growth of a country.

To the most casual observer it must seem that there is a link between scientific advance and the way in which education has facilitated the development of knowledge. Education is needed for people to benefit from scientific advance as well as to contribute to it.

Perceptions of Economists

Economists have established the fact that education affects economic growth of a country. Education influences the economy of a country directly through employment, composition of Labor forces, mobility and division of labor and productivity. Educated persons are preferred for employment rather than uneducated people. The proportion of educated and uneducated workers, the level and kind of education that the educated workers have, decide the composition and division of labor force with education opportunities for mobility of labor increases, and with more education, better training, and higher level of competence the productivity of workers increases and as productivity increases, the economy develops.

Education influences indirectly the economic development through increased savings, small families and by developing right kind of attitudes and skills and by removing some of the obstacles to social change, innovations and progress. More education means more earnings and small family and more earnings lead to more savings and mobility to higher social levels. Education is an agent and also a condition for change. Educated people are more likely to adopt innovations and thereby to increase productivity.

A number of studies undertaken by economists and educationalists in the Indian context have proved the influence of education on economic growth. Educated persons are relatively in scarce supply. So the employers are willing to pay them more at the time of recruitment and also for the rest of their working life, in economic terms the marginal productivity of the educated worker is higher than the marginal productivity of uneducated worker.

Economic Characteristics of Education

The economic characteristics of Education have been enumerated by economists in their writings as follows.

- It yields a host of direct and indirect benefits
- It is a non- controversial fiscal tool

Education is not an arguable or debatable financial tool, as it is clear that education brings economic development.

- It brings technological change.

The Scientific and technological findings of the researches made in the field of education brings various changes in the technological tools in order to increase the growth in production and development.

- It increases productivity.

Internal productivity is a measure of input-output ratio over a period of time, given the educational system and its characteristics with reference to specific operation of the educational system. Where as External productivity is the relationship between the cumulative benefits derived from it over a given period and the corresponding investment in producing these benefits. This relationship is what is meant by an educational system's cost-benefit ratio.

- Education can exchange the skills, ideas etc.

Education can exchange the skills, ideas and knowledge through training and orientation programmes.

- It is both a consumption as well as an investment.

The merit of education is that it yields both consumption as well as investment benefits. For example the person who bought a book and read that gets consumption as well as investment benefits at the same time.

HRD and Economic Development

It is a known fact that in most of the developing countries, there has always been a relatively low amount of investment in human capital, which gets manifested in terms of low labour efficiency, factor immobility, limited specialisation in occupation and trade, a deficient supply of effective entrepreneurship and management, customary values and traditional social institutions. Many studies of economic growth (both in developed and developing countries) confirm the importance of non-material investment. And hence, HRD plays an important role in the whole process of economic growth and also in economic development.

Education and Human Resource Development

Education is powerful means in developing human resources of a nation. This development can take place through out the life of every individual human being. In order to sustain the economic progress all the members of the nation must be developed.

In essence, development of human resources is closely related to the process of development and both move in the same direction, and both supplement each other. For example, investment in education accelerates the process of development because, amongst other things, it promotes economic growth, reduces income inequalities, accelerates rural development and also helps in population control.

- Education helps to develop knowledge, skill and other innate abilities. The productive capacity of labor depends on the extent of human capital the labor possesses and human capital is created by investment in Education.
- The productivity of an individual increases as he moves through the different levels of Education.

- Improvement in health is also a way of developing human resources. A good health will enable the worker to improve his working capacity. An educated person can maintain good health.
- Human capital formed by education is a contributing factor to Economic Growth.
- Even in developed countries economic growth depends on education and Science with research playing a key role in development.

Education and Economic Growth

Basing on the above concept it is clear that the education acts as a powerful means of Human resource Development which in turn helpful in Economic Growth. Education leads to the skilled and talented human resource, research in different fields of education sector causes the rapid development and also increases the efficiency of the financial operators and tools which in turn helpful for the economic growth.

Conclusion

A good education system, if it responds to the requirements of the economy of a country, will aid productivity and innovation. Education preserves and transmits knowledge and through this function helps remove some of the obstacles to economic and social development. Education develops the reasoning power and the ability to analyze and relate facts and events in proper sequences, to draw inferences and apply conclusions to new situations, and these mental abilities indirectly contribute to productivity.

Human Resource Development helps to increase the economic growth by increasing the production of essential goods and services and also helps to preserve and enhance the human dignity, freedom and worth of individuals. Human resources are developed through formal, informal, In-service, Organized, Self motivated education, Health and Nutrition Programmes.

Every nation or country needs education. The need for education of a nation involves many economic and non-economic factors. Of all the economic factors involved, manpower requirement is the prime indicator of educational need. There is a significant relationship between Educational Planning and production of Man power. Proper educational planning and finance allocation should be made on education. This also stresses the importance of universalisation of education. Education leads to HRD which in turn useful for Economic Growth.

REFERENCES

1. Chalam, K.S. *Education and Socio-Economic Development, Economic Foundations of Education.* pp. 149-153, Andhra University, VSP, AP.

2. William E. Becker, Darrell R. Lewis, *Higher Education and Economic Growth,* Indiana University.

3. Bruce Robert Morris, *Problems of American Economic Growth.*

8

COST DIFFERENTIAL IN SECONDARY EDUCATION OF RAYALASEEMA REGION IN ANDHRA PRADESH

I. Narendra Kumar, V. Kodandarami Reddy** & V. Balakrishnama Naidu****

In ancient period, India was known as Viswa Guru, Golden bird, a country of milk and curd, etc., it was the model of developed country in that period. But today, India is among the developing countries. It is the second most populous country of the world. If the population growth will be continued at the present rate, India will be the most populous country of the world around 2031. Education is a basic component of Human Development. It captures capability of acquiring knowledge, communication and participation in community life. According to Human Development Report (1993) literacy is a person's first step in learning and knowledge building and as a result literacy indicators are essential for any measurement of Human Development.

---

* Academic Consultant, Dept. of Econometrics, S.V.University, Tirupati - 517 502, A.P.

** Professor & Chairman of BOS, Dept. of Econometrics, S.V. University, Tirupati - 517 502, A.P.

*** Professor & Head, Dept. of Econometrics, S.V. University, Tirupati - 517 502, A.P.

Fifty years after Independence witness the slow progress of education, particularly secondary education in India. The plan outlays on secondary education show that the state provided 91 per cent of the total expenditure on secondary education. In India secondary education is the lintel of the entire education edifice of a country. This sector has grown much faster than all other sectors of education and is poised for a bigger leap with success in universal primary education.

The secondary education sectors prepare students in the age group of 11-16 for entry into higher education as well as for the world of work. There had been a steady increase in the spread of secondary education in the country. Although education is free up to secondary which children belonging to SC/ST get free education in all states and union territories, but it has not enabled a good number of children to avail secondary education. 64 per cent of the children in the age group of 11 to 16 years enrolled for secondary education in 2006-2007. In contrast, the overall gross enrollment ratio at the secondary stage was quite high in South Korea (100 per cent), Sri Lanka (92 per cent) and Philippines (78 per cent). Moreover, girls have not been discriminated in these countries in respect of secondary education. In fact female gross enroll at secondary stage is higher than the overall gross enrollment ratio in Sri Lanka and Philippines and only a 2 percentage lower in South Korea.

Many schools are strictly private whereas other used government grants-in-aid but are non-privately (aided schools). Schools run by church, missionary societies and muslim societies (madrasa) are common forms of private schools. In India 70 per cent of population depending on agriculture sector, highest ratio of high class people sent their children private schools and corporate schools, while the middle class and lower class people sent their children to municipal and village schools. Now-a-days the education system tough entrance, interview for admission, long class room hours, heavy homework assignments and high tuition fee rates in the mid-1990's, led to charges of lost childhood for pre-school children and acknowledgement of both the social cost and enhanced social benefits for the families involved.

The present study covered the behaviour of cost and expenditure incurred i.e. cost and payment made i.e. fee or price of secondary education in Rayalaseema region of Andhra Pradesh. The cost and fee are important deciding factors of the secondary education and determine the employment and income generation after attainment of quality education in the economy. The main objective of the study that the behaviour of cost structure i.e., fixed and variable and realized and determine the price of education.

Andhra Pradesh geographically divided into three regions are namely Coastal Andhra, Rayalaseema and Telangana. Anantapur, Chittoor, Kurnool and Kadapa districts come under Rayalaseema region. Four secondary schools comprising of two from the rural and two from the urban were selected at randomly from each district. In total 16 secondary schools were chosen as sample of the study comprising eight rural secondary schools and eight urban secondary schools in Rayalaseema region of Andhra Pradesh. The primary data was collected from the selected secondary schools by the interview method. The data included cost with its constituents-fixed and variable and fee collected from students on various items are tuition fee, admission fee, transfer fee, fines, donation for buildings, etc. and secondary information was obtained from the published and unpublished books, reports, journals and other magazines. The collected data were tabulated and analyzed with the help of simple statistical tools like averages, percentages and tested the't' values. The total fee and cost structure of secondary schools in Rayalaseema region are presented in Table-1.

Table-1

Total Fee and Cost Structure of Secondary Schools in Rayalaseema Region of Andhra Pradesh

S.No.	*No.of Schools*		*No. of Students*	*Total Cost (TC)*	*Total Fee (TF)*	*Average Cost (AC)*	*Average Fee (AF)*	*Net Cost (AC-AF)*
1	Anantpur	School-I	1180	53,10,000	10,03,000	4,500	850	3,650
		School-II	1210	58,08,000	12,70,500	4,800	1050	3,750
		School-III	1070	44,94,000	8,82,750	4,200	825	3,375
		School-VI	1120	51,52,000	10,36,000	4,600	925	3,675
2	Chittoor	School-I	1220	67,10,000	15,25,000	5,500	1250	4,250
		School-II	1150	66,70,000	11,78,750	5,800	1025	4,775
		School-III	1250	67,50,000	17,18,750	5,400	1375	4,025
		School-VI	1170	69,03,000	12,69,450	5,900	1085	4,815
3	Kadapa	School-I	1240	52,08,000	13,08,200	4,200	1055	3,145
		School-II	1350	59,40,000	13,97,250	4,400	1035	3,365
		School-III	1160	54,52,000	10,73,000	4,700	925	3,775
		School-VI	1070	51,36,000	9,79,050	4,800	915	3,885
4	Kurnool	School-I	1020	43,86,000	8,31,300	4,300	815	3,485
		School-II	1290	67,08,000	13,54,500	5,200	1050	4,150
		School-III	1130	54,24,000	11,01,750	4,800	975	3,825
		School-VI	1210	54,45,000	13,31,000	4,500	1100	3,400
		Total	18840	9,14,96,000	1,92,60,250	4856	1022	3834

Source: Field Data

Table-1 shows that total fee and cost of urban and rural schools in Rayalaseema region of Andhra Pradesh. Especially from 16 secondary schools students enrolled were 18,840, the total fee collected from them was Rs.1,92,60,250/- and average fee Rs. 1026/-, the average net cost observed was Rs. 3834/-. Thus, maximum fee of Rs. 4815/- in Chittoor dist and minimum was Rs. 3145/- in Kadapa district. These schools were divided into two types viz. rural and urban. The total fee and cost of rural schools in Rayalaseema region of Andhra Pradesh are presented in Table-2.

Table-2

Total Fee and Cost Structure of Secondary Schools in Rural Areas in Rayalaseema Region of Andhra Pradesh

S.No.		No.of Schools	No. of Students	Total Cost (TC)	Total Fee (TF)	Average Cost (AC)	Average Fee (AF)	Net Cost (AC-AF)
1	Anantapur	School-III	1070	44,94,000	8,82,750	4,200	825	3,375
		School-VI	1120	51,52,000	10,36,000	4,600	925	3,675
2	Chittoor	School-II	1150	66,70,000	11,78,750	5,800	1025	4,775
		School-VI	1170	69,03,000	12,69,450	5,900	1085	4,815
3	Kadapa	School-III	1160	54,52,000	10,73,000	4,700	925	3,775
		School-VI	1070	51,36,000	9,79,050	4,800	915	3,885
4	Kurnool	School-III	1130	54,24,000	11,01,750	4,800	975	3,825
		School-VI	1020	43,86,000	8,31,300	4,300	815	3,485
		Total	8890	4386000	831300	4300	815	3485

Source: Field Data

Table-2 shows that the total fee and cost of rural secondary in Rayalaseema region in Andhra Pradesh. The enrolled students in rural schools were 8890. The total fee collected was Rs. 8,31,300/-, with average fee as Rs.815/-, the average net cost observed was (AC-AF) of Rs.3,485/-. It was maximum of Rs. 4,815/- in Chittoor District and minimum was Rs.3,375/- in Anantapur district of Andhra Pradesh. Fee and cost structure of secondary schools in urban area in Rayalaseema region of Andhra Pradesh are gives in Table-3.

Table-3

Total Fee and Cost Structure of Secondary Schools in Urban Areas in Rayalaseema Region of Andhra Pradesh

S.No.		No.of Schools	No. of Students	Total Cost (TC)	Total Fee (TF)	Average Cost (AC)	Average Fee (AF)	Net Cost (AC-AF)
1	Anantapur	School-I	1180	53,10,000	10,03,000	4,500	850	3,650
		School-II	1210	58,08,000	12,70,500	4,800	1050	3,750
2	Chittoor	School-I	1220	67,10,000	15,25,000	5,500	1250	4,250
		School-III	1250	67,50,000	17,18,750	5,400	1375	4,025
3	Kadapa	School-I	1240	52,08,000	13,08,200	4,200	1055	3,145
		School-II	1350	59,40,000	13,97,250	4,400	1035	3,365
4	Kurnool	School-II	1290	67,08,000	13,54,500	5,200	1050	4,150
		School-VI	1210	54,45,000	13,31,000	4,500	1100	3,400
		Total	9950	47879000	10908200	4812	1096	3716

Source: Field Data

Table-3 represents the total fee and cost of urban secondary schools in Rayalaseema region of Andhra Pradesh. The numbers of students enrolled were 9950 in secondary schools. The total fee collected from them was Rs.1,09,08,200/- with average fee of Rs.1,096/-, the average net cost observed was Rs.3,716/-. It was maximum Rs. 4,250/- in Chittoor district and minimum of Rs.3145/- in Kadapa district of the region. The total fee and cost structure in Aided secondary school in rural and urban areas are presented in Table-4.

Table-4

Total Fee and Cost Structure of Aided Secondary Schools in Rural and Urban Areas in Rayalaseema Region of Andhra Pradesh

S.No.		No.of Schools	No. of Students	Total Cost (TC)	Total Fee (TF)	Average Cost (AC)	Average Fee (AF)	Net Cost (AC-AF)
1	Anantapur	School II	1210	58,08,000	12,70,500	4,800	1050	3,750
		School-III	1070	44,94,000	8,82,750	4,200	825	3,375
2	Chittoor	School-III	1250	67,50,000	17,18,750	5,400	1375	4,025
		School-VI	1170	69,03,000	12,69,450	5,900	1085	4,815
3	Kadapa	School-II	1350	59,40,000	13,97,250	4,400	1035	3,365
		School-VI	1070	51,36,000	9,79,050	4,800	915	3,885
4	Kurnool	School-I	1020	43,86,000	8,31,300	4,300	815	3,485
		School-II	1290	67,08,000	13,54,500	5,200	1050	4,150
		Total	9430	46125000	9703550	4891	1029	3862

Source: Field Data

Table-4 shows that the total fee and cost of aided secondary schools in the region. The numbers of students enrolled were 9430 in the schools. The total fee was collected of Rs.97,03,550/- with an average fee of Rs.1,029/-, the average net cost was (AC-AF) Rs.3,862/-. It was maximum Rs.4,815/- in Chittoor District and minimum was Rs.3,365/- in Kadapa District in the region. Fee and cost structure of unaided secondary schools in rural and urban areas of Rayalaseema region are presented Table-5.

Table-5

Total Fee and Cost Structure of the Un-Aided Secondary Schools in Rural and Urban Areas of Rayalaseema Region of Andhra Pradesh

S.No.	*No.of Schools*	*No. of Students*	*Total Cost (TC)*	*Total Fee (TF)*	*Average Cost (AC)*	*Average Fee (AF)*	*Net Cost (AC-AF)*
1 Anantapur	School-I	1180	53,10,000	10,03,000	4,500	850	3,650
	School-VI	1120	51,52,000	10,36,000	4,600	925	3,675
2 Chittoor	School-I	1220	67,10,000	15,25,000	5,500	1250	4,250
	School-II	1150	66,70,000	11,78,750	5,800	1025	4,775
3 Kadapa	School-III	1160	54,52,000	10,73,000	4,700	925	3,775
	SchoolL-VI	1070	51,36,000	9,79,050	4,800	915	3,885
4 Kurnool	School-III	1130	54,24,000	11,01,750	4,800	975	3,825
	School-VI	1210	54,45,000	13,31,000	4,500	1100	3,400
	Total	9240	45299000	9227550	4902	999	3903

Source: Field Data

Table 5 shows that fee and cost structure in the Rayalaseema region of A.P. The students enrolled as 9240 in the schools. The total fee was collected from them was Rs. 92,27,550 with average fee of Rs. 999. The average net cost was (AC-AF) Rs. 3,903. It was maximum Rs.4,775 in Chittoor district and minimum was Rs. 3400 in Kurnool District in the region. Total fee and cost structure by district wise in Rayalaseema region are presented in Table 6.

Table-6 reveals that the total fee structure of secondary schools in Rayalaseema region of Andhra Pradesh. The total fee collected from the secondary schools in rural areas was Rs.83,52,050/- the lowest percent of fee contributed in Anantapur district (22.97 per cent) and highest percent fee was contributed in Chittoor district (29.31 per cent) followed by 24.56 per cent in Kadapa district and 23.14 per cent in Kurnool district.

Table-6

Total Fee and Cost Structure in Secondary Schools in Rayalaseema Region of Andhra Pradesh

Districts	*No. of students (Rural)*	*No. of students (Urban)*	*Total No. of students*	*Fee (Rural)*	*Fee (Urban)*	*Total Fee*
Anantapur	2190	2390	4580	1918750 (22.97)	2273500 (20.84)	4192250 (21.76)
Chittoor	2320	2470	4790	2448200 (29.31)	3243750 (29.73)	5691950 (29.55)
Kadapa	2230	2590	4820	2052050 (24.56)	2705450 (24.81)	4757500 (24.71)
Kurnool	2150	2500	4650	1933050 (23.14)	2685500 (24.61)	4618550 (23.97)
Total	8890	9950	18840	8352050. (100)	10908200 (100)	19260250 (100)

Source: Field Data

In urban areas the total fee collected from all the secondary schools in the study area was Rs.1,09,08,200/-. The lowest per cent of fee collected in Anantapur district (20.54 per cent) and highest percent in Chittoor district (29.73 per cent) followed by 24.81 per cent in Kadapa district and 24.61 per cent in Kurnool district.

The total fee and cost structure collected (rural +urban) in secondary schools was Rs.1,92,60,250/- from the students (18840). The lowest per cent contributed in Anantapur district (21.76 per cent) and highest per cent in Chittoor district (29.55 per cent) followed by 24.71 per cent in Kadapa district and 23.97 per cent in Kurnool district.

Table-7

Total Fee and Cost Structure Differences in Rayalaseema Region of Andhra Pradesh

S.No.	Districts	't' – value Between Rural and Urban Schools	t-value
1.	Anantapur	2.08**	2.41**
2.	Chittoor	0.78@	
3.	Kadapa	0.66@	
4.	Kurnool	1.99**	

Source: Field Data

From the Table-7 it is observed that total fee and cost structure in secondary schools between rural and urban schools of Chittoor (0.78) and Kadapa (0.66) districts are not significant while Anantapur (2.08) and Kurnool (1.99) districts are significant at 5 per cent levels. Totally the total fee and cost structure among the district are significant (2.41) at 5 per cent levels.

Conclusion

The analysis of price and cost structure has shown the necessity of determination of price on the basis of cost structure. The positive difference in average cost and average fee (AC-AF) is observed in all schools which need to be corrected. The possible way to overcome such residual would be the increase in average fee. Average fee may be manipulated by increasing the average fee charged by each student or number of enrollment should increase to reduce the average cost. Schools in Chittoor district could meet most of their expenses fixed and running with the fee collected where as other districts could not cover their running expenses with the fee collected.

Thus the study has revealed inconsistency in the behaviour of schools in managing their variable operations in terms of teacher-students ratio. Both number of students enrolled and fee per student were insufficient. Therefore, some positive and effective actions are needed in such direction.

REFERENCES

1. *Census Reports*, Govt. of India, New Delhi, 2001.
2. Mehta, P.L., & R. Poonga, *Free and Compulsory Education*, Deep and Deep Publication, New Delhi, 1999.
3. Mohanty, B. *School Administration and Supervision*, Deep and Deep Publication, New Delhi, 2001
4. Natarajan, S. *Introduction to Economics of Education*, Sterling Publishers Pvt. Ltd., New Delhi, 1999.
5. R.Natarajan, *Internationalization of Education in the New Millennium*, University to News, 2005.
6. *Report of the Education Commission (1964-66)*, Govt. of India, Ministry of Education, New Delhi, 1967.
7. Singh, B. *Education and Human Resource Development*, Deep and Deep Publication, New Delhi, 1995.
8. *Statistical Abstracts*, Govt. of Andhra Pradesh, Hyderabad, 2005.
9. *Statistical outline of India*, Tata Publications, New Delhi, 2006.
10. Thakur, D. & D.N. Thakur, *Educational Planning and Administration*, Deep and Deep Publication, New Delhi, 2004.
11. Thakur, D. & D.N. Thakur, *New Education Policy*, Deep and Deep Publication, New Delhi, 2004.
12. UNDP - *Human Development Report*, 2006.
13. World Bank, *Global Economic Prospectus and the Developing Countries*, World Bank, Oxford University Press, Washington D.C.

9

FINANCIAL RESOURCES AND COST EFFECTIVENESS ANALYSIS IN PRIMARY EDUCATION

*Gara Latchanna**

Introduction

It is obvious that investments on education are crucial for the sustained economic development, since it contributes to increased worker productivity, more rapid technological adaptation and innovation and creating knowledge-based economy. That is why, provision of education especially that of primary education is becoming a top priority in almost all governments' endeavours. Moreover, education is indispensable to raise productivity, level of living and tackling poverty. For example, the private returns of primary schooling are 41%, secondary education 27% and higher education is 28% (Psacharopoulos, 1994).

The global experiences also have shown us that no country has sustained economic progress without literacy rates above 50 per cent. This implies that unless the base is so strong and well founded at the pre-primary and primary levels of education, when humane values and values of education are fostered, the super-structure in the form of all levels, of education including professional disciplines, would remain weak, puerile and socially

---

* Professor, Department of Education, Andhra University, Visakhapatnam

not meaningful. Besides the efforts made to universalise primary/elementary education many developing countries of the world didn't achieve 100% literacy rate and the system of their education lagged behind due to various impediments. This raises doubts to public and policy makers whether resources allocated to primary/elementary education are sufficient or the allotted resources utilized judiciously for achieving desired targets.

Financial Allocation and Utilization for Primary Education, Conceptual Frameworks

Among other factors, the availability of financial resources determines the performance of education sector. For the sake of an insight, financial resources invested in primary education by selected developed countries is presented in Table 1 below.

As reflected in Table 1, developed countries allocate high share of national resources to education. Research findings witnessed that GNP and GDP has link with educational provision and quality. Global comparison shows that aggregate expenditure on education nearly always increase with GDP and educational outcomes broadly improve with educational expenditure, although such relations are not so smooth. However, one can infer that the input for education has implication in combating illiteracy or social exclusions or competent citizens. Thus, good inputs result in good outputs.

Table 1

Country	Public Expenditure for Education as % GDP	Annual Expenditure Per Student in USD
Australia	4.6	3121
Finland	6.6	4253
Germany	4.5	3361
Spain	4.8	2628
Sweden	6.6	5189
UK	4.6	3328

Source: World Education Report (UNESCO, 1998)

Some of the reasons that create motivation in developed countries to change pattern of their education system since early 1980's were the need for increased efficiency, improved financial control, reduction of bureaucratic systems, increased responsiveness to local communities, improved innovation and provision of conditions for improving the quality of schooling. Hence, such efforts and others contributed to their development in every aspect.

However, wider variations exist in educational outcomes and spending efficiency among countries with similar incomes/level of educational expenditure. The extent of investments in primary education and the effectiveness of utilizing these available resources give an insight into quality, access or both. Available data has shown that the expenditure made over the period of 1975-1999 in Sub Saharan Africa and South/West Asia has been devoted to expanding primary education enrolments, whereas countries in East Asia, Latin America and Caribbean spent on higher levels of spending per student. As a matter of fact, there is no single optimal mix of quality and access, and no best way of ensuring equitable growth. What matters is that each country addressed the issue in its own context.

Educational finance directed to education sector can be assessed using various techniques. In this regard, the following discussion highlights how the resource utilization is assessed and the cost-effectiveness is analyzed.

Who bears the cost of primary education? What are the sources of meeting these costs? What are the determinants of these costs? Is it possible to determine the optimum size of institution on the basis of educational costs? What are the optimum size of inputs and outputs in primary education? These pertinent questions are to be examined by researchers, planners and administrates, employing the method of cost-effectiveness, which is a vital tool for assessing the resource utilization to know the school output/efficiency.

The effective utilization of school inputs can be measured by either cost-benefit analysis or cost-effectiveness analysis. The former attempts to measure both the costs and benefits of a project in financial terms by means of rate of return. The latter attempts to assess the public policy in the field of education where the objectives are clearly definable and measurable and but not in monetary terms.

A brief summary of the concepts, costs/expenditure, cost analysis, and cost effectiveness analysis are given below. A cost refers to the total opportunity cost of a project (real resources used up) it is used for long term planning. Opportunity cost is sacrifice of alternative opportunities to use the resources either for present consumption or for other forms of investment (foregone earnings). *Expenditure* represents purchase of services and goods, school buildings, equipments and others. Expenditure is valid for allocation analysis.

Cost Analyses are critically important for deciding how to allocate funds within a program and for understanding the relationships between costs and outcomes. Examining cost figures for the program as a whole (or for parts of it) is a basic form of cost analysis.

Cost-Effectiveness Analysis is the relationship between program costs and program effectiveness. Costs are measured as dollars spent, whereas effectiveness or outcome is measured as changes. Cost effectiveness attempts to assess what is the lowest cost method of achieving a given target benefit. The benefit can be specific in terms of its scale. But cost effectiveness has its own problems in terms of choosing what will be the target. The targets need to be relatively easily observable, but also sufficiently abstract and developmental to have multiple method of hitting it. Cost effectiveness analysis refers to the considerations of decision alternatives in which both their costs and consequences are taken into account in a systematic way. It is decision oriented tool, in that it is designed to ascertain which means of attaining particular educational goals are most efficient. Cost effectiveness analysis is closely related to cost benefit analysis in that both represent economic evaluation of alternative resources use and measure costs in the same way. However cost benefit analysis is used to address only those types of alternatives where the out comes can be measured in terms of their monetary values. The purpose of cost effectiveness analysis in education is to ascertain which program or combination of programs can achieve particular objectives at the lowest cost. The assumption is that different alternatives are associated with different costs and different educational results. By choosing those with least cost for a given outcome, society can use its resource more effectively. That is the saved resources can be devoted for the expansion of other programs. There is no single standard for cost-effectiveness. Generally, the term is used loosely as a way of saying that something probably costs less, or is more effective, than something else. Cost-effectiveness indices can be compared for different programs, different treatment modalities. The overall cost-effectiveness of a program can be improved by first finding that parts of the program contribute most to effectiveness and then discovering which of those program components have the lowest cost. It may be possible to improve cost-effectiveness by enhancing use of these more effective and less expensive components while decreasing use of less effective and more expensive components.

How Financial Utilizations for Primary Education are Assessed?

According to John Vaizey et al, the main purpose of the cost-effectiveness analysis is to identify which school, which type of teaching method produces the output at lowest cost. This method can take two different forms.

1. A comparison is made between alternative ways of achieving the same objective in order to identify that with the lowest cost. This is defined as the most cost-effective method of achieving the same objective. This technique can be employed in the primary educational system to compare different institutions, schools, different methods of teaching etc. Alternatives share the same objectives but have different costs.

2. A comparison is made between two schools or among many schools with similar level of cost structure in order to find out which achieves the highest level of efficiency/output.

The most cost-effective institution is the one, which maximizes the output/efficiency achieved for a given level of cost.

Output/Efficiency Assessment

The Output/efficiency is measured in primary education in terms of the number of pupils who leave school each year. It may be a poor measure of educational effectiveness since it ignores the quality of education and it does not measure the knowledge or skills acquired by pupils. A comparison of per pupil costs in different costs in different schools, which are attempting to achieve same objectives, may be the first step in applying cost-effective method in primary education.

As Atmananda Mishra (1967) clearly pointed out, the lower costs does not mean greater efficiency of an institution per pupil costs shifts with price level, salaries and enrolment.

In the second step, attempt is made to measure the achievement of those objectives in terms of test scores, examination results or some other quantifiable measure of educational achievement. The measure chosen will depend on the objectives of the program. For example, if the cost-effectiveness method is used to compare the method of teaching, then the effectiveness may be measured in terms of pupil scores on comprehension tests. On the other hand, the cost-effectiveness of A.P.P.E.P., the aim of which is to improve the quality in primary education, might reduce the wastage, stagnation, and absenteeism and increase the enrolment. Leslie and Jamison (1980) used the method to compare and choose among traditional methods and educational media. They explored the use of T.V. and Radio in classrooms in Mexico, Dominican Republic and Nicaragua. They found that T.V. worked no better than Radio.

These illustrations are noted to show that this method can be applied to variety of educational programs, using many different measures of educational output/effectiveness. The main aim is to measure the extent of differences in costs and effectiveness of primary education in different regions and between different racial groups but it provides the data for cost-effectiveness in the form of costs and scores in achievement tests.

Input Specification and Quantification

Material inputs such as buildings, equipment, furniture etc. can be quantified with the appropriate rates of depreciation/ discount. The inputs like teacher services, parental attitudes, family background, Socio-cultural background, and school environment bearing potential of the pupils can be reduced to numbers for estimating input-output rations. All these difficulties sought to be surmounted by having conceptual design as different from empirical design with appropriate adoption of concepts and measurement techniques. Empirical designs with all its hedging in the form of assumptions may not come up to the ideal of conceptual design but it may form part of a pragmatic approach for analyzing the reality so as to present approximations of what is happening in the process of learning at the primary educational level.

Closing Remarks

Provision of primary education in developing countries especially is very challenging. The goals set to universalise primary education are at risk given the current trends. What can be done is that, lower costs to students and their families improve the quality of school, increase the efficiency of the school system and other options should be sought. On top of these, developing countries should enforce and renew their political commitment and resource commitment as well as cost effective methods of utilizing the available resources.

Moreover, the problem of assessing the utilization of resources in education is particularly an unexplored area in the economics of education. Studies on input-output/cost-benefit, cost-effectiveness approaches in primary education might provide insights into the scope for increased efficiency of resource use. The economics of education, which is essentially a policy-oriented discipline, would deserve the attention that it is now receiving by researchers in the sector.

REFERENCES

1. Atmananda Mishra, (1967). *The Financing of Indian Education.* Asia Publishing House, Bombay.

2. Blaug.M. (1965). *Economics of Education, Vol.2.* Penguin, London. Carnoy, Martin (1999).*Globalisation and Education Reform.* Paris: UNESCO.

3. Fourth Survey of Research in Education, 1983-88, NCERT, 1991.

4. Gara Latchanna. (2005). *Economics of Tribal Primary Education.* The Associated Publishers: Ambala Cantt.

5. Griver, R.P. (1996). *Education For All.* Ambala Cantt: The Associated Publisher.

6. Mayor, Federico (1995), *Memory of the Future.*Paris: UNESCO.

7. NIEPA and Government of India (2000).*Year 2000 Assessment, Education For All (India).*NewDelhi: Thomson Pres Service.

8. Psacharopoulos, George (1994).Returns to Investment in Education: global Update. *World Development* 22 (9).

9. Rathaiah, L. and Bhaskara Rao (1997).*International Innovations in Education.* New Delhi: Discovery Publishing House.

10. Sethi, Vinita (1997). *Educational Development and Resource Mobilization.* New Delhi: Kanishka Publisher.

11. Vaizey J. et al. (1972). *The Political Economy of Education.* Gerald Duckworth & Company Limited: London.

12. UNESCO (2002). *Education for All Year 2002 Assesment, Statistical Document,* UIS2OOO. UNESCO.

13. World Bank (2002). *Education for All; the Lessons of Experience, The Impact of Policy in 20 Countries Case Study.* Amsterdam: World Bank.

14. __________ (2000b). *Entering the 21st Century; World Development Report1999/2000.* Oxford University Press.

15. __________ (2000). *Can African Claim the 21st Century?* Washington D.C.: World Bank.

10

TRENDS IN THE GROWTH OF HIGHER EDUCATION IN INDIA: 1950-51 TO 2005-06

A. Vamsi Krushna & D. Pulla Rao***

Introduction

Higher Education provides an opportunity to critically reflect upon the social, economic, cultural, moral and spiritual issues facing humanity. It contributes to national development through dissemination of specialized knowledge and skills. It is a crucial factor for survival. It is indeed difficult to conceive of a plan for building up a sustainable and prosperous society without the development of human resources, as the system of education and various socio-economic and cultural aspects, which influence national development, are inextricably linked with one another. For instance, while the economy provides for necessary resources for promoting the system of higher education, the system prepares in turn a cadre of manpower with varying degrees of specialization and levels of skills for increasing productivity of various factors of production, which consequently enhance income and improve quality of life of people. Education is universally recognised as an investment in human resources. The importance of higher education has been pointed out by the International Commission on Education for 21st Century: "Higher education is at one and

* Research Scholar, Dept. of Economics, Andhra University, Visakhapatnam.

** Professor, Dept. of Economics, Andhra University, Visakhapatnam.

the same time one of the driving forces of economic development and the focal point of learning in a society. It is both repository and creator of knowledge. Moreover, it is the principal instrument for passing on the accumulated experience, cultural and scientific, of humanity." In developing societies, higher education is considered to be a speedy vehicle for upward social mobility, especially for the socially and economically deprived sectors.

Historical Background

In ancient India Takshashila, Nalanda, Vikramshila, Nadia, Vallabhi, etc., were the centres of higher learning. They attracted scholars from various parts of the world. Higher intellectual atmosphere was the important characteristic of these centres. Some of these centres were of the residential character and may be compared with the modern universities in some respects. Nalanda was one of them and it is believed that about four thousand students were once residents there. Some of the centres faced neglect during the Muslim rule in the country. These rulers as they consolidated their rule in India, they started their own centres of learning called *Madrasas*.

Higher education in modern India began with the establishment of Hindu College at Calcutta in 1817 by Raja Ram Mohan Roy with his friend David Hare. East India Company was basically a commercial company, therefore it took little interest in the education of Indian masses. But in 1824 the Company established the Sanskrit College in Calcutta. Several social reformers and intellectuals of the time opposed the move, because they felt that Indian masses should receive education in modern/western/useful science through the medium of European Languages. Later, Elphinstone College at Bombay in 1834 and Madras Christian College at Madras in 1837 were founded. Two groups arose at this time, one was Orientalists and other was, Anglicists. Orientalists favoured the policy of teaching through the medium of classical Indian Languages like Sanskrit, Arabic and Persian while Anglicist favoured the policy of teaching through the medium of European Languages. This controversy gave rise to the famous minutes of 1835 of Macaulay. Some people regard Macaulay as "torch-bearer in the path of progress" while, some others dislike him for his violent condemnation of Indian languages, culture and religion. (Naik & Nurullah, 1974:75). He decided in favour of Anglicists. Thus the system of English education came to be encouraged by the government. Female education though neglected earlier received some encouragement from the Christian Missionary Societies in Bombay, Madras and Calcutta.

The Wood's Education Despatch (1854) was the most important educational document under the Company's regime and is referred to, by some historians, as the "Magna Carta of English Education in India" (Naik and Nurullah, 1974:114). Wood's Despatch for the first time prescribed an educational policy for India in detail. On its recommendation three universities were set up in the Presidency towns at Bombay, Calcutta and Madras in 1857 on the model of London University. The main functions of these universities were to conduct examinations and to award degrees. At the end of the nineteenth century there were five universities in India. Two other universities were later founded at Lahore (1882) and Allahabad (1887). As of 1901-02, there were 191 colleges in the country and the students enrolled in them numbered 23,009.

Government appointed the Calcutta University Commission (1917-19) to study and report on the problems of the University. But the problems facing the Calcutta University were also similar to those facing other Indian Universities of the time. The report of the Commission had far reaching consequences upon the development of University education in India as a whole. It led to the creation of a large number of universities in the period between 1917-22. These were Banaras Hindu University, Patna University, Osmania University, Lucknow University and Aligarh Muslim University. A report of the Central Advisory Board of Education on Post war Educational Development in India, the Sargent Report of 1944, was an effort to develop a national system of education in India. It suggested the formation of University Grants Committee. The UGC therefore came into existence in the year 1945. At the time of independence in 1947, there were twenty universities in the country. Most of these were teaching universities.

Education in Post-Independence Era

Education Commission (1948-49)

On the eve of Independence, Government of India, in November 1948, appointed the University Education Commission known as Radhakrishnan Commission to offer suggestions for enabling the Indian Universities to meet the new responsibilities. The Commission felt that all universities should be constituted as autonomous bodies, they should be teaching institutions rather than affiliating ones. It is also suggested that the University Grants Committee should be reconstituted and the University Grants Commission should be set up for allocation of funds. The Commission pointed out "Democracy depends for its very life on a high standard of general, vocational and professional education. Dissemination of learning, incessant search for new knowledge, unceasing effort to plumb the meaning of life, provision for professional education to satisfy the occupational needs of our society are the vital tasks of higher education". The planners in the First Five Year Plan 1951-56 received valuable guidance from the Report of the University Education Commission in the respect of the resource and the overall needs of the country with regard to the re-organisation of University Education.

Education Commission (1964-66)

In July 1964, Government of India appointed an Education Commission generally known as Kothari Commission, to survey and examines the entire field of education in order to establish a well designed, balanced, integrated and adequate system of national education capable of making a powerful contribution to national life. The Commission emphasised the need for expansion of higher education, enhancing quality of Higher Education and research and finally the use of dynamic techniques of management and organisation suited to special functions and purposes of higher education.

National Policy on Education (1968)

The National Policy on Education adopted in 1968 was based on the recommendations of the Kothari Commission (1964-66).

The adoption of the 1968 policy led to considerable expansion of the educational facilities all over the country at all levels. More than 90 per cent of the country's rural habitations developed schooling facilities within the radius of one kilometre. There was sizeable augmentation of facilities at other stages also. While these achievements were impressive by themselves, the general formulations incorporated in the 1968 Policy did not, however, get translated into a detailed strategy of implementation. Problems of access, quality, quantity, relevance and financial outlay accumulated over the years, as no plan of action was prepared for effective implementation.

National Policy on Education (1986)

As a consequence of the non-implementation Education Policy of 1968, a new National Policy on Education (NPE) had to be adopted by Government of India in May 1986. The policy laid great emphasis on the elimination of regional disparities in the educational system. It says, "Steps will be taken to facilitate inter-regional mobility by providing equal access to every Indian of requisite merit, regardless of his origins". The universal character of universities was underscored. The establishment of network arrangements between different institutions in the country to pool their resources and participate in projects of national importance was emphasised. The policy further focused upon enhancing support to research in the universities for ensuring high quality. For securing a synthesis of knowledge, inter-disciplinary research was encouraged.

Ramamurti Committee Report (1990)

On 7th May 1990, Government of India appointed a Committee to review the 1986 National Policy on Education. Government accorded the highest priority to education both as a human right and as a means for bringing about a transformation towards a more humane and enlightened society. Ramamurti Committee (1990) emphasised that the quality of higher and technical education is to be improved in real terms not only to make it relevant to the society but also to cater to the needs of competitive industry.

Structure of Education in India

India, being a union of states, has accepted a uniform structure of school and college education popularly known as "10+2+3" pattern of school and college education. This pattern visualizes 10 years of general education including 8 years of Elementary, 2 years of Secondary Education and 3 years of College Education leading to the award of first degree. The higher education structure includes three years of general education in arts, sciences, and commerce as a part of 10+2+3 structure. These programmes lead to the award of the degrees of B.A., B.Sc. or B.Com. Alternatively, the students may go for first-degree courses in medicine, engineering, and other professional courses at first-degree level. After completing these courses, the students are awarded M.B.B.S. or other equivalent degrees in medicine, or B.E. /B. Tech. or other equivalent degrees in engineering and technology.

The first degree courses in general education are followed by two years of post-graduate studies leading to Master's degrees in Arts, Sciences, and Commerce. These degrees are abbreviated as M.A., M.Sc., and M.Com respectively. Similarly, there exist postgraduate courses in professional and technical education leading to M.D. /M.S. and M.E./M.Tech. Degrees in medicine, and engineering and technology respectively. The professional courses in Law may also be pursued after the first degree in Arts, Science, and Commerce, which leads to the award of the degree of LL.B., followed by LL.M. at the post-graduate level. Similarly, the professional courses in Education or Teaching may be pursued after the first degree courses in general education leading to the award of B. Ed. degree after undergoing a one-year course in the science of teaching. This is followed by a two-year post-graduate programme leading to the award of the degree of M.Ed. Up to this stage a student will have studied for a period of about 17 years. After this, a selected group of students goes for research degrees leading to the degree of Ph.D. The minimum duration of research degree programmes is of 3 years; including 1 year of M.Phil. programme being offered in some universities. Research degree programmes are available in all streams including Medicine, Engineering, Law and Education. Briefly, the structure of formal education in India consists of about 20 years from class I to the research degree - 8 years up to elementary, 10 years up to secondary, 12 years up to senior secondary, and 20 years up to university education.

Growth of Institutions of Higher Education

After independence the growth of higher education was rapid. Centre and State governments took serious steps and established many universities and colleges. Various kinds of institutions of higher education came into existence. Institutions of higher learning in Technology, Medicine, Agriculture, Electronics and Engineering were established. During a period of three years from 1947 to 1950, 7 new universities were created raising the total number to 27. By 2000 the number of universities increased to 256. Further it has been increased to 490 by the year 2005-06. By looking at the Table-1, one would agree that there has been a commendable progress in the expansion of higher education. Taking the whole system of higher education, the Indian higher educational system is the second largest in the world, next only to the United States. The government policies and the opportunities that are created by the government for higher education have made the system very huge. Of all the university level institutions, 20 are central universities, 216 are State Universities, 101 are Deemed Universities, 13 are Institutions of National Importance and 140 are Research Institutions.

The affiliated colleges have a very important role in higher education in India with most of the undergraduate and postgraduate teaching being done in them. Ultimately the number of colleges increased from 695 in 1950-51 to 11,831 in 1999-2000. Thereafter, increase of the number of colleges accelerated to 20,769 at the end of the year 2005-06. The enrolment in the colleges increased from 1,74,000 to 12,859,239 between 1950-51 and 2005-06. The quality of colleges has a very significant bearing on the quality of higher education. The index of growth of universities and colleges taking 1950-51 as the base shows that the increase is not substantial as compared to the enrolment of students in universities and colleges. The index of growth of colleges is much higher than the index of growth of universities. The annual compound growth rate of universities and colleges during 1950-51 and 2005-06 was 5.41 per cent and 6.37 per cent respectively. As may be seen the annual compound growth rate of colleges is higher than that of universities. Table - 1 below shows the growth of higher education.

Table-1: Growth in Universities and Colleges in India

Year	*No. of Universities*	*Index*	*No. of Colleges*	*Index*
1950-51	27	100	695	100
1955-56	33	122	1,025	147
1960-61	47	174	1,542	222
1965-66	75	278	2,572	370
1970-71	100	370	3,604	518
1975-76	120	444	4,395	632
1980-81	144	533	4,722	679
1985-86	164	607	5,816	837
1990-91	180	667	7,346	1057
1995-96	226	837	9,252	1331
1999-2000	256	948	11,831	1702
2005-06	490	1815	20,769	2988
Annual Compound Growth Rate	5.41		6.37	

Sources: 1. UGC Annual Reports, 1993-94, 1995-96, 1998-99, and 1999-2000

2. Ministry of Human Resource Development, Govt. of India, Annual Report, 1996-97, 2000-2001, 2006-07.

5. Growth Of Enrolment Of Students Of Higher Education

Table-2 provides data on the number of students enrolled in higher education for selected years between 1950-51 and 2005-06. The total enrolment in higher education was 1,74,000 in 1950-51. The enrolment of students increased to 35,71,000 in

1985-86 and to 77,37,000 in 1999-2000. Finally the enrolment of students stood at 12,859,239 by the year 2005-06. The annual compound growth rate of enrolment over a period of our study was 8.14 per cent.

Table-2: Growth of Enrolment in Higher Education

Year	*Enrolment (in 000s)*	*Index*
1950-51	174	100
1955-56	295	169
1960-61	557	320
1965-66	1,067	613
1970-71	1,954	1123
1975-76	2,426	1394
1980-81	2,792	1604
1985-86	3,571	2052
1990-91	4,425	2543
1995-96	6,426	3693
1999-2000	7,737	4446
2005-06	12,859	7390
Annual Compound Growth Rate	8.14	

Sources: 1. UGC Annual Reports, 1993-94, 1995-96, 1998-99, 1999-2000

2. Ministry of Human Resource Development, Govt. of India, Annual Report, 1996-97, 2000-2001, 2006-07.

Of the total enrolment in universities and colleges, 92.97 per cent students are enrolled in the undergraduate classes, 6.75 per cent in the postgraduate classes and only 0.28 per cent at the research degree level. The faculty-wise enrolment shows that:

(i) About 59.51 per cent enrolment is in general education – 55.16 per cent in Arts, 23.71 per cent in Science and 21.13 per cent in Commerce;

(ii) The remaining 40.49 per cent enrolment is in professional and technical education and others – 32.12 per cent in

Engineering and Technology, 5.88 per cent in Medicine, 4.71 per cent in Education and 57.27 per cent in others.

With phenomenal expansion during the post-independence period, higher education system in India has become one of the largest in the world. If the progress continues at the same pace, we may surpass even USA and Russia within a decade or so.

Growth in Number of Teachers

Teachers play an important role in the institutions of higher learning. The role of the teacher is crucial in the educational system. Perhaps there may not be sufficient incentives for better performance and there may be no scale to measure the efficiency of the teacher, but he plays a distinctive role in the life of a student. The quality of the student reflects the quality of a teacher. The quality of an institution can be elevated if the teacher is a person of distinction and calibre but if he is incompetent and inept, he can bring disrepute to it.

The teacher plays an important role in the implementation of educational programmes. In the recent past, there has been a big growth in the number of teachers engaged in teaching students of higher learning.

So far, we have examined the growth of institutions and enrolment in higher education during the period of five decades in the country. But, growth does not really indicate the quality of education. One indicator of the quality is the student-teacher ratio. So we, as a first step, examine the number of teachers employed in the higher educational institutions, universities and colleges in the country and the rate of growth of the teachers during the period of the study.

Table-3 shows that there were 21.3 lakh teachers employed in higher educational institutions in 1950-51. The number of teachers increased to 227.0 lakh in 1985-86. The number reached 351.0 lakh in 1999-2000. Further, it has gone up to 488.0 lakh in 2005-06. It is interesting to note that the increase in the number of teachers in the country is not commensurate with the increase in the number of students enrolled. This has resulted in the increase in the student-teacher ratio over time except in 1975-76 and 1980-81. It shows that the ratio was 8:1 in 1950-51 and it increased continuously up to 15:1 in 1970-71. The student-teacher ratio decreased to 14:1 in 1975-76 and the same ratio continued in 1980-81 also. It then increased continuously and reached 22:1 in 1999-2000. Afterwards, it rose to 26:1 in 2005-06.

Table-3: Number of Teachers Employed In Higher Educational Institutions in India

Year	*Number of teachers (in 000s)*	*Index*	*Student-teacher ratio (No. of student per teacher)*
1950-51	21.3	100	8
1955-56	33.2	156	9
1960-61	55.5	260	10
1965-66	84.7	398	13
1970-71	128.8	605	15
1975-76	167.6	787	14
1980-81	193.3	907	14
1985-86	227.0	1066	16
1990-91	263.1	1235	17
1995-96	300.6	1411	21
1999-2000	351.0	1648	22
2005-06	488.0	2291	26
Annual Compound Growth Rate		5.86	

Sources: 1.UGC Annual Reports, 1993-94, 1995-96, 1998-99, 1999-2000.

5. Ministry of Human Resource Development, Govt. of India, Annual Report, 1996-97, and 2000-2001.

Note, however, that the number of teachers has not increased in the country in consonance with the increase in the number of students enrolled. This has resulted in an increase in student-teacher ratio over time except in 1975-76 and 1980-81. The increase in the ratio will adversely affect the quality of education at higher level. The index of growth of teachers taking 1950-51 as the base shows that the increase is not substantial as compared to the enrolment of students. The annual compound growth rate of teachers over a period of our study was 5.86 per cent.

Conclusions

India achieved freedom from the British imperialism on 15th August 1947. Many decades have elapsed since. Yet in matters of higher education the country is unenviable placed. Economic backwardness of the country may have to do with mass illiteracy and ignorance of the people. But economic backwardness alone cannot explain educational backwardness. The population explosion in the country could not have been unrelated to the illiteracy of its people.

We examined here the effect of the initiatives of the government in the field of higher education. More specifically, we examined the genesis of higher education in this country and later touched upon its trends since 1950-51. The focus is on (1) number of institutions (2) enrolment of students (3) the size of the teaching staff and (4) the student-teacher ratio in higher education.

Our data shows that growth in enrolment of students has exceeded growth of the number of institutions and teachers. To reflect upon the quality of education we arrived at student-teacher ratios. The student-teacher ratio in higher education as it stood in 2005-06 was 26:1. The student-teacher ratio in higher education is less than the ratios at primary and upper-primary stage. It is along the expected lines and is a positive sign. As the student goes into the higher and higher educational institutions there will be a greater demand on the quality of teachers, of buildings of the institution, of other infrastructure including toilets. These need to be strengthened. Mere increase in the number of teachers does not satisfy the demands of the students. One important reason of the downfall in the quality of higher education during the recent decades may be the lack of coordination between enrolment, number of teachers and number of institutions, with student enrolment growing faster than the other two. Though, there has been a massive expansion of institutional facilities during the last 55 years, the goal has moved farther with the number of students pursuing higher education increasing. Moreover, there are glaring disparities based on caste, sex, religion, region etc., in what has been achieved. These are disturbing.

Higher education has to play on all-pervasive role in restructuring our present society and in improving the 'socio-economic status' of the people. Higher education should directly benefit the students, through its specially developed software and educational programmes. To sum up, every effort should be made to see that higher education spearheads the development of our economy and transforms our society self-reliant and ever learning society.

REFERENCES

1. Chalam, K.S. (1993): *Educational Policy for Human Resources Development* Rawat Publications, Jaipur.

2. Chauhan, C.P.S. (1990): *Higher Education in India: Achievements, Failures and Strategies,* Ashish Publishing House, New Delhi.

3. Chauhan, C.: .S. (2000): 'Contemporary issues in Higher Education', *University News,* AIU, New Delhi, December 2004.

4. Government of India. *National Policy on Education,* 1968, Ministry of Education and Culture, New Delhi, 1968.

5. Government of India. *National Policy on Education* (NPE), 1986 and its revised version 1992, MHRD, New Delhi, 1986 and 1992.

6. Nurullah, S and Naik, J.P. (1943): *History of Education in India during the British period,* Macmillan & Co. Ltd., Bombay.

7. Power, K.B. (2000): 'Higher Education in the Twenty-First century', *University News,* AIU, New Delhi, December 4.

8. University Grants Commission. *Annual Reports,* 1959-60, 1993-94, 1995-96 and 1998-99, UGC, New Delhi.

SUB-THEME: B
HUMAN DEVELOPMENT

11

DIMENSIONS OF ECONOMIC GROWTH AND HUMAN DEVELOPMENT IN INDIA: AN ASSESSMENT

*T. Nirmala Devi**

The Indian economy has emerged as one of the fastest growing economies of the world. The GDP growth rate during the 10th plan period (2002-07) averaged to 7.6 per cent and accompanied with a significant growth rate in macro-economic stability (Naik, S.D, 2008). With a growth rate of above 9 per cent in recent years, India also experienced the consequences of rapid economic growth without equity, viz; persistent poverty, accounting for nearly one-fourth of the world's poor; high child and maternal mortality rates, which are worse than those of the sub- Saharan countries; growing unemployment and poor health care, posting highest number of undernourished people in the world as well as one-third of the world' under-weight children. Further, there are sections of population that continue to be excluded from development benefits. Having known the fact that progress in human resources, particularly in education and health indicators, acts as both cause and effect of the development process, India's contribution in that direction is not significant. While its smaller neighbouring countries are performing better at the Human Development Index (HDI), India with the second highest growth rate in the world ranked poorly and slipped further from 126th

---

* Professor & Director, Centre for SAARC Studies, Andhra University, Visakhapatnam-530 003

in 2006 to 128th rank in 2007 among 177 countries. There are large disparities across different states and regions of India, in terms of human development and the indicators are much worse in some of the states in the country. The low quality of life reflects not only the burden of human deprivation, but also the difficulty in eliminating the poverty. The human deprivation is strikingly visible in the country, as majority of people are deprived of the basic necessities, i.e. inadequate access to safe drinking water, sanitation and health facilities. Food insecurity is another pressing problem among the rural and urban masses.

The sixty years of self- governance has not improved the quality of life significantly in the country. Even though the government introduced several programmes in the past for removing income inequalities and raising the welfare levels of the people, they could not be implemented properly and the economic vulnerability remained the same. This poor display revealed a long way to reach the inclusive growth which emphasizes more equitable distribution of income, besides building capabilities in terms of attainment of better health and education. Thus, the core of the paper focuses on the increase of social spending as well as the proper implementation of social services, which in turn, largely ensures human development. It also attempts to examine the dimensions of economic growth and human development, in the light of the social protection.

Economic Growth and Human Development

India's growth story is revolving around the growth of the services sector which is 55 per cent in GDP in 2006 (World Bank 2008). The country also witnesses the resurgence of manufacturing sector, in contrast to the loss of dynamism in the agriculture and allied sectors. The trickle down process of growth has been weak in India, since growth is not located in sectors like agriculture, where labour is not concentrated (Radhakrishna, R, 2008). The Indian economy is basically characterized as agricultural and the majority of people live in rural areas. Hence, the declining priority of agriculture in the country, particularly from the early 1990s further deteriorated the levels of standard of living of the rural masses. The low contribution of agriculture to the GDP and the low share of public investment in this sector lead to an increasing tendency to move out of agriculture sector. The flow of bank credit towards the agriculture sector was also declined and causing concern. Statistics show that growth is not visible in the agriculture sector, which has the potential to alleviate poverty through productive employment. Growth is also not seen in states like Bihar, Orissa, M.P. and U.P. where poverty is concentrated. Evidence suggests that India achieved poverty reduction by 17 percentage points in two decades, i.e. from 1981 to 2001, in contrast to China by 45 percentage points, i.e. from 53 per cent in 1981 to 8 per cent in 2001 (Radhakrishna, R. 2008).

The expansion of productive employment is required to reduce the poverty incidence, however, it is not increasing in consonance with the GDP growth. The unemployment rate in India has shown an increase from 7.31 in 1999-2000 to 8.28 in 2004-05, owing to the fall in employment in the public sector. The job opportunities in the public sector registered a negative growth of 0.70 during the period from 1983-94 to 1994-2005, notwithstanding the moderate growth recorded in private sector during the same period (Govt. of India 2007-08). This is because the growth in the employment in the private sector is not sufficient to erase the negative growth in the public sector.

Incidence of Poverty

The incidence of poverty has spread unevenly among the regions of the world and is deeply rooted in India. As social challenge in India remains quite acute, the progress in eliminating poverty is found to be difficult in most of the states of the country. As per the national estimate, about 36 per cent of population lived below poverty line during 1993-94, which reduced to 28.6 per cent during 1999-2000. The rural poverty was higher at 37.3 and 30.2 per cent, while the urban incidence of poverty was well below the rural poverty, i.e. 32.4 and 24.7 per cent in the above periods respectively. According to the international poverty line, above one-third of population (34.3 per cent) was living below one dollar per day during 2004-05. If measured in two dollars per day, the extent of poverty was strikingly visible at 80.4 per cent in the country (World Bank 2008). There is an uneven spread of poverty among the regions of the country and is deeply rooted in the BIMARU States, despite the continued efforts of these state governments. The human deprivation in several forms associated with poverty incidence is conspicuous in most of these provinces. The states like Kerala, Tamil Nadu and West Bengal achieved poverty reduction at a rate more than the national average.

The severity of chronic poverty was seen in rural and urban households in Orissa with 28 and 26 per cent; in U.P with 12 and 18 per cent; in M.P with 19 and 25 per cent; in West Bengal with 19 and 6 per cent; in Bihar with 19 and 19 per cent respectively. Only Jammu and Kashmir and Punjab witnessed the low poverty incidence. The chronic poverty varied significantly across social and occupational groups; and recorded the highest for SCs in rural areas (Radhakrishna, R, 2008). This type of conditions forced the people to limit their current ability to perform. Various wage employment programs like Jawahar Rojgar Yojana, Employment Assurance Scheme, Public Distribution System, Antyodaya and other social security programmes have been implemented in the past, but met with limited success. These programmes were viewed as nearly providing relief type employment, rather than regular employment (Mahendra Dev, 2008). The human poverty index also confirmed the backward status of the country, in terms of both rank (62) and value (31.3 per cent), relative to most of the other developing countries (UNDP 2007-08).

Status of Millennium Development Goals

Out of the eight Millennium Development Goals (MDGs) set by the United Nations as global measures towards inclusive approach, six are directly relevant to the concept of human development. There are very large disparities across different states and regions of India, in terms of their performance. Table.1 presents the national average of six MDGs of India in 1991 and 2005, which reveals the wide gap in attaining these goals.

These indicators are much worse in the northern states – Bihar, U.P. Orissa, Rajasthan and M.P. – than in the southern and western states, however progress in indicators overtime show that Bihar managed to reduce its infant mortality rate (IMR) at a much faster rate than Karnataka and Andhra Pradesh during 1981-2000. Similarly, child under-weight rates declined at a much faster pace in U.P. and Bihar than in Gujarat, Maharashtra and Kerala. The national average of India does not reveal the intra-state variations, as there is a huge heterogeneity among most of the Indian states. In some states like Kerala, M.P. etc, there are large variations in IMR and net primary enrollment rates among various provinces. This pointed out the need for state-specific approaches that allow for greater flexibility in addressing problems of various regions in the country. (Mahendra Dev. S, 2006)

Gender inequalities can be reduced through targeting by gender, as in the case of regional disparities through geographical targeting. The inter linkage between/among various MDGs are clearly established. The examples are : the association of a reduction in the proportion of under weight children with a reduction of child mortality; reduction in maternal mortality rates (such as tetanus immunization, expansion of antenatal care coverage) with an increase in the rate of professionally attended deliveries which will also reduce IMRs; reduction in child malnutrition with increase in schooling, and above all the association of female adult schooling with virtually the major indicators (like IMR, Under-5 mortality rate, underweight children, gender disparity in school enrollment, primary completion rate) and even in the incidence of poverty (Gibson and Lepcha, 2007).

Health Status

The significant improvement in health status in India is seen only in the decline of crude death rate and the control of communicable diseases. The mortality rates among infants, children and mothers did not show considerable decline, indicating the inadequate health services available to the people. Though an overwhelming proportion of people lives in rural areas, health care are mostly inaccessible to the rural residents.

Table-1

Millennium Development Goals in India

MDGs	*Indicators*	*1991*	*2005*
Eradicate extreme poverty and hunger	Prevalence of Child Malnutrition (%)	53a	47d
Achieve universal primary education	Primary Completion Rate (%)	68	90
Promote gender equality	Gross Parity Ratio in Primary and Secondary School	70	89
Reduce child mortality	Infant Mortality rate (per 1,000 live births)	90	56
	Under-5 Mortality rate (per 1,000 live births)	123	74
Improve maternal health	Maternal Mortality Ratio (per 1,00,000 live births)	570	540b
	Births attended by Health Staff (% of total)	34a	43c
	Contraceptive Prevalence Rate (% of 15-49 married women)	-	47c
Combat HIV/AIDS and other diseases	HIV Prevalence (% of popn. ages 15-49)	-	0.9

Source: World Bank (2008), *World Development Report*, New York: Oxford University Press.

Note: a =1990-95; b =1990-2005; c =2000-06; and d =1995-2003.

The health scenario in the country is not impressive, notwithstanding the moderate increase in life expectancy at birth in total and in females from 1990 to 2004. There is some progress in the availability of safe drinking water and sanitation facilities from 1990 to 2004. Still a considerable section, i.e. nearly 14 per cent of people did not have access to safe water in the region, and two – thirds were denied access to sanitation facilities. The health crises were also severe in India apparently

Table-2
Health Status in India

Healthcare Indicators	*1990*	*2004*
Life expectancy at birth (years)	59.0	63.6
Female Life expectancy at birth (years)	60.1	64.7
Probability at birth of surviving to age 65 - Females (%of cohort)		66.1 e
Probability at birth of surviving to age 65 - Males (%of cohort)		57.4 e
Population undernourished	25a	20 b
Children under weight for age (% under age 5)		47 c
Children under height for age (% under age 5)	....	51 c
Physicians (per 100,000 people)	....	60 d
Public Health Expenditure(% of GDP)	....	0.9

Source: UNDP (2007-08), *Human Development Report*, New York: Oxford University Press.

Note: a =1990-92; b =2002-04; c =1996-05; d =2000-04 and e=2000-05.

with one-fifth of undernourished population; a well below one-half of under-weight children and about one-half of under-height children. In all, the public spending on health is not even one per cent of the GDP of the country (table.2). This country has to perform better in time to come to attain a reasonable health standards, as the reduction in negative parameters like undernourishment and IMR during the above period is not appreciable, when compared to smaller neighbouring countries like Bangladesh and Nepal. Another characteristic of the country's health scenario is the absence of the same quality of services to all. The poor, rural population, the less educated women and children were deprived from the health facilities in the country. These people are ignored by the health care system, due to the absence of adequate infrastructure, as seen from the lower number of physicians and nursing staff per one lakh people and the availability of services in the public health centre's and also in the rural sector. Thus, the country, by and large, has always

Table-3
Literacy and Enrollment in India

Adult Literacy Rate (% aged 15 and above)		*Net Primary Enrollment Rate (%)*		*Girls to Boys Ratio at Primary Level (%)*		*Primary Completion Rate*		*Youth Literacy Rate (% aged 15-24)*		*Public Expenditure on Education (as % of GDP)*	
1985-94	1995-05	1991	2005	1991	2005	1991	2005	1985-94	1995-05	1991	2002-05
49.3	61.0	-	89	0.76	0.93	68.2	89.8	61.9	76.4	3.7	3.8

Source: As in table.2

lacked a proper health care system which ensures human development.

Literacy and Enrollment

Education is the most important enabling factor in fostering economic progress, however, the neglect of education, particularly at primary level is unfortunate, in view of its strong bearing on the overall development. During the last six decades, the efforts of the government could not bring significant improvement in the literacy levels. The low literacy levels continue to impede the development process by affecting the general quality of life in the country.

The percentage of illiteracy was still alarming in adults in some of the states of the country. However, the adult literacy rate as well as youth literacy rate in recent years was somewhat considerable, besides the net enrolment ratio at primary level in India, as seen in table.3. The adult literacy rate is strikingly visible in females, as they registered an increase of 14 percentage points from 1985-94 to 1995-05 (not shown in the table), relative to the increase of nearly 11 percentage points in total adult literacy rate. In general, the ratio of girls to boys at primary level was also impressive in recent years. The progress in net enrolment ratio at primary level, primary completion rate, and youth literacy rate has also shown considerable progress. Though education goals will require considerably more effort from the government, the public expenditure on education registered only a marginal increase from 1991 to 2002-05. Available information suggested that above one-fifth of tertiary level students in India were in science and technical disciplines, suggesting an inclination towards them (World Bank).

Gender Justice

Gender inequity is among the sharpest social disparities in many developing countries, despite the growing concern for its reduction all over the world. It is not a single homogeneous phenomenon, but a collection of interlinked problems. Though women do not enjoy the same opportunities as men, women's reduced access to health care, education and other basic needs in the country is a reflection of their worse off conditions than men. Even in the present years of globalization, women in India remain far behind men in enjoying basic human rights, let alone participating on equal footing with men. The level of gender disparity in health and education is high in most of the states in India. The gender gap which is largely attributed to low socio-economic status and deep-rooted patriarchal values is quite strong and conspicuous in a number of fields. The disparity in some of the above areas is comparable with that of sub Saharan Africa. No doubt, there is some progress in women's participation in the development process. Notwithstanding this, the male-female gap is conspicuous in vital areas like health, literacy, labour participation and political representation. The state should pay necessary attention to substantially reduce the gender gap in these areas through increased investments in providing basic social services to women. It is a known fact that the reduction of gender disparity would help in the attainment of a majority of MDGs.

Concluding Observations

The human development approach is still to make a concrete impact on the development policy of India. The country has not paid adequate attention to the human development indicators over the past six decades, which suffered mainly from low investment and poor monitoring. It is often argued that India is contracted by inadequate resource flows and as such, the country could not focus upon the core issues of human development, hence, its achievement in poverty reduction and improvement in social infrastructure is meager. However, evidence shows that inclusive growth can be achieved through firm commitment and good governance in countries like Sri Lanka, where the economic growth is not an obstacle. Even poor countries like Nepal and Bangladesh have showed greater dynamism in recent years in improving the social sector and in reducing the negative rates. The public expenditure on social services in India is, however, lower, as compared to many other developing countries. Particularly, public spending on health is very meager. The current social fabric of India calls for a significant share of GDP for human development indicators.

The post-reform period witnessed significant widening of regional disparities and the rural-urban divide. Concerted efforts are required for universal access to education and to empower the huge population of India to get their due share. The thrust of the educational system should be on skill formation through vocational and technical training particularly among the rural youth for productive employment opportunities. Despite the grim situation, the poor states like Rajasthan and Bihar should be able to meet the MDGs with a combination of interventions. Unless there is an improvement in the delivery system and improved people's participation in the laggard states, it is difficult to accelerate the growth and poverty reduction in India.

It is a known fact that the human capabilities can clearly be enhanced by economic growth, only when the nature of growth should be equitable and employment-intensive. Hence, the present economic scenario of India addresses a better monitoring and acceleration in people's participation in the development process. Better governance is the most essential thing to reap the benefits of social security nets like PDS and other related ones in the education and health sectors, which were limited earlier by the poor implementation. Care should also be taken in improving the social and physical infrastructure, in order to attain the MDGs. A study by Mahendra Dev indicates that faster and inclusive growth can be achieved simultaneously through implementation of pro-poor and people-centric policies. In the present context, there is an urgent need to strengthen the agriculture sector to increase its productivity, which in turn provide livelihood to the majority of rural masses and reduce inequalities to a large extent. The country should take steps to create productive employment, which is the effective means to ensure food security and poverty reduction.

REFERENCES

1. Elizabeth Gibson and Pasang D Lepcha (ed. 2007), *Measuring India's Progress on the Millennium Development Goals- A Citizen's Report,* pp.8-14.
2. Govt. of India, Ministry of Finance (2007-08), *Economic Survey,* pp.247-9

3. Mahendra Dev. S. (2006) "Economic and Social Development of Andhra Pradesh: Retrospect and Prospect" in R.S. Rao, V. Hanumantha Rao and N. Venugopal (eds.), *Fifty Years of Andhra Pradesh: 1956-2000*, Hyderabad: Centre for Development Research and Communication, pp. 73-78.

4. Mahendra Dev. S (2008), *Inclusive Growth in India – Agriculture, Poverty and Human Development*, New Delhi: Oxford University Press, pp. 276-91.

5. Naik, S.D (2008), "The Indian Story: Growth without Equity", *Business Line*, Feb 8.

6. Radhakrishna. R (ed. 2008), *India Development Report*, New Delhi: Oxford University Press, p.18.

7. *Ibid.*, pp. 8-18.

8. *Ibid.*, p. 7.

9. UNDP (2007-08), *Human Development Report*, New York: Oxford University Press, table.3, p.239.

10. World Bank (2008), *World Development Report*, New York: Oxford University Press, table.2, p. 336.

11. *Ibid.* table. 4, p. 340.

12

MILLENNIUM DEVELOPMENT GOALS (MDGs) – INDIAN SCENARIO

V.Krishna Murthy & R.V.L.N. Ratnakara Rao***

Introduction

The United Nations declared eight Millennium Development Goals (MDGs) to be achieved by 2015, which include women development indicators and battle against starvation. In fact, starvation is the furtive enemy of development. The report on the State of Food Insecurity in the World 2008, has come out with stark revelations which cannot be overlooked. The report says that by the end of 2009 the number of hungry people will reach one billion. At present the number of chronically hungry people is 963 million. India, China, the Democratic Republic of Congo, Bangladesh, Indonesia, Pakistan and Ethiopia account for two-thirds of these people, nearly (642 millions). According to the FAO report that overall hunger situation in India continues to be one of suffering, though it varies from one state to another state. Madhya Pradesh's hunger level is worse than even Ethiopia's. Though Punjab's rank in India is number one, it comes at 34 in the developing countries list. According to the FAO report food insecurity has increased due to rising global food prices and the deteriorating financial situation. The worst affected are the poor, the landless, women and children it says. The situation is growing worse day by day and it seems difficult

* Retd. Professor, Dept. of Education, Andhra University, Visakhapatnam.

** Dept. of Phisical Education, Andhra University, Visakhapatnam.

that Millennium Development Goals to halve the number of the hungry by 2015 will be achieved, as agriculture has logged only a nominal 2.3 per cent annual growth. Substantial policy initiates should be taken and small farmers should be encouraged. While the poor are victims of malnutrition due to non-availability of food and nutrients, it has plenty of land that can be cultivated. All we need is expansion of cultivated area, particularly for foodgrains eg. Our country's north-eastern part remaining the most untapped and it should be used for food grain production. The policy-makers should understand the exigencies of the situation and make useful amends to satisfy the needs of hungry.

Women Development Indicators

The United Nations Millennium Development Goals have explicitly linked economic progress to the equilisation of opportunities for women. These goals thus recognize the importance not only of raising the status of women, but also of narrowing disparities between women and men. The gender disparities are often greatest in the poorest countries. More women are gaining access to education, but equality in education is still far from reality in some regions. i) one way to bring women into productive labour is by increasing their participation in education, equipping them with skills necessary to compete in the labour markets. Accessibility of education, labour markets and decent and productive employment is vital for creating equality between men and women, one of the thrust areas of Millennium Development Goals i.e. achievement of gender equality as MDG indicators put strong focus on poverty, employment, education, health, and civic and political participation. ii) in fact, women development indicators like literacy ratio, sex ratio, life expectancy, age at marriage and couple protection rate are also health indicators and also included under the UN Millennium Development Goals.

Eight Goals: 8 MDGs

The following are the eight goals and India's performance in each one of terms as per information available in recent reports and MDG Website.

1. Eradicate extreme Poverty and Hunger.
2. Achieve Universal Primary Education.
3. Promote Gender equality and empower women.
4. Reduce Child Mortality.
5. Improve Maternal Health.
6. Combat HIV/AIDS, Malaria and other diseases.
7. Ensure environmental sustainability.
8. Develop a Global partnership for development.

Goal 1: Eradicate Extreme Poverty and Hunger:

The problem of hunger persists in India with over 200 million people lacking access to enough food to meet their basic nutritional needs. Over 50 per cent of the children in the country are malnourished and of those about 20 per cent are severely malnourished.

Goal 2: Achieve Universal Primary Education

In India lack of access to water and sanitation has an adverse effect and girl's attendance at secondary schools. Since almost two-thirds of the World's 110 million children out of school are girls (over 73 million) ensuring their education is a top development priority.

Goal 3: Promote Gender Equality and Empower Women

In India, socially debilitating customs and patriarchal mind sets curtail women's basic rights. Also, the gap between men and women is higher among rural areas and for scheduled castes and scheduled tribes. Fear and shame prevent many women from speaking out against the declining sex ratio, foeticide, infanticide, domestic violence, dowry deaths, rape, sexual harassment, HIV/AIDS, vulnerability issues, and trafficking in women and children.

Goal 4: Reducing Child Mortality

In India, 1.7 million infants die every year and in addition one million die before they reach their fifth birth day. More than 64 per cent of infant deaths occur in the first month of life and a majority of them die in the first week. The main killers are asphyxia, premature birth, diarrhea, pneumonia, and other respiratory infections. Around 30 per cent of new born babies have low birth weight and, therefore, face high risk of death. In 2006, 2.1 million children under five years of age died in India, the biggest number after China.

Goal 5: Improve Maternal Health

Reduction of maternal mortality depends on the availability of skilled attendants at birth. Currently in India, skilled providers attend only 42 per cent of birth. While the target value of maternal mortality is 109, the 2001-03 figure was 301. By current trends, India is not expected to reach the goals of improving maternal health.

Goal 6: Combat HIV/AIDS, Malaria and Other Diseases

Tuberculosis (TB) is a major public health problem in India; each year over 1.8 million people contract TB and about 450,000 die from it. Also, one in 630 people is infected by malaria. According to reports or the National Aids Control Organisation (NACO), Indi had 2.3 million people infected with HIV.

Goal 7: Ensure Environmental Sustainability

Around 40 million households in rural areas do not have a safe source for drinking water and over 100 million rural households live without access to sanitation facilities. The Indian government has released recently the National Action Plan and Climate Change. However, challenges remain. Increasing population, falling water tables, coupled with serious drought conditions have dire consequences for health, nutrition and the over all development, especially of children.

Goal 8: Develop a Global partnership for development

India in the past few years has seen the initiation of Multilateral Debt Relief Initiative and with recent findings in developed countries to increase development assistance to meet committed targets by $18 million a year till 2010. India may meet its financial aid requirement.

UN Development Goals Not Easy to Achieve: Indian Scenario

In view of the prevailing conditions in India, UN Development Goals are not easy to achieve, among which the following may be cited.

1. Dependency on Welfare Schemes

India will find it difficult to achieve the Millennium Development Goals (MDGs) set for 2015 by the UN, as people have engaged in traditional jobs were becoming dependent on welfare schemes. Giving a mid way assessment on the MDGs drawn up in 2000, Planning Commission Member Syada Hameed told that traditional livelihoods were facing slow death and people engaged in them were being forced into despair eg. Artisans, agricultural sector etc. The skills are fading and with it the skilled, eg. Handloom. They are becoming more and more dependent on what in government terminology are called welfare schemes, making the achievement of MDGs more difficult.

2. Highest Maternal Deaths (25% of the World Total)

Even though India is emerging as a global economic leader (eg. GDP), it has the highest number of maternal deaths during child birth or a fourth of the world total (25%).

a) Diseases and Nutrition Deficiency (20% of the World Total)

India also contributes to a fifth of the World's share of diseases and nutrition deficiency (20%) and has the second largest number of HIV and AIDS cases.

b) Benefits have not trickled down to the poorest

The fact is that the benefits of our growth have not trickled down to the poorest of the poor and they are unable to access even the most essential of services like drinking water, sanitation, schools and basic health facilities.

c) Malnutrition on among Women and Children

With malnutrition among women and children becoming the most insidious problem faced by India, the government will have to examine some of the flagship programme in the light of national and international experience in tackling it.

d) Need for inputs from UN agencies

In tackling this problem, there was need also for inputs from UN agencies. Further, we need to work together because we are serious about meeting UN MDG targets.

e) Need to ensure a healthy and happy future

More importantly, we have to ensure a healthy and happy future for men, women and children and to the next generation.

f) Sanitation

Another major challenge is sanitation as the report reveals that 62 per cent of Indians do not have access to improved sanitation, while 43 per cent of South Asian urban population lives in slum conditions.

In order to meet the MDG target, an addition 1.6 billion people across the globe need access to improved sanitation. But if the current trend continues, the world is likely to miss the sanitation target by 600 million people.

g) Need for well planned actions

Though South Asia in general and India in particular is emerging as a global political and economic force, there is need to implement well planned actions to improve the delivery of essential services to the people.

To achieve the MDGs, the governments (Central, State and Local bodies), UN and donors in the region must make some important commitments, set aside their personal, political or geographical considerations and work for the global welfare.

Education and Health slow down in India's millennium march:

The Central government's primary education programme Sarva Siksha Abhiyan (Education for All) may be helping India get close to the millennium development goal of ensuring primary education for all by 2015, according to the United Nations Millennium Development Goals (MDG) report, 2008.

Areas of Slow Down

(i) Secondary education, maternal and infant mortality rates

But India needs to do a lot more for the secondary education sector and health indicators like maternal and infant mortality rates.

(ii) Non-enrolment in primary schools

Though the enrollment ratio among young children moved up to above 90 per cent across south Asia, more than 18 million children of primary school age (6-14 years) are still not enrolled in schools, the report found, the MDG target is to ensure 100 per cent enrolment across the world by 2015.

(iii) Gender parity

Within primary schools, gender parity is at 95 per cent in six out of 10 regions. Only Sub-Saharan Africa, Ocenia, Western Asia and Northern Africa and developing countries as a whole are marginally behind on gender parity.

(iv) Poverty

The Centre's initiatives in the social sector such as the National Rural Employment Guarantee Scheme have helped India achieve 27.5 per cent decline in Poverty. India is well on track to meet the MDG poverty target of 19 per cent by 2015 Olson said.

In India, poverty decreased from 52 per cent to 41 per cent between 1990 and 2005 but due to population growth, the number of people living in abject poverty rose by 20 million during the periods, the report said.

(v) Measles deaths and vaccination rate

Deaths from measles have been cut in one-third between 2000 and 2006, and the vaccination rate among the developing world children has reached 80 per cent.

(vi) Drinking Water

More than one and a half billion people have gained access to clean drinking water since 1990, but due to stress on fresh water resources, nearly three billion people now live in regions facing water scarcity (twice the number or two-thirds).

(vii) Medicines

Private sector initiatives and the advent of mobile telephony have helped improve access to essential medicines in the poorest countries.

(viii) Child birth and pregnancy, under nourished children and sanitation

But not all targets are on track. The Centre has been able to do precious little to reduce complications relating to child birth and pregnancy.

About a quarter of the developing world's children are under nourished (25%) and half of the developing world population still lacks improved sanitation facilities (50%). More than one-third of the urban population is living in slums (33%).

MDG: Asia richer, healthier, but only in its Cities

Asia's record of progress on MDGs remains impressive, although uneven.

1) China and India

The remarkable growth figures from Asia, driven primarily by China and India, no doubt have helped lift millions out of poverty, but rising food and fuel prices, and population growth in India have reversed these gains.

2) Vietnam

Vietnam has surpassed the MDG poverty reduction goal of halving the number of people living below the poverty line and is planning to go even further by another 40 per cent by 2010.

3) Bangladesh

Bangladesh too is well on track of poverty reduction, with a 40 per cent drop (2005 figures). But in recent months/years, rising food and fuels have reversed some of these gains.

4) East Asia

East Asia is generally on track and though South Asia is behind, it is making progress on many goals. But the individual countries progress across the MDGs is disparate, with health and environmental sustainability being the slowest areas for progress. Eg. Global warming up and Himalayan constructions.

5) Afghanistan

Operating in one of the most challenging security environments in the world and assisted by other development partners, Afghanistan has rolled out a basic package of health services, covering nearly 85 per cent of the population. This is reported to have led to a 26 per cent drop in under-five mortality and a 23 per cent reduction in infant mortality between 2002 and 2006.

6) Bhutan

The Bhutan government, working closely with the UN and other partners, has ahead reached the goal of halving the number of people without access to adequate drinking water and sanitation.

7) Decline in Poverty in East Asia and China

While most of the decline in poverty occurred in East Asia, particularly China, and other regions had much smaller decreases in the poverty rate, and only modest falls in the number of poor.

8) Variations in meeting the MDGs

a) One of the striking features of the growth story in the Asia-Pacific region is the increasing gap between countries. Eg. While the larger, rapidly growing economies like China, and may be India, have advanced by leaps and bounds, there is a widening gap between these faster growing economies and those being left behind. Particularly, the least developed, land locked and the small island developing states. These are mostly off-track in meeting the MDGs.

b) Even within the well-performing countries, too, particularly regions and groups are falling behind. The rapid economic growth in these prospering countries is not automatically translated into tangible improvements for the majority of people or directly improved the lot of those at the lowest rungs of society.

c) In equalities are increasing dramatically, especially in the fast growing economies. This is painfully evident, when we note that the indicators for maternal mortality have barely improved across the region, despite remarkable progress on economic indicators.

9. The benefits of Asia's growth have remained largely concentrated in its urban centre's. Rural populations, which still comprise majority of the regions populace, have typically been by passed.

10. Moreover, these dramatic growth rates (that have been given wide publicity) have not been accompanied by commensurate increases in employment opportunities or investment in human development, there by increasing the number of poor (aam admi) and the lower middle class.

To do more to improve

1) Olson, the UN's India representative made a suggestive observations, when he said "India would have to do more to improve the secondary education system and in health sector to reduce the maternal and infant mortality rates, control the spread of HIV/AIDS as well as providing clean drinking water and sanital facilities to its population". P.N. Kulkarni, one of the researchers who compiled the report said "targeted interventions and improvement in the institutional delivery mechanism are imperative for India to meet the MDG targets".

2) Though there has been some improvement in the levels of poverty in South Asia, child's malnutrition, a key indicator of hunger and poverty remains remarkably high in most parts of Asia, including India.

3) **Rising Prices:** The UN's Annual Report, a yard stick for measuring the achievement of the MDGs, has warned that rising prices of food is expected to add another 100 million people to the list of those living in absolute poverty in countries like India.

4) **Global Poverty, larger than previously thought:** Globally, there had been a strong and sustained progress in reducing extreme poverty. But improved estimates of poverty from the World Bank show that the number of poor in the developing World is larger than previously thought, of 1.4 billion people in 2005.

5) Sub-Saharan Africa and the former Soviet Republics: Increase in Poor

Sub-Saharan Africa and the former Soviet Republics actually saw the number of poor increase between 1990 and 2005.

Latin America

Conditional cash transfers, which have been pioneered and tired with some success in Latin America, can provide much needed focus on specific MDGs, especially those related to education and health. Schemes in which mothers are provided cash incentives to ensure that their children especially girls, go to school or to ensure that children are vaccinated, can make a major difference in achieving the MDGs. Asian countries, with some exceptions, have not used such schemes as widely as other regions where they worked very well, especially in rural areas. At the UN Development Programme, administrators have seen and helped drive some progress in this region, even in countries that are land locked and emerging from conflict. Finally, as has already been said, MDGs are achievable, and essential, but it will take concerted, creative and decisive action from the global community in helping the backward and developing communities. Will the global community accept such responsibility and respond positively is the million dollar question now.

Achievements of UN MDGS by 2015

The Eleventh Plan (GOI, XI Five Year Plan, 2007-12) proposes a five fold agenda for gender equity. This includes: economic empowerment, social empowerment, political empowerment, strengthening mechanism for effective implementation of women-related legislations, and augmenting delivery mechanisms for mainstreaming gender for children. It adopts a right frameworks based on the principles of protection, well-being, development and participation. Recognising the women and children are not homogenous categories, the eleventh plan aims to have not just general programmes, but also special targeted interventions catering to the differential needs of different groups. Thus, during the plan period, specific pilots for girl children and Muslim women will be taken up. Inclusive growth in the Eleventh Plan envisages respecting the differential needs of all women and children and providing them with equal access to opportunities. This can only happen when women are recognized as agents of socio-economic growth and autonomy of decision-making and the rights of children are respected.

During the 11th Plan period, utmost care was given to specify for the development of Dalits, tribal and marginalized women through financial inclusion, to attain gender equality and to receive their rightful share from all the women related general development sectors. For example, to ensure a gender responsive health care system maternal health services have to be improved and emerging and compulsory obstetrics care will be made available within a travel time of two hours.

- Targets for halving prevalence of anaemia and malnutrition along women and children have been set and the ICDS (Integrated Child Development Scheme) is being restructured and reoriented towards this end.

- A new component of conditional monitoring benefits is proposed to target foetal malnutrition, ensure better care for pregnant women and encourage breast feeding.

- Universalisation of Anganwadis will be carried out and Panchayats and mother's group will be given resources to ensure effective implementation of the scheme.

- Need based, community run crèches will be introduced to tackle malnutrition and cater to child care.

Similarly, the Union Budget has brought out statements which indicate Budget Provisions for 100 per cent women specific programmes and 30 per cent women specific programmes.

a) 14 ministries/departments indicate Rs. 87,953 million as 100 per cent allocation and 13 ministries indicate Rs. 2,23,825 million as 30 per cent allocation.

b) The 100 per cent allocation ministries are traditional sectors with women related programmes (2007-08).

Conclusion

The present millennium is witnessing phenomenal global changes, and no nation can isolate itself from the process of growth and change, hence achievement of the UNMDGs is a must for India. In fact, the interim Budget presented by the Pranab Mukherjee as in charge Minsiter for Finance made allocations to sectors like women development, primary education, mid-day meals scheme, rural employment generation programmes, pension scheme etc. under the broad umbrella of welfare for the Aam Admi is a right step in this direction.

REFERENCES

1. *Business World*, 20 August, 2007.
2. *Career & Competition*, Monthly Chronicle, August, 2007.
3. *Civil Services Chronicle*, August, 2007, October, November, 2008.
4. *Competition Success Review*, February, 2009.
5. *Deccan Chronicle*, 23 September, 2008.
6. Neelam Raj, *Sunday Times of India*, October 19, 2008.
7. *Outlook*, 22 September, 2008.
8. Raja J. Chelliah and K.R. Shanmugam, "A Strategy for Poverty Reduction and Narrowing Regional Disparities", *Economic and Political Weekly*, August 25, 2007.
9. *The Financial Express (Economic Bureau)*, September 12, 2008.

13

HUMAN RESOURCE DEVELOPMENT AT NATIONAL LEVEL

K.V.V. Devi Prasad & G. Syamala Rao***

Introduction

The term Human Resources refers to the knowledge, skills, creative abilities, talents, aptitude, attitude, values and beliefs of human beings. In general, Human Resource Development defined as those learning experiences, which are organized for a specific time and designed to bring the possibility of behavioral change. The most convenient classification to talk about HRD is on the basis of macro and micro context i.e. we could talk about HRD at the national and organizational levels. HRD in organizational context is a process by which the employees of the organization are helped in a continuous planned way to sharpen their capabilities required to perform various functions associated with their present or expected future roles. At organizational level, the aspects of human resources like knowledge, skills, creative abilities, talents play major role in deciding the efficiency and effectiveness of the organization. HRD in national context, HRD defined as the process of enabling people to make things happen. It deals with both the competency development in people and creation of conditions to help people

---

* Asst. Professor, Dept. of Management Studies, G.V.P. P.G. College, Rushikonda, Visakhapatnam, A.P.

** Asst. Professor, Dept. of Management Studies, G.V.P. P.G. College, Rushikonda, Visakhapatnam, A.P.

apply these competencies for their own benefit and that of others. At macro level, the aspects of human resources like culture, aptitude, attitude, values and beliefs play major role in over all development of the country. The objective of this paper is to discuss the significance of HRD at National level and draw solutions for overall development of the country through Human Resource Development.

Need for HRD at National Level

HRD is exploring new frontiers and is coming out from the domain of organizations to national and global level, but the thrust is still the same that treats human as resource to attain organizational objectives. The fundamental truth is that economic development is for mankind is lost and there is a mad race for achieving economic goals at any cost. At national level, humans treated as ends rather than a resource.

- HRD enables people to make things happen. If people have to make things happen, they need circumstances to make them happen.
- HRD deals with both competency development of people and creation of better living conditions.
- To help people to apply these competencies for their benefits and that of others. There are many things included and implied as competencies and benefits.
- Competencies may include knowledge, skills and values. These may be developed in individuals, groups, communities or collectives.
- Competencies may deal with any field like agriculture, science and technology, management, various professions like medicine, law, engineering, teaching, politics, public administration, home science, cooking, Tourism, telecommunication, Research and Development etc.
- The competencies may be simple like learning alphabets or complex involving technology applications to medicine, space, defense, environment studies etc.

- The competencies so developed would enable people to act and improve their own lives and those of others. These are further simplified and suggested that HRD at national level means competence building, commitment building and culture building.

Human Development

Human development is the process of enlarging people's choices so that they can live a long and healthy life, be educated, have access to resources for a decent standard of living, enjoy political, economic, social and cultural freedoms, and have human rights, self-esteem and opportunities for being creative and productive.

Human Development has two basic aspects:

1. The formation of human capabilities – improved health, knowledge, skills and wisdom.
2. The use of acquired capabilities – for productive purposes, for leisure or for being active in cultural, social and political affairs.

Role of United Nations Development Programmes (UNDP) in NHRD

According to United Nations Development Programmes (UNDP), HRD means enhanced competency in terms of healthy living, long living, skill base that contributes to productive activities and enhances quality of life through creation of purchasing power.

HRD therefore deals with competency building in the people. It is a creation of a set of capabilities and skills. The Human Development reports of UNDP take a view that Skills help to generate economic activities. Economic activities lead to an enhanced purchasing power by these individuals. The purchasing power acquired from economic activities leads to skill base, healthy living and long living. From over the last decade UNDP has been using these three main indicators of HRD at Macro Level. The Human Development Index (HDI) is a combination of all these three.

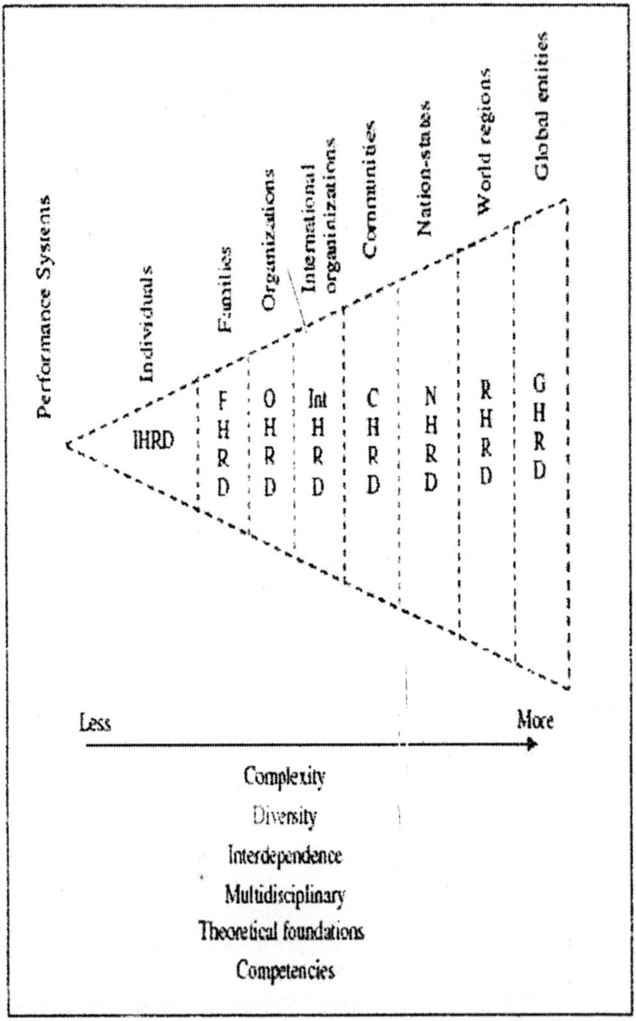

FIGURE 1: A Collaborative Layering of Human Resource Development (HRD) Performance Contexts

Source: Informed by Ahn & McLean (in press) and McLean (2005).

· The method of Calculation of HDI may vary from year to year but the essence of HRD remains the same. Human development is most frequently measured with the United Nations (UN) Human Development Index (HDI), which includes indicators for health, education, and standard of living. Countries are classified into three levels of human development based on their scores—low (< .500), Medium (.500-.800), and high (.800-1.000) (UNDP, 2004).

Role of Ministry of Human Resources Development (HRD)

The Ministry of Human Resources Development (HRD) is an Indian government ministry, responsible for the development of human resources. The ministry is divided into two departments: the Department of School Education and Literacy, which deals with primary education and literacy, and the Department of Higher Education, which deals with secondary and post-secondary education. The Ministry of Human Resources Development is headed by a minister of cabinet rank as a member of the Council of Ministers. The minister is assisted by two Ministers of State, one for each department.

Prerequisites of National HRD

The primary goal of HRD is competency building among people of the country. There are also other goals like creation of culture, quality of Life etc. so that the competencies should be developed on a continuous basis. Achieving HRD goals therefore requires the following.

- There should be specialized people to help in achieving the HRD goals by using various interventions, tools and technologies, processes etc.
- The people called as HRD Professionals/HRD Facilitators should integrate National needs and Individual needs.
- Identifying people developmental needs should be carried out on research basis.
- There should be Value Addition in competency building

through continuous learning.

- Use of latest technology and information systems that can facilitate HRD.
- Formation of national level HRD policies should match the developmental needs of people.
- The outcomes of National HRD Programmes should be evaluated from time to time.
- Formation of culture that should make country a continuous learning nation.
- There should be HRD Auditing procedure for Value Added HRD at National Level.

HRD Facilitators at National Level

In addition, the most important sources required is a material or economic source that facilitates the acquisition of some of the above. This also needs the top management commitment to HRD or a vision of the head of the country - Prime Minister, President etc. that can help to achieve national goals and put it to competitive advantage. In the national context, the trained people required who can facilitate HRD are Teachers, Media People, Several Experts, Social Workers, Adult Educators, OD facilitators, Consultants, Coaches, Learning Managers, several others and the count y leaders are also important.

HR Professionals may work in any one of the four locations. (a) Site / Plant (b) Corporate HR (c) Business Unit / Up Country (4) Out Side HR function. He may be specialist or Generalist. He may be contributor or working alone, integrator, or a strategist. For structuring HRD at national level, it could be structured as a separate department or a ministry. Most of the countries in the developing world had done this. In fact, a regular convention of ministries and others associated with HRD in the Asia Pacific Region. In some countries the Prime Minster himself may be handling the HRD Portfolio. In some countries, specialized task forces to look after human development education and the life. They can also be a dedicated full scope HRD Ministry in the country. The Union Minister of HRD / Education and the State minister of HRD constitute the HRD team. National level working groups committees and task forces are common factors in practice. The following subsystems have been extensively used in the last 25 years of HRD in the country - Training, Performance Appraisal, Feedback and Counseling System, Career Planning and Development, Potential appraisal.

Proposed HRD Policies at National Level

Education Policy: Education seems to have the ability to influence many other variables. Investment in primary education makes people more productive, improves rural, urban self-employment.

Educating girls and developing women: Several studies have indicated that women play a strategic role in developing human resources as mothers they are the primary agents of HRD. Children learn from mothers and foundations for the mothers laid their later development. Investing on women and development by giving them access to education, training and credit for employment generation is therefore likely to raise productivity of all sectors.

Health Policy: Providing basic health services to the people will result in healthy and long living. Providing safe drinking water, nutritious food, population control programmes, health awareness programmes, availability of medicines will result in improving quality of life and increase in life expectancy rate.

Entrepreneurship Development as a policy: Entrepreneur as a person brings overall change through innovation for maximum social good by satisfying needs in the society. Entrepreneur skills like creative problem solving, persuading, selling, decision-making, strategic planning etc yield in establishing successful enterprise. Use entrepreneur skill development as a strategy for Income and Employment generation.

Technological Policy: Invest in science and technology to build technological capability and lay foundations for economic growth and improved standard of living. Investment should be made in building knowledge base and skill base.

Community Development: Encourage community participation and local involvement through decentralization and other processes. People should be encouraged to participate in local development programmes.

Current issues in National Human Resource Development:

- Human Resource Development (HRD) should be redesignated as Human Development (HD).
- Proactive HD policies at the global, national and the unit level must be made and properly implemented.
- At the global and national level appropriate policies on population, health care, education, literacy, nutrition, etc are to be designed and implemented to achieve the objectives of HD.
- At the unit level also human beings should be given prime importance treating them as the centre of all concerns by empowering them.
- Innovative systems should be developed and implemented. The latest innovations in the field were deliberated and the following were appreciated.

HRD Interventions at National Level:

(i) Management of Culture and Cross Cultural Management Techniques.

(ii) Quality Circles and its impact on HD.

(iii) 360 degree appraisal.

(iv) TQM and its impact on HD.

(v) Concentration on Core Competency.

(vi) Redesigned Management Principles based on Indian Ethos.

(vii) Allowing and Encouraging individuals to discover their self.

(viii) Role of Information Technology in developing people.

Outcomes of HRD at National level:

- Economic growth and helps to reduce income inequalities.
- Rural Development.
- Improves the skills and capabilities of people.
- Helps in reduction of illiteracy.
- Provide good Health Services and Nutritious food
- Improves Basic, Higher and Technical Education.
- Political Stability
- Encourages lawful behavior of citizens.
- HRD Programmes helps to meet skilled manpower requirements of the growing economy.
- Increase in GDP, PPP and HDI.

Suggestions to HRD Facilitators while implementing NHRD

- Recognize the facilitating role of Private and Non Governmental agencies can play in HRD and support their participation. Promote Corporate Social Responsibly Programmes by giving some financial relaxations to those agencies.
- Mobilize resources needed for HRD Programmes using a variety of unconventional methods. Some alternative financial schemes may be included like cost sharing by beneficiaries, health insurance, community support, increasing taxes - reallocating resources, other than those from national taxes and duties.
- Improve the efficiency and effectiveness of various government agencies and institutions through development of professionalism and cost effectiveness, improvement in interdepartmental coordination and other methods.
- Improve the effectiveness of population policies and programmes to ensure the practice of small family norm

and population control.

- Invest on environmental education to create a healthy environment where people can live healthy and for sustainable growth.
- Strengthen agriculture industry other infrastructure and institutional base through HRD improvement. Support for small-scale industries, cottage industries, farming, dairy and other rural business, which results in increased in Purchasing Power Parity.
- Another important focal point for HRD interventions are the institutions in every country that provide services and implement public policy programmes which include educational institutions, hospitals, cooperative banks, insurance, security agencies and law enforcing institution etc. The effectiveness and efficiency of these institutions play a very crucial role in the help on any state. Any decline in these is the beginning of decline of nay country.

Conclusion

The difference between two nations largely depends on the level of quality of human resources. Thus, HRD at national level plays very significant role in development of the country. HRD enables the people of the country in terms of healthy living, long living, increased skill base and employment, attracting FDI, increase in PPP, GDP, HDI (Human Development Index), decrease in illiteracy, decline in crime rate, improved standard of living, technical education, political stability and encourages lawful living of individuals. Ultimately HRD at national level concentrates on competency building, commitment building and culture building.

REFERENCES

1. Ajay Kumar Singh, "HRD Perspectives in 21st century", *The Indian Journal of Commerce*, Vol 51, No.4, Oct – Dec 1998, pp 167, 176.
2. Ben Cox. J, Khadija Al Arkoubi and Samuel D. Estrada, "National Human Resource Development in Transitioning Societies in the Developing World: Morocco", *Advances in Developing Human Resources* 2006;Vol. 8, No. 84, *SAGE Journals Online and HighWire*

Press platforms, pp. 87,88 http://adh.sagepub.com/cgi/content/refs/8/1/84

3. Murthy M.G.K., "Globalization and HRD", *The Journal of Commerce,* Vol 51, No.4, pp 179,186.
4. Subba Rao .P, *Human Resource Management and Industrial Relations,* Himalaya Publications 2006, 195-205.
5. Rao T.V., "HRD Audit", Vol 9, ResponseRoles Publishers, pp 17-35.
6. Rao.T.V, K.K.Varma, Anil K Khandelud, and Abraham SJ 2006,pp 399-405.
7. "Rapporters report on HRD Perspectives in 21st Century", *The Journal of Commerce,* Vol 51, No.4, pp 165,166.
8. Susan A. Lynham and Peter W. Cunningham, "National Human Resource Development in Transitioning Societies in the Developing World: Concept and Challenges", *Advances in Developing Human Resources,* 2006; Vol.8; No.116, *SAGE Journals Online and HighWire Press platforms,* pp. 120-125 http://adh.sagepub.com/cgi/content/refs/8/1/116,
9. *UNPD Reports* 1997,2004 published by Oxford.
10. Vasant Desai, *Dynamics of Entrepreneurial Development and Management,* McEditon 2005, Himalaya Publishing House, pp: 13-14.
11. www.dwaf.gov.za/Docs/Other/RISDP/Glossary.doc

14

HUMAN RESOURCE DEVELOPMENT PRACTICES IN UNIVERSITY SYSTEM

Jagannath B. Kukkudi & Ramesh B. Agadi***

Introduction

The concept of human resource development relates to development of persons to their maximum potential and the conservation of talent for development. HRD has been defined as "the process of increasing the knowledge, skills and the people in society". But today, there is a little awareness of the fact that HRD is a contributing factor for the economic growth of the country, without qualitative improvement of human resource. The possibilities of an improvement in the standard of living of the masses are remote. An organization is known not by concrete and bricks but by the type of its human resource. It is constructed or destroyed by quality and behaviour of its people. It has growingly been realized that improvement in manpower in key to both micro and macro developers.

Development is important in every sphere of life and educational institutes are no exception to it. Development of university education depends much upon the quality of its human resource, i.e., teachers. In modern times knowledge is increasing at very rapid rate both horizontally and vertically. So, a high degree of knowledge is basic requirement for the success of teacher, and that knowledge teachers involve themselves in

*&** Faculty, Dept of MBA, Gulbarga University, Gulbarga, Karnataka.

research oriented activities, which indicate the degree of sincerity, diligence and creativity.

University Commission under the chairmanship of Dr. S. Radhakrishnan in 1948 emphasized on the role of universities in the advancement of the frontiers of knowledge, viz., research and especially pure or fundamental research. Teaching human resources of university ought to be motivated and persuaded to put their heart and mind in research work. It is the quality of research work, which governs the academic standard of the institute and its faculty. It is teaching human resources, which shape the destiny of teeming youth and steer the whole nation towards development and prosperity.

Teaching and research have been wedded to each other. Both the activities are means to development of university teachers. Research activities are more important at higher educational level. Creativity first erupts in mind and then is transformed in the shape of valuable writings. Hence, teaching should be creative. It is rightly said that application is soul of knowledge.

The present study of human resource development (HRD) in university system is restricted to self development process of university teachers. The objective of the study is to examine the nature and magnitude of self development concept of HRD. It is studied by undertaking randomly selected 100 teachers from various department of Gulbarga University, Gulbarga in Karnataka, which comprises 42 Lecturers, 36 Readers and 22 Professors. Here, the parameters of development includes their creative activities like writing books, papers and undertaking research projects funded by UGC, ICSSR, ICAR, etc.

Training and Resources in University

HRD is one of several departments on campus that provide educational services for University employees. If the department provides training-related services that will enhance the personal and professional development of University staff and faculty and the services listed here assist staff and faculty in meeting their training needs.

- Faculty and Staff Services
- Other University Services
- Information Resources.

Faculty and Staff Services are available for all staff and faculty.

a) **Building Great Places to Work:** A new learning resource for Building Great Places to Work (BGPTW) provides online access to tools for creating best possible working climates.

b) **Work/Life Resource Center:** The Work/Life Resource Center (WLRC) assists f culty, staff, and students with helping to balance their work lives and personal lives. WLRC can help with:

1. Finding child care
2. Sick and emergency back-up care
3. Elder and dependent care
4. Flexible work arrangements
5. Resources for expectant parents
6. Seminars, workshops and brown bag presentations.

c) **Faculty and Staff Assistance Program:** The Faculty and Staff Assistance Program is a confidential resource providing assessment and problem resolution service (up to five FASAP sessions per issue) and referrals to University or community resources, if necessary. FASAP counselors assist with such issues as emotional concerns (depression, anxiety, etc.), family/marital partner concerns, grief and loss, alcohol or other drug problems, and life transition issues.

FASAP offers 45-minute educational presentations to any faculty and/or staff group or organization upon request. Each presentation consists of a brief topic overview and allows time for questions and discussion. The Brown Bags can be held at the requestor's site. Some of the Brown Bag topics available include:

1. Humor for the Health of It
2. Emotional Intelligence: What is it?

3. Creative Thinking
4. Dealing with Grief and Loss
5. Happiness Is...(Examining Job Satisfaction)
6. Remember This! (Memory Improvement Tips)
7. S.O.S.: Stop On-going Stress
8. Talking with Elderly Relatives About Difficult Issues
9. Understanding Generations at Work.

HS Employee Assistance Program

The Employee Assistance Program (EAP) is a confidential, no cost service for Faculty, Staff, and their families. Our goal is to inspire ongoing individual and organizational development, while contributing to the health and well-being of the Health System community. We do this by providing brief counseling and coaching services, mediation services, crisis intervention, assessment and referral, educational and training programs, and supervisory, staff, and team consultation.

1. Resiliency and Stress Fitness in the Workplace
2. Work-Life-Family Balance
3. What Positive Emotions Can Do for You
4. Emotional Intelligence in the Workplace
5. Building High Trust Relations at Work
6. Cultivating Respect, Appreciation, and Inspiration Across the Generations
7. The Good, the Bad, and the Ugly: Managing Emotion As We Manage Our Conflicts
8. Improving Interpersonal Conflicts
9. Mental Health, Stress, and Productivity in the Workplace
10. Depression: What It Is and the Help That Is Available
11. Loss and Grief in the Healthcare Profession: Doorway to Empathy

12. Above All "Do No Harm": Exploring Substance Abuse and Addiction in the Workplace.

Mediation Services

Mediation Services provides individual consultation about workplace disagreements, and professional mediation for two or more parties who want to resolve a work-related dispute. In an individual consultation, the mediator helps you to explore the concern off the record and think through alternatives for resolving it.

The Office for Institutional Equity

This office delivers programming and services for University of Michigan faculty, staff, students and management to support diversity, equal access, affirmative action, equitable treatment, and cultural understanding and competency; and to prevent discrimination, sexual harassment and discriminatory harassment.

Health System Human Resources

Health System Human Resources Department presents *The EDGE: Strategies for Cutting Edge Leadership*. *The EDGE* is a multi-program series for a variety of employees ranging from all staff to executive leadership. *The EDGE* originated from the Work Force Investment Plan which recommends providing leadership development opportunities, training and resources. There are four components to *The EDGE*:

- Leaders at All Levels
- Foundations for Successful Leadership
- Masters Series
- Executive Series

Fit Healthy Lifestyle Programs

Fit offers a broad range of programs devoted to teaching, motivating, and supporting individuals in making healthy lifestyle choices.

Weight Management Program: teaches healthy habits for life, focusing on diet, exercise and health psychology.

Healthy Cooking Classes: make high-fit, low-fat cooking and eating tastier, healthier, and easier than ever.

Exercise and Relaxation Classes: including yoga, body sculpting, step aerobics, Pilates and more are offered once a week for 45 minutes.

Personal Training and Fit-Script programs which are designed to meet participants' individual exercise needs and focus on patients with special health needs.

Tobacco Cessation -helps individuals quit smoking through private and group programs.

Alcohol Management- teaches people how to make better decisions about how much alcohol they consume.

Health Education Resource Center - helps people with any health challenges they may encounter in life.

Risk Management Services

Risk Management provides essential insurance coverages, contract review, and loss prevention services to the University Community. Insurance areas include: Auto, Property, General Liability, Medical Professional Liability, and other coverages.

Assistance and training areas include: claim reporting, addressing issues related to mold exposure, and specific topics tailored to the needs of individual departments. RMS also sponsors quarterly seminars addressing topics of Employee Background Checks, Preparing For Disasters, IT Security Issues in Higher Education, Dealing with Student Interns, etc.

Challenge Program

University Challenge Program uses experiential learning activities to help University departments and subgroups, as well as businesses and community organizations, learn more about themselves and how they can work together more effectively. Your Challenge Program can be designed to address any of the following topics.

1. Improving communication, listening, and feedback skills

2. Strengthening group cohesion and camaraderie
3. Developing practical decision-making and problem-solving techniques
4. Enhancing trust in self and others
5. Recognizing and understanding individual strengths
6. Practicing effective goal-setting
7. Exploring leadership issues
8. Getting to know each other better
9. Demonstrating commitment and support

Information Resources

The Askwith Media Library

The Askwith Media Library (formerly the Film and Video Library) offers extensive information on professional and organizational development.

Kresge Business Administration Library

Kresge Business Administration Library has a large collection of Human Resources books, journals, and information in electronic format.

Occupational Safety and Environmental Health

Occupational Safety and Environmental Health (OSEH) has an extensive library of health and safety training videos available for your use.

IT Education Services Non-Credit Courses

IT Education Services offers a comprehensive program of non-credit computing and computing-related courses for computer users of all levels and learning styles. Instructor-led courses cover topics such as project management, Microsoft Office products, FileMaker Pro, Web publishing, Brio Query, digital photography, desktop publishing and more.

Occupational Safety and Environmental Health

The University of Michigan's Occupational Safety and

Environmental Health (OSEH) Department is a vital link in the enhancement of a healthy and safe University environment.

Division of Research Development and Administration

DRDA assists faculty and staff members in all aspects of externally funded research projects and other scholarly activities – from the identification of a potential sponsor and the preparation of a proposal. DRDA offers the following training courses:

1. Research Administrator's Network (RAIN) Meetings, held quarterly
2. Introduction to Sponsored Projects Administration"
3. Industry Sponsored Projects: Working with DRDA
4. Developing Budgets for Sponsored Projects
5. DRDA and CFR: Gifts vs. Grants, Who Does What
6. Arts, Humanities and Education Grants: An Overview
7. Finding Funding Opportunities
8. Research Proposal Writing Workshop

Web-based learning: The IS Learning & Information Center (MAIS LINC) is an integrated, web-based solution for administrative systems training, documentation, and communications.

Classroom training: Instructors are functional experts from the central business offices, academic units, and MAIS who understand the business processes supported by the systems.

Faculty Exploratory: The Faculty Exploratory was designed specifically for faculty at the University to enhance lecturing, research and publishing skills. Whether you already use technology and just need a few tips or are just starting out and need a whole new skill set.

Habit of Writing Text Books

Text books written with utmost care in the light of socio-economic requirements of the society are prescribed for the graduate and post graduate courses. They are the most critical source of knowledge to both learners and teachers. Those who have ideas, experience and concept in their mind write such books. Thus, the information summarized in Table 1 about this habit or teachers of Gulbarga University, Gulbarga reveals that majority of them (87%) don't write text books as they feel that this activity doesn't get much weight in their career advancement. This aspect of non-linkage with their promotion has also been confirmed by the opining of those who wrote some books only during lectureship as they stopped writing of textbooks thereafter due to indifferent attitude of selection committees at the time of their immediate promotion. The table under reference, provides that only 6% of lectures; 18% of readers and 14% of professors have shown interest in this type of creative work. Thus, on an average only one after four university teachers appears to be busy in producing this source of knowledge.

Table -1

Text Books Written

No. of books	*Percentage of Lecturers*	*Percentage of Readers*	*Percentage of Professors*	*Total Teachers*	*Total No. Books*
0	94	82	86	87	0
1	4	10	5	7	7
2	2	8	3	4	8
3	-	-	3	1	3
4	-	-	3	1	4
Total	100	100	100	100	22

Source: Field Survey.

Habit of Writing Reference Books

Reference books are the original source of knowledge based upon the research project reports. Such books, as respondents reported, bring name and better prospects to the authors. Unlike textbooks, these books remain in libraries for further consultation by academicians. Career oriented teachers feel more interested in writing these books, as this habit serves as method of self-development. They also get due encouragement and weight for promotion. However, it may be stated that teachers take up this activity at an advanced stage of their career. Table - 2 reveals that only 15% of lecturers working in Gulbarga University, Gulbarga having teaching experience above 8 years, have written such books in their area of interest.

Table-II

Cadre wise Teachers writing Reference Books

No. of Books	*Percentage of Lecturers*	*Percentage of Readers*	*Percentage of Professors*	*Total Teachers*	*Total No. Books*
0	85	38	27	56	-
1	15	32	22	22	22
2	-	21	26	14	28
3	-	3	5	2	6
4	-	3	5	2	8
6	-	3	5	2	12
9	-	-	5	1	9
12	-	-	5	1	12
Total	100	100	100	100	97

Source: Field Survey

As against 32% of Readers and 22% of Professors indicating the majority of even senior people also don't like to involve themselves in this sound academic mechanism of self development. The proportion of respondents having written more than one such book has arrived at 21%. Moreover, on the whole, the teaching community in university system is more inclined towards this form of work due to its linkage with their career development.

Publication of Papers

Research papers published in standard journals by the university teachers serve as an important source of academic communication on the one hand their self development on the other. This process of self development in the university system is well taken care of as due weightage to such activity is ensured in the career advancement and promotion of the teachers. In fact research papers are an outgrowth of teaching and research experience of the teachers through which they become visible to others, and this process of interaction makes more and more involvement of the academicians for continuing the chain of information dissemination and development. It is in this context that writing habit of Gulbarga University, Gulbarga teachers were examined.

Table-III reveals that about 96% of university teachers are quite conscious about their development.

Table-III
Publication of Research Papers

No. of papers	*Percentage of Lecturers*	*Percentage of Readers*	*Percentage of Professors*	*Total Teachers*
Nil	9	-	-	4
2-4	16	-	-	7
5-6	19	13	0	13
7-10	7	9	-	6
11-14	28	35	10	27
15-18	18	30	30	25
19-30	3	13	35	13
31-40	-	-	5	1
41-44	-	-	10	2
45-50	-	-	5	1
Above 50	-	-	5	1
Total	100	100	100	100

Source: Field Survey

The proportion of teachers getting as many papers published in journals of national repute as 2-4, 5-6, 7-10, 11-14, 15-18, 19-30, 31-40, 41-44, 45-50 above 50 papers has arrived as 7, 13, 6, 27, 25, 13, 1, 1, 2 and 1 percent respectively which indicates quite sincere involvement of teaching fraternity in this process of development. It may further be pointed that except 9% of lecturers all the respondents have got some papers published.

Research Project

Lot of money is being invested by the Government of India through the national level academic institutions like ICSSR, ICAR, UGC, etc. for the research and innovation in education. These institutions are financing the research projects undertaken by the teachers so that cadres of qualitative research scientists are developed in Indian universities. These research projects are not the part of their routing work assigned, yet they are given due weight age for such activities at the time of selection for higher positions. It is through this process of self development and appraisal, by which the teachers in Indian universities learn about themselves. The findings of these projects become the basis of policy formulation. It has been observed that very fewer teachers are interested in these activities, say they have to complete and self ability to get involved in such creative and valuable process of self development and development of the system as a whole.

Table-IV
Research Project

No. of Research Project	*Percentage of Lecturers*	*Percentage of Readers*	*Percentage of Professors*	*Total Teachers*
Nil	95	82	40	79
1	3	15	20	10
2	2	3	-	2
3	-	-	12	3
4	-	-	18	4
5 and above	-	-	10	2
Total	100	100	100	100

Source: Field Survey

The present study of Gulbarga University, Gulbarga teachers proves the aforesaid hypothesis as many as 79% of the teachers have not shown any interest in research projects funded by the autonomous bodies like UGC, ICSSR, ICAR, etc. It has been observed that this is a very time consuming process.

Table-V

Fellowship and Awards

No. of Organization	*Percentage of Lecturers*	*Percentage of Readers*	*Percentage of Professors*
Nil	58	62	55
UGC	24	22	28
CSIR	7	6	9
ICSSR	9	6	3
ICHR	2	-	5
IIT	-	4	-
Total	100	100	100

Source: Field Survey

The self-development activities of Gulbarga University, Gulbarga teachers on an average have brought recognition to them as 42% of respondents have earned either post doctoral fellowships or other such awards announced by the reputed national bodies like UGC, ICSSR, CSIR, IIT. However, majority of these teachers have obtained fellowship from UGC and CSIR. Thus, it may be stated that the teaching work and research activities of Gulbarga University, Gulbarga are quite of high standard.

Conclusion

The information personally gathered and on the spot assessment about Gulbarga University, Gulbarga teachers work life indicate that they do not get much incentive for their academic growth from the existing system, i.e., to a great extent they pursue self-development oriented research activities on the basis of their own perception and priority. Therefore, it is suggested that the existing state university system be thoroughly examined and needed changes be made to evolve a culture of development of human resource in such seats of learning so that social responsibility be duly acknowledged.

REFERENCES

1. Kohli, Updesh & Gautam Vijayshil, *HRD & Planning Resources in India*, Sanjay Printers, Delhi, 1988, p. 1.
2. Khan, Farooq, "Management of Human Resources", *Economic Times*, Delhi, September 22, 1984, p. 8.
3. Ganchi, D. A. "New Directions of Teaching at Higher Level", *University News*, Delhi, Feb. 1990, p. 1.
4. Internet services.

15

INTER-STATE VARIATIONS OF HUMAN DEVELOPMENT INDEX IN INDIA

M. Kumar Raju C. Gungulappa** & A. Reddappa****

"Economic growth contributes most to poverty reduction when it expands the employment productivity and wages of poor people and when public resources are channeled to promoting human development ..... A virtuous cycle of economic growth and human development arises when growth is labour using and employment generating and when human skills and health improve rapidly."

– *UNDP, Human Development Report 2005.*

"We have a collective responsibility to uphold the principals of human dignity, equality and equity at the global level. As leaders we have a duty therefore, to all the world's people, especially the most vulnerable and, in particular, the children of the world, to whom the future belongs."

—*Human Development Goals 2000*

Introduction

The accepted notion of what constitutes economic development has undergone a paradigm shift in recent times. The concept of development has been extended to be more comprehensive and go beyond the mere material dimension of increase in per capita income, complemented by the non-material dimension (like levels

---

*, ** & *** Research Scholars, Dept of Economics, S.V. University, Tirupati, Andhra Pradesh.

of education, status of health and access to basic amenities). Thus development, apart from income, relates to general well-being and economic capabilities of the people. Sen (1999) says that besides income and wealth we have reason to value many things which ensure real choices and opportunities to lead the kind of life we would value living.

It is argued that development should facilitate every human being to live, as she/he likes: expanding the potential capabilities[1]of every human being[2] (HDR, 1990). After consistent debates and discussions, this development approach has been converging with the notion of human development.[3]

Advances in Human Development Report in India Snapshot

Looking back over the past decade the long-run trend towards progress in human development has continued on average, people born in a developing country today can anticipate being wealthier, healthier and better educated than their parents 'generation. They are also more likely to live in a multiparty democracy and less likely to be affected by conflict. The gender gaps in primary school enrolement, admittedly a limited indicators for gender equity, have narrow, through girls still account more than half of children out of school.

The scale of human development gains registered over the past decade should not be underestimated - nor should it be exaggerated. They also hide differences across dimensions of human development. Progress towards human development has been uneven across and within regions. Human development is the enlargement of the range of choice and it is an end itself (Streeten, 1994). There has been a significant improvement in states has always been in the middle. The Levels of human development across the districts vary significantly. A welcome feature of the trends between the last two decades is the convergence of human development across districts.

Andhra Pradesh in All India Contexts

Andhra Pradesh Human Development Report 2007 the single goal of the human development approach is to put people, ignored so far, back at the center of the development process with their involvement and participation in terms of economic debate, policy and advocacy. The goal is massive but simple; the aim is to assess the level of long-term well-being of the people and to bring about development of the people, by the people and for the people. The United Nations Development programme (UNDP) initiated the process and first brought out a Human Development Report in 1990 in which the status of human development of a country/region was indicated.[4]

The UNDP has also urged individual nation states to bring out human development reports at the national level, across sub-regions within the country, for instance states in India, within the states across districts or sub-regions (i.e. cluster of districts based on specific criteria of homogeneity).Consequently, there are a number of countries, both developed and developing, that have prepared HDRs at the national levels.[5] The Planning Commission of India prepared and published the first HDR of India in 2001 in which all the Indian states are ranked in the order of their achievement in terms of the indicators that reflect human development. Thereafter the Planning Commission has also been encouraging state governments to prepare their own Human Development Reports.

The Role of UNDP in Human Development Index Preparation

The United Nations Development Programme (UNDP) initiated the process and first brought out a Human Development Report in 1990 in which the status of human development of a country/region was indicated. In fact, Madhya Pradesh was the first state in India to produce a HDR long before the Planning Commission. The other Indian states[6] have come out with their state level reports, one by one. As mentioned before, the Andhra Pradesh Human Development Report (APHDR) is one of these state level human development reports. Against this background, this paper compares the levels of the single goal of the human development approach is to put people, ignored so far, back at the center of the development process with their involvement and participation in terms of economic debate, policy and advocacy. The goal is massive but simple; the aim is to assess the level of long-term well-being of the people and to bring about development of the people, by the people and for the people.

Human Development Index Concept

The Human Development index is a simple composite measure that gauges the overall status of a region in terms of three basic dimensions - long and healthy life, knowledge and decent standard of living - of human development. According to UNDP methodology, literacy rate, enrolment rate, life expectancy and per capita GNP are the representative indicators for these basic dimensions.

Human Development in India

The Planning Commission of India considered the following indicators for three dimensions of HDI in NHDR: literacy rate (7+ years of age) and adjusted intensity of formal education for education, life expectancy at age one and infant mortality rate (IMR) for health, and consumption expenditure (per capita per month) for command over resources (NHDR, 2001).

The components of the human Development index are concentrated in which medium developed and low developed states. In the way of more concentrated in development of rural infrastructural facilities. Particularly in rural areas rural energy. Energy is the key input of their development of living standards these will be helpful to improve their quality of life and health conditions such as Rajasthan, Madhya Pradesh and Uttar Pradesh.

According to NHDR 2001, the performance of Andhra Pradesh appears to be lagging among the 15 major Indian states (See Table 1). Though the state improved the level of human development over the period, its relative position slipped as the other backward states began to perform better, especially in the 1990s. The HDI value of AP increased from 0.298 in 1981 to 0.377 in 1991 and further to 0.416, but the rank of the State was 9 in 1981 and 1991 and 10 in 2001. The HDI value in the State has been consistently lower than the All-India average and the other South Indian States.

Human Development Index (HDI) across Major Indian States Table-1

S.No	States/UTs	1981		1991		2001	
		Value	*Rank*	*Value*	*Rank*	*Value*	*Rank*
High Human Development Index (HDI) States in India							
1	Kerala	0.500	1	0.591	1	0.638	1
2	Punjab	0.411	2	0.475	2	0.537	2
3	Tamil Nadu	0.343	7	0.466	3	0.531	3
4	Maharashtra	0.363	3	0.452	4	0.523	4
5	Haryana	0.360	5	0.443	5	0.509	5
Medium Development Index (HDI) States in India							
6	Gujarat	0.360	4	0.431	6	0.479	6
7	Karnataka	0.346	6	0.412	7	0.478	7
8	West Bengal	0.305	8	0.404	8	0.472	8
9	Rajasthan	0.256	12	0.347	12	0.424	9
10	Andhra Pradesh	0.298	9	0.377	9	0.416	10
Low Development Index (HDI) States in India							
11	Orissa	0.267	11	0.345	12	0.404	11
12	Madhya Pradesh	0.245	14	0.328	13	0.394	12
13	Uttar Pradesh	0.255	13	0.314	14	0.388	13
14	Assam	0.274	10	0.348	10	0.386	14
15	Bihar	0.237	15	0.308	15	0.367	15
	India	0.302		0.381		0.472	

Note: Rural and Urban Combined.

***Source*:** National Human Development Report 2001, Planning Commission of India

The HDI value of Andhra Pradesh was lower than the all-India average, (0.302) in 1981 as well as 2001(0.472). The percentage change between two points in A.P is higher than in all-India but indices. We refer to the early 1990s as period I and early years of this decade as period II. The above table shows that in 1981

Tamilnadu state, has reached to 7th position but, in 2001 the result was admired and hoisted to 3rd position But in 1981 the state of Andhra Pradesh position was in 9th, but it is deterred, the condition of A.P decreased to 10th place We can observe the growth of Human Development Index in Kerala; it has strict progress during the 1981-2001.

The HDI value of AP increased from 0.298 in 1981 to 0.377 in 1991 and further to 0.416, but the rank of the state was 9 in 1981 and 1991 and 10 in 2001. The HDI value in the state has been consistently lower than the all-India average and the other south Indian states. When compared to BiMaRU [7] states, the state was ahead in the 1980s but in the 1990s the state was lagging behind Rajasthan, which was one among the poorer states in India. Based on the analysis of development radar, the comment of NHDR on Andhra Pradesh was that "on the whole, the attainment on the indicators seems reasonably balanced, though the attainment levels are less than half of the norms for most indicators even in the early 1990s" (NHDR, 2001: 16) lower in the most backward states like Bihar and Uttar Pradesh.

Need for the Study

To know how the human development indicators in India and Andhra Pradesh such indicators long and healthy life, knowledge and decent standard of living - of human development. According to UNDP methodology, literacy rate, enrolment rate, life expectancy and per capita GNP are the representative indicators for these basic dimensions. This will be helpful to increase the development of basic needs and Infrastructural and sanitation facilities which is the lowest indicators of various states and regions and districts in the Country.

Sample Design

For the present study a three - Stage Sampling method employed in selecting level of Human development index. They are classified into three categories ***1. Developed 2.Medium Developed** 3. **Low Developed**,* taking into three indicators long and healthy life, knowledge and decent standard of living - of human development. According to UNDP methodology, literacy rate, enrolment rate, life expectancy and per capita GNP are the representative indicators for these basic dimensions.

Period of the Study

The present study made an attempt at evaluation of Human development Index .the secondary data is used for the present study. The secondary data covers from 1981 to 2001.

Human Development in Andhra Pradesh

There are significant inter-district disparities in the index values. The values across districts vary from 0.717 in Hyderabad to 0.397 in Mahaboobnagar in period II (See Table 2). A comparison of levels in the early years of this decade (period II) shows that 11 districts had lower Levels of human development as compared to the index value for the state of 0.537 (Table 2). Out of these, five districts (Warangal, Nizamabad, Adilabad, Nalgonda and Mahabubnagar) are in Telangana, three (Kadapa, Kurnool, Anantapur) in Rayalaseema and three (Srikakulam, Vizianagaram and Prakasam) in North and South Coastal Andhra. In most districts of South Coastal Andhra the index of human development was higher than the state average. In Telangana, districts like Hyderabad, Rangareddy, Karimnagar, Khammam and Medak had higher levels of the two periods for education and health indicators relate to 1991 and 2001 respectively, while per capita income at the district level refers to 1993-94 and 2003-04 respectively, literacy rate and school attendance rate (of 5-14 age children) for education; life expectancy and infant survival rate (ISR) for health; and inequality adjusted per capita consumption expenditure for the economic dimensions.

Over time, the index values of human development for A.P. increased from 0.402 in period I to 0.537 in period II (Table 2) The index value has improved for all the districts but the rate of improvement varies from district to district. The ranks have improved significantly for Visakhapatnam, East Godavari, West Godavari and Warangal in period II as compared to period I. On the other hand, the ranks of Nellore, Chittoor and Kadapa have declined.

Human Development Index and Ranking of Districts (Period I: Early 1990s and Period II: Early years of this decade) Table-2

Sno	*Districts in A.P*	*Index value*		*Rank*	
		Period1	*Period11*	*Period1*	*Period11*
High Development Human Development Index and Ranking of Districts					
1	Hyderabad	0.591	0.717	1	1
2	Krishna	0.510	0.623	2	2
3	Ranga Reddy	0.452	0.610	5	3
4	West Godavari	0.448	0.607	7	4
5	Guntur	0.490	0.599	3	5
6	East Godavari	0.411	0.586	11	6
7	Karim Nagar	0.448	0.573	8	7
8	Nellore	0.452	0.565	4	8
Medium Development Human Development Index and Ranking of Districts					
9	Khammam	0.360	0.481	10	9
10	Chittoor	0.451	0.558	6	10
11	Visakapatnam	0.383	0.553	15	11
12	Medak	0.385	0.550	13	12
13	Kadapa	0.447	0.536	9	13
14	Prakasam	0.409	0.532	12	14
15	Warangal	0.349	0.514	18	15
Low Development Human Development Index and Ranking of Districts					
16	Nizamabad	0.383	0.504	14	16
17	Adilabad	0.361	0.488	16	17
18	Nalgonda	0.360	0.481	17	18
19	Kurnool	0.327	0.473	20	19
20	Anathapur	0.343	0.458	19	20
21	Srikakulam	0.269	0.453	21	21
22	Vizianagaram	0.236	0.402	23	22
23	Mahaboob nagar	0.249	0.397	22	23
	Andhra Pradesh	0.402	0.537		
	C.V :	20.98	1[illegible].89		

Note: CV - Coefficient of Variation.

Source: 1. computed using Economic Survey of Andhra Pradesh 2005-06 for Per Capita District Income;

Census data for Adult Literacy and School Attendance; and Irudaya Rajan's Study for in mortality rates.

The rate of change in HDI values during 1991-2001 was higher in those districts which had lower HDI levels in 1991 .This indicates that the backward districts improved more than the relatively better developed districts in the state. Therefore, there is some convergence of districts in terms of HDI. The co-efficient of variation (i.e., measure of inequality) shows that it declined from 20 per cent in period I to 14 per cent in period II indicates decline in regional disparities in human development across districts of Andhra Pradesh. The components of human development index show that there is no correlation between income and health / education for some of the districts. The rank in terms of per capita income is much higher than the rank for education and health for three districts viz, Visakhapatnam, Medak and Khammam. On the other hand, the rank for education is higher than for per capita income in West Godavari, Krishna, Nellore, Chittoor, Kadapa and Nalgonda. Similarly, the rank for health is higher than the rank for income in Krishna, Guntur, Kadapa, Nizamabad and Karimnagar. It is clear that apart from looking at aggregate HDI the components of the index have to be examined in order to have more effective policies.

Conclusion

Improvement is seen in the human development in the state. However, its relative ranking among the major states has always been in the middle. The Levels of human development across the districts vary significantly. A welcome feature of the trends between the last two decades is the convergence of human Development across districts. Two major conclusions can be drawn from the analysis in this paper. One is that there has been notable improvement in human development of Andhra Pradesh. But the relative performance of the state remained stagnant as shown by its ranking in human development across states. Second, there seems to be some convergence across Districts in human development in Andhra Pradesh, indicating that the more backward districts are catching up with the developed districts.

NOTES

1. However, the capabilities approach goes far beyond individual attributes to analyze the role of the social environment on human choice and agency (Rains, 2004).

2. Sen, (1999) says that development is a process of expanding the real freedoms that people enjoy. Therefore, development can be seen in terms of expansion of the real freedoms where the expansion of human capability can be seen as the central feature of the process of development.

3. Consequently, the role of social variables in the fostering of economic progress received much attention. The human development approach says that human beings are both ends in themselves and means of production.

4. It, in fact, indicates the relative status of the country/region in question in the set of countries/regions.

5. The UNDP supports the HDRs of nation states at many levels: funding, technical assistance, setting the methodology, publication etc. After National Human Development Report (NHDR) units were set up, it has developed a series of tools to contribute to excellence in sub-national, national and regional HDRs.

6. So far reports have been prepared by the states of Punjab, Maharashtra, Tamilnadu, Kerala, West Bengal, Gujarat, Orissa, Karnataka, Rajasthan, Himachal Pradesh, Assam and Nagaland. Recently Uttar Pradesh and Tripura.

7. The term refers to Bihar, Madhya Pradesh, Rajasthan and Uttar Pradesh.

16

GLOBALIZATION AND HUMAN RESOURCE DEVELOPMENT

A. Naga Raju & I.B. Raju***

Economic Growth and Human Development

The relationship between economic growth and human development is complex. The rapid economic growth induces the globalization patterns and gives the competitive advantage. This competitive advantage is a prerequisite for the attainment of success in globalized environment. The roots of the concept of human development can be traced in many cultures and religions of the human history. These will promote economic growth, reduce income inequalities, and accelerate rural development and helps in population control. In order to devise an effective policy we have to rely on HRD indicators. These indicators reflect all such human activities that add to human productive Capacity and once human productive capacity goes up, it automatically adds to HRD. Over the 30 years all the countries in general and developing countries in particular, significantly registered progress in key indicators of human development like health, education, life expectancy, child mortality, poverty and deprivation despite all the economic maladies. The

* Head, P.G.Department of Commerce, DNR College, Bhimavaram-534202, West Godavari Dist., Andhra Pradesh.

** Faculty Department of Management Studies, DNR College, Bhimavaram-534202. West Godavari Dist., Andhra Pradesh.

human capabilities that are the central focus of human development, however, are much broader than purely the productive abilities and human capital that are central to the new growth patterns and differ from the concept of human resource development.

The basic difference between the means and the ends. While human resource development considers human beings merely as means of generating greater output of goods and services, human development, by contrast, identifies people as ends- their well being as being the ultimate and sole purpose of development. Human development to growth depends on two factors – on accumulation of human capital through investments in education and skill formation, health and nutrition and research and development and on accessible opportunities for people to contribute to economic development through Social, political and economic development.

There is always a critical trade-off between the human resources growth and material resources potential in every country. The relation of population resources has been thought of as one of restricting the size of the former with the availability or the possibility of harnessing of the latter. The most important indicators of human resource development fall in two categories- First, those which measure a country's stock of human capital and Secondly, those which measure the gross or net additions to the stock or more precisely, the rate of human capital formation over a specified time period. While the stock of human capital indicates the level of human resource development which has been achieved by a country, the rate of human capital formation indicates its rate of improvement.

HRD Implications in India

According to Economic Survey 1996-97, The on going economic reform process should be reappraised and revitalized to give the entire national development effort a more human face. The eradication of poverty and unemployment must be abiding goal of our development policies and programmes. The achievement of this goal will require sustained and rapid economic growth combined with well functioning public programmes for social services, rural development and employment generation to provide an effective safety net for all those millions at the margins of the growth process. As a result, peoples' choices were enlarged and accordingly a favorable environment has created for people to enjoy long, healthy and creative lives. Generation of more income for the people and for investment in economic and social infrastructure have a pervasive influence. If higher incomes are available to the people and if the basic minimum needs are met, it would provide the pre-conditions for improving the quality of life. The high incidence of poverty impedes sustainable human development.

In order to secure both growth and human development in India, it is essential to create an ideal situation in which economic development and social opportunity may be linked up. There should be political commitment in deliberate policy actions. It is possible to achieve high human development at relatively low levels of income. India has been categorized as low human development country on the basis of weak links between growth and social opportunity. Late 2000, there has been remarkable attainment in the field of education and health in India.

The correlation between income and non income indicators like life expectancy, literacy rate and female-male ratio is lower than the correlation between the non income indicators. The progress in human development in India is marked by unevenness and stagnation. Public policy both at the state and at the central level has to be designed to meet different kinds of challenges in different parts of the country.

REFERENCES

1. Nanjundappa, D.M. (1997), "Formulating a Development Paradigm", *The Hindu- Business Line,* April 22.
2. Kumar A.K. Shiva (1991), UNDP's Human Development Index, *Economic and Political Weekly,* October, 12.
3. UNDP Human Development Reports Various Issues.
4. ADB's Asian Development Outlook.

17

CLIMATE CHANGE: A THREAT TO HUMAN DEVELOPMENT

*A. Ranga Reddy**

The paper highlights the impact of climate change on human development, especially on India. The scientific study of human development began with studies on childhood during 19th century. Adolescence was not considered a separate phase of development until the 20 century, when scientific interest on aging also began.[1] In fact, the development of human resources contribute to sustained growth and productive employment.

Human Development is about people. It is about expanding people's choices and the substantive freedoms - the capabilities- that enable them to lead lives that they value. Choice and freedom in human development mean something more than the absence of constraints (Amartya Sen, 1997). People whose lives are blighted by poverty, ill-health or illiteracy are not in any meaningful sense free to lead the lives that they value. Neither are people who are denied the civil and political rights they need to influence decisions that affect their lives. As per the UNDP's Global Human Development Report 2007, in spite of the absolute value of the human development index for India improving from 0.577 in 2000 to 0.619 in 2005, the relative ranking has not changed much. India ranks at 128 among the countries with medium HDI out of 177 countries of the world for 2005 year.[2]

Professor, Department of Economics, Sri Venkateswara University, Tirupati - 517 502, Andhra Pradesh.

Climate change will be one of the defining forces shaping prospects for human development during the 21st century. Though its impact on ecology, rainfall, temperature and weather systems; global warming will directly affect all countries. Nobody will be immune to its consequences. However, some countries and people are more vulnerable than others. In the long term, the whole of humanity faces risks but more immediately, the risks and vulnerabilities are skewed towards the world's poorest people. Climate change could further adversely affect food security and exacerbate malnutrition at low latitudes, especially in seasonally dry and tropical regions.[3]

The share of the population living in developing countries on less than US $ 1 a day has fallen from 29 *per cent* in 1990 to 18 Per cent in 2004. Over the same period, child mortality rates have fallen from 106 deaths per thousand live births to 83 and life expectancy has increased by 3 years. Fortunately, Globally, the primary school completion rate rose from 83 Per cent to 88 Per cent between 1999 and 2005.

Human Development in India

More recently, the emergence of India as a high growth economy, with *per capita* incomes rising at an average of 4-5 *per cent* since mid - 1990s, has created enormous opportunities for accelerated human development. Rapid economic growth has produced modest progress in poverty reduction and in nutrition but not under-nutrition. One half of all rural children are under-weight for their age - roughly the same proportion as in 1992 (Govt. of India, 2007).

Research in India has found that girls nutrition suffers most during periods of low consumption and rising food prices and that rainfall shortages are more strongly associated with deaths among girls than boys. Children in poor households work on farms, tend cattle or engage in other tasks in exchange for food during periods of stress. Manmohan Singh, Prime Minister calls the nation from Red fort on August 15, 2008 to bring down the malnutrition as a curse, that must be removed.[4]

Micro-level climate research for Andhra Pradesh shows temperatures rising by 3.5°C by 2050, leading to a decline of 8-9 *per cent* in yields for water – intensive crops such as rice. In Andhra Pradesh, one survey covering eight districts in dryland areas found that droughts occurred on average once every 3-4 years, leading to losses in output value of 5-10 per cent. This is enough to push many farmers below the poverty line. Models for farm income in India as a whole suggest that a 2-3.5°C temperature increase could be associated with net farm revenue reduction of 9-25 per cent.

Future of Water Shortage and Diseases

Himalayas is a Sanskrit word that translates as "abode of snow". Today the glacial abode, the largest mass of ice outside of the polar caps, is shrinking at a rate of 10-15 metres a year. The evidence shows the pace of melting to be uneven. But the direction of change is clear. Ice caps melt", affects south west Monsoons."

The Ganges could lose two-thirds of its July-September flow, causing water shortages for over 500 million people and one third of India's irrigated land area. Projections for the Brahmaputra point to reduced flows of between 14 and 20 per cent by 2050. Many rivers in the east and west are on threat in reducing their flow. Change of Agrarian Zones affects agriculture production and crop productivity. Famine and acute hunger at the tunnel end are to be seen. Urbanisation is at an increased level as rural regions are on dry up. Water table is on decline as more ground resources are being tapped. Growth in slums, diseases and skin disorders are common. Indian region will be more cyclone-prone as sea water hots up. There is a threat for tropical forests and green cover.[5] In developing countries, women are the worst sufferers in betching drinkable water, in curing diseases and giving food to children.

The health status of millions of people is projected to be affected through, for example, increases in malnutrition, increased deaths, diseases and injury due to extreme weather events;

increased burden of diarrhoeal diseases, increased frequency of cardio-respiratory diseases due to higher concentrations of ground level ozone in urban areas related to climate change; and the altered spatial distribution of some infectious diseases.

Human Health and Extreme Weather

Climate change will affect human health through complex systems involving changes in temperature, exposure to extreme events, access to nutrition, air quality and other vectors. Many of the emerging risks for public health will be concentrated in developing countries, where poor health is already a major source of human suffering and poverty where public health systems lack the resources to manage new threats.

Malaria gives rise to some of the greatest cause for concern. This is the disease that currently claim around one million lives annually, over 90 *per cent* of them in Africa. Rainfall, temperature and humidity are three variables that most influence transmission of Malaria and climate change will affect all three.

Climate change (characterized by temperature increase, sea level rise and precipitation changes) will continue into the foreseeable future and intensify with potentially disastrous consequences for the planet and its inhabitants. The most vulnerable groups will be the poor, the elderly, and children, including those living in rich countries. The most affected regions will be the Arctic, Sub-Sahara Africa, small islands, and Asian megadeltas. High risks will be associated with low lying Coastal areas, water resources in dry tropics and subtropics, agriculture in low latitude regions, key ecosystems (such as coral reefs) and human health in poor areas. Moreover, extreme weather events will worsen, especially tropical cyclones and heat waves. The result is that prospects for achieving many of the eight 2015 millennium development goals which include poverty reduction, better health and education, gender equality and saving the environment - will become even more remote.[6]

The Centre for Global development (CGD) said that India is figured third in the list of biggest CO_2 emitters through power generation after China and United States. As many as 16 power plants operated by NTPC were in CGD's red alert category for spewing out the deadly gas in the country.[7]

Although climate change and sustainable development are complex, interlinked problems that pose a challenge to humanity, they could be solved together by integrating adaptation and mitigation response measures into the broader rubric of sustainable development strategies. The countries political will certainly brings a safer and brighter future to the Global people, flora and fauna.

Climate Change and Human Development

Human development itself is the most secure foundation for adaptation to climate change. Policies that promote equitable growth and the diversification of livelihoods, expand opportunities in health and education, provide social insurance for vulnerable populations, improve disaster management and support post emergency recovery all enhance the resilience of poor people facing the climate risks. That is why climate change adoption planning should be seen not a new branch of public policy but as an integral part of wider strategies for poverty reduction and human development. So far adoption planning has been a fringe activity in most developing countries. To the extent that strategies for adaption are emerging, the focus is on climate - proofing infrastructure. Accountable and responsive government and the empowerment of people to improve their own lives are necessary conditions for successful adoption, just as they are for human development. The successful foundation for adoption planning was four "i"s - information, infrastructure, insurance and institutions.

India is experiencing rapid health transition, with large and rising burdens of chronic Non-communicable diseases (NCDs) especially cardiovascular diseases, Diabetes Mellitus, Cancer, stroke and chronic Lung diseases. It is estimated that in 2005 NCDs accounted for 5,466,000 (53%) of all deaths (1,03,62,000) In an average coastal and hinterland area people are capable to meet the challenges of climate change.[8]

Planet with Fever

People do contributing to warming. It is man-made invisible disaster. When we use an air conditioner, turn on a light, ride in a car, play a video game etc. whatever it is, we are unknowingly contributing to the quantum of green house gases in the air. The regions that are likely to be hurt the most by climate change include Africa, South Asia and Latin America. India and Europe are exposed to catastrophic risk from a change in monsoon patterns and the reversal of the Atlantic thermohaline circulation, respectively.[9]

Table 1

Measuring the Global Carbon Footprint

	Carbon dioxide emissions			CO_2 emissions per capita (t. CO_2)		Population Share
	1990	*2004*	*1990-2004*	*1990*	*2004*	*2004*
1 United States	4818	6046	25	19.3	20.6	4.6
2 China	2399	5007	109	2.1	3.8	20.0
3 Russian Federation	1984	1524	-23	13.4	10.6	2.2
4 India	682	1342	97	0.8	1.2	17.1
5 Japan	1071	1257	17	8.7	9.9	2.0
6 U.K	579	587	1	10.0	9.8	0.9
7 Thailand	96	268	180	1.7	4.2	1.0
8 Malaysia	55	177	221	3.0	7.5	0.4
9 Egypt	75	158	110	1.5	2.3	1.1
10 United Arab Emirates	55	149	173	27.2	34.1	0.1
11 Netherlands	141	142	1	9.4	8.7	0.2
12 Germany	980	808	-18	12.3	9.6	1.3

Source: UNDP (2008) Human Development Report 2007/ 2008, p. 69.

Today, we dumped another 70 million tons of globule warming pollution into the thin shell of atmosphere surrounding our planet. Tomorrow, we will dump a slightly larger amount, with the cumulative concentrations now trapping more and more heat from the sun. As a result earth, has a fever.[10]

Emissions from India are on a rising trend. Even so, its *per capita* carbon foot print is less than one tenth of that in high income countries. Based on the Industrial development, the country would release emissions of CO_2, SO_2 NO, CH_4 etc. Their contribution is quantified below.

The Table 1 above presents a picture that U.S. is the first, which has been producing high quantum of emissions. Next comes, recently the China. In Asia- Malaysia, Thailand, United Arab Emirates emerged as fast generators of emissions. Germany, Russion Federation are taken strong measures in reduction of gases. When comes to *per capita* emissions, in fifteen years UAEs become the first, U.S. is the second and Japan stand third, respectively. China and India are in forefront in population, but in contribution of emissions, they are after U.S. only. In overall, it is true that emissions are accelerating over sky.

Impact of Climate Change

Extreme climate events provide another set of threats. Floods, droughts and storms bring in their wake increased health risks, such as cholera and diarrhoea among children. During 2005, Bangladesh, India Pakistan faced temperatures 5-6°C above the regional average. There were 400 reported deaths in India alone, though unreported deaths would multiply this figure many times over. The heat wave that hit Europe in 2003 claimed between 22,000 and 35,000 lives, most of them elderly. In Paris, the worst affected city, 81 *per cent* of the victims were aged over 75 years. Summer heat related mortality could increase 55 per cent by the 2020s, more than double by the 2050s and more than triple by the 2080s.

Climate change could also contribute indirectly to at least three classes of wider health problems such as west nile virus,

Lyme disease and Malaria may rise; water born disease organisms may become more prevalent; and photochemical air pollution may increase. Strategies are being developed to address the risks.

Setbacks for human development will bring losses in agricultural productivity, will reduce income, diminishing access to health and education. In turn, reduced opportunities in health and education will restrict market opportunities and reinforce poverty. At a more fundamental level, climate change will erode the ability of the world's most vulnerable people to shape decisions and processes that impact on their lives.[11]

Strategies for Mitigation of Climate Change

Approaches to mitigation will determine the outcome. The more we delay action, the more atmospheric concentrations of green house gases will rise, the more difficult it will to be stabilize below the 450 parts per million (ppm) CO_2 target – and the more likely the 21st century will experience dangerous climate change.

Dangerous climate change is not a short term emergency amenable to a quick fix. The current generation of political leaders cannot solve the problem. Over the next few decades, the World needs an energy revolution that enables all countries to become low carbon economics. The revolution has to start in the developed world. Living within a sustainable 21st century carbon budget requires that rich countries cut emissions of green house gases by atleast 80 per cent by 2050, with 30 Per cent cuts by 2020. Developing countries will also have to chart a low carbon transition pathway.

There are three foundations for success – putting a price on carbon emissions – behavioural change of consumers and investors in shifting demand to low carbon energy sources – Rich countries have to take lead.

Carbon budgets can also play an important role in increasing public awareness and holding governments to account and their multi-lateral mitigation efforts. Developed countries that have not ratified the Kyoto protocol have relied on voluntary targets: voluntarism is clearly not delivering the required income. In United States, California and Texas now established as global leaders in wind power generation. In Denmark, the wind power sector has been encouraged and increased to 20 *per cent* of total power. In 1998, Japan complied with Kyoto reduction commitment and introduced energy efficiency standards and gained 50 *per cent,* including cars, fridges, freezers and televisions. Several countries have successfully changed the national transport sector fuel mix. India and Pakistan have seen a major expansion of CNG use. Forests are the most visible ecological resource on mitigation through international cooperation. Going solar and wind energies in day today economic activities are highly needed.

In India, till Feb. 28, 2007, National Clean Development Mechanism Authority has approved 526 projects in the various fields of bio-mass based cogeneration. The authority has so for approved many projects mainly in the field of Renewable Energy, Municipal Solid waste, Hydro floro carbons (HFCs), small Hydro and energy efficiency, etc. Implementation of these projects would attract foreign investment and efficient technologies, which improve climate change and Human development.[12]

Conclusions

Man is inventing on one side and other side creating always problems of his own on this planet. At present, planet is on hot and bringing miseries to lives, due to climate change. The more emissions of gases led to warming up of globe, which creates disasters like droughts, famines, cyclones, forest fires, unseasonal rains, spread of diseases. These economic disasters are already present over earth since billion years but they are today intensified by warming of air. The girl and women are the worst sufferers in this development. These can be controlled by using multilateral and multi-dimensional measures like afforestation, reducing carbon use transport, taxes on carbon producers, using wind and solar power, riding on cycles, eating vegetarianism. Government of India had approved 526 projects to bring relief and rehabilitation from climate change and human Development. Anyhow, countries' and environment saints wise counsel will prevail over it and makes this global people as a happier to live by man, *flora* and *fauna*, for some more billion years.

REFERENCES

1. Diane E. Papalia, Sally Wendkos olds, Ruth Duskin Feldman (2004), *Human Development*, Tata McGraw Hill, New Delhi, p. 22.
2. Govt. of India (2008), *Economic survey* 2007-08, p. 239.
3. R.K. Pachuri (2008) Every year of Delay means Greater Climate Change, *Span*, March/ April, p. 7.
4. Special correspondent (2008) All promises fulfilled, says Manmohan, *The Hindu*, August, 16, p. 12.
5. V. Jaydev (2008) Global Warming, *Manorama Year Book*, p. 287.
6. Mohan Munasinghe (2008), Rising Temperatures, Rising Risks, *Finance & Development*, March, p. 37.
7. *The Hindu* (2008) India third biggest CO_2 emitter in the world, says Data, Sept. p. 11.
8. Govt. of India (2008) Ministry of Health and Family Welfare, *Annual Report*, 2007-08, p. 4.
9. Natilia Tamirisa (2008) *Climate Change and the Economy, Finance & Development*, March, p. 19.
10. Al Gore (2008) It is time to make peace with the planet, *Span*, March/April, p. 3.
11. UNDP (2008) *Human Development Report* 2007/2008, p.107.
12. Publication Division (2008) *India 2008*, p. 316.

APPENDIX

1. Human Development Index

The human index has three components, life expectancy at birth, educational attainment comprising adult literacy with two-third weights and a continued primary, secondary and tertiary enrolment ratio with one third weight and income.

2. Kyoto Protocol (1997)

Specifies that, by 2012, Annex. 1 (industrial) Countries will collectively reduce their emissions by 5 *per cent* relative to 1990 levels and Non-annex I (developing) Countries are exempt from mandatory emissions reductions. Currently, 174 countries have ratified this agreement, although the United States the largest green House gas (GHG) emitter has rejected it. Neverthless, global GHG emissions rose by more than 70 per cent from 1970 to 2004, with major increases since Kyoto.

3. Evolution of Carbon Dioxide

For more than 10,000 years, carbon dioxide concentrations in the atmosphere were stable at about 280 parts per million by Volume (ppmv) but following the Industrial revolution, these concentrations rose rapidly and now exceed 380 ppmv. As a result - and with the help of other minor green house gases, (GHGs), such as methane and nitrous oxide over the past 100 years, the planets surface has warmed by an average of 0.75°C and the rate is accelerating. Other evidence of global climate change includes a systematic rise in the mean sea level (about 16 centimeters during the past century), the melting of ice in polar areas and glaciers, increased damage to wet areas, shifts in ecological cycles and animal behaviour. By 2100 year Co_2 concentration may reach 550 ppmv and temperature will increase to 3°C sea level to 30-40°C.

4. Nobel Prize for Peace

The award of 2007 Nobel prize was shared and given to Dr. Rajendra Kumar, Pachuri, of India, IPCC and Al Gore of formerly Vice President, U.S.A.

18

HUMAN RESOURCE DEVELOPMENT AND QUALITY OF LIFE

R. Ranganathan & M. Yogeswari***

Introduction

Education is the key to human development. Education is a fundamental right of every child. Article 26 of United Nations' declaration for human rights highlights the right to education. Article 45 of constitution of India notes free compulsory education for children under the age of 14 years. Further, Article 41 emphasizes right to education for persons including those with disabilities. Under the constitution, persons with disabilities have been guaranteed the fundamental rights as available to other citizens of the country Viz., equality of opportunity, non discrimination, no untouchability, freedom of religion, right to the language, script or culture, right to franchise, right to property, right to enforce fundamental rights, access to education in any educational institution, and right to work.

Biwako Millenium Framework (2002) for action towards an inclusive, barrier-free and rights-based society for persons with disabilities in Asia and the Pacific was adopted in the 58th session at resolution 58/4 on 22nd May, 2002 in Japan. The

* Professor of Special Education, Department of Education, Andhra University, Visakhapatnam, A.P.

** Research Scholar, Department of Education, Andhra University, Visakhapatnam, AP.

resolution proclaimed extension of the *Asian and Pacific decade of disabled persons 1993-2002*, for another decade, 2003-2012.

Government of India is a signatory to various UN resolutions concerning persons with disabilities. *The UN resolution 37/52* of 3rd December, 1982 is a significant UN instrument, aimed at achieving full participation and equality and protection of rights of persons with disabilities, which followed the declaration of International Year of Disabled Persons in 1981. Subsequently, *the Asian and Pacific decade of disabled persons (1993-2002)* was observed. The Asia and Pacific decade has focused on 12 policy areas, one of which is education. Children with disabilities include those with visual impairment, hearing impairment, mental retardation, locomotor disabilities and multiple disabilities.

Historically, India has been an inclusive society. Persons with disabilities were always part of the society. The origin of Special Education in India can be traced back to the era of "Gurukula" education which adhered to fundamental educational principles of Special Education like determining the strengths and needs of each pupil, individualization of teaching targets and methods to match the skills and interests and preparing the pupils for meeting the social expectation of their prospective interests. Though the learners were not labeled as 'disabled', they were provided assistance on the basis of their individual needs.

The development in Special Education over the years has been slow but steady. Before 1900, institutions for persons with disabilities were mostly managed by voluntary efforts and missionaries. The charity approach was predominant during those days. After independence in 1947, the human rights approach started gaining ground and provision for services to persons with disabilities found place in the constitution itself. Special school approach was considered to be the most effective strategy. As a result, scores of special schools emerged. The Governments started committing to education of persons with disabilities thereby starting special schools in various states and also in districts. Even today, special schools are increasing in number and this approach will remain as one of the models to serve persons with disabilities, especially to meet the needs of children with severe disabilities.

Education of persons with disability did not have a special focus until recent years. India, crossing a billion population has about 200 million school aged children, among whom nearly 4 million children require special needs education. A starting figure indicated in the seminar on Special Education, at *the Asia pacific programme of Education and Information Development Japan (November 6-10, 2000)* states that only 5% of children with disabilities are enrolled in schools. Moreover, 40% of children with disabilities are found to be not completing the further 3 years of compulsory education. Children with disabilities in rural areas do not have access to special education services, as most of the services are concentrated in urban areas.

Population of Children with Disabilities

The projected child population in the age group 0-6 years for 2001 was 157.86 million with boys accounting for 51.88% of the population and girls constituting 48.12%. Uttar Pradesh (19.3%) stands high in child population among the states followed by Bihar (10.3%), Maharashtra (8.35%), West Bengal (7.05%), Madhya Pradesh (6.73%), Rajasthan (6.62%), and Andhra Pradesh (6.13%). North eastern states have less child population when compared to other parts of the country. In all the states, male child population exceeds 50 percent which was higher than that of the female child population (Census, 2001).

Approximately 6% of persons with disabilities belong to the age group 0-14 years in rural areas and 5.4% to urban areas. In the case of number of persons with mental retardation, the NSSO (2002) reveals a low number, through many other reports present a high percentage of persons with mental retardation. It is possible that child with mild mental retardation were not covered in the NSSO 2002 survey. As children with mental retardation do not always have visible characteristics, they could have been missed out. In addition, perception of mental retardation by enumerators and informants also is a major factor in including or excluding such persons in the enumeration.

When compared to the total child population, those with disabilities form a very small percentage. Yet, every child has a right to equal opportunity. Further, considering the population of our country, the child population with disabilities is proportionately large, requiring attention.

Quality of Life and Human Resource Development

In early civilization the societies were simpler, the life skills and vocational skills were also simpler. The disabled persons could be easily assimilated in the simple social system. Only severely disabled persons carried a stigma and faced even orchestration because of the deterministic outlook. Those without observable disabilities were integrated into the society with ease. As the societies grew complex and skilling of vocations started with the advent of industrial revolution, even moderately and mildly disabled found it increasingly difficult to cope with the disability and increasing societal demands. The efforts to universalize education heightened the concern for mild and moderately disabled children who entered the system but dropped out because of the lack of sensitivity of system to their educational needs (Jangira, 1986). The concern resulted in the establishment of remedial classes and special schools for the disabled.

Education and rehabilitation of the disabled received increased attention in the postwar years when prevalence of disability showed marked increase in the war ravaged countries. The war itself caused orthopedic, hearing and visual impairment. This spurt in disability was in addition to the incidence of disability already prevalent in the countries. The humanitarian current flowing after the war to rehabilitate victims touched the disabled too. This is the period when socio-political conscience awakened to make amends for the neglect of services to the disabled for long.

There is another dimension of the concern for education of the disabled. Although the industrial revolution had inducted an element of economic competition wherein earning capacity determined the survival and the quality of life an individual qualified for, the war raved economies accentuated the process. Decolonization further contributed to this accentuation. The standard of living enjoyed by the western countries as fruits of colonization could not sustain it with decolonization and economic recession. The situation demanded each individual's contribution to economic growth.

Optimally low dependent - independent population ratio became the cherished goal. The low dependent - independent population ratio in developed countries bears testimony to this fact. The education and training of each and every citizen with fuller employment became indispensable. Every individual came to be recognized as a human resource. Naturally, the efforts to make every disabled person independent economically through programmes of education, habilitation and rehabilitation were recognized.

Yet another dimension of the change in education and rehabilitation of the disabled refers to the quality of life. In the post-war years, the UN charter of human rights provided another landmark in the pursuit of quality of life for every citizen. Education being one of the essential inputs to quality of life, its universalisation in the population of the disabled also assumed significance. However, the parameters of the quality of life in the disabled group of persons needed addition to those for the others. For example, one parameter of the quality of life for the disabled is that once the disability is identified, it should not be allowed to deteriorate. Nor should secondary disorders be allowed to develop in the disabled person. The extent of the success a society can achieve through its relevant structures and agencies determines the quality of life of the disabled. The earlier the identification, the better will be the effectiveness of the provision. The quality of provision of orthetic and prosthetic aids comprises another parameter. Provision of special learning aids, materials and equipment duly supported by the trained personnel in as normalized an environment as possible determines the quality of education for the disabled. Special education provision, therefore, refers to another parameter of the Quality of Life Index for the Disabled (QLID). Vocational preparation and employment of the disabled form yet another parameter of QLID. The level of adjustment and safety devices in production of instruments determine the quality continuum of these parameters. During late fifties and sixties, the improvement in the quality of life of the disabled as a part of the overall improvement of the quality of life of all citizen became one of the goals of national development. So, development of the disabled as human resource came to be linked to the quality of life.

The Human Resources Development approach has a philosophy of its own. Each and every individual has to be developed for optimum contribution to the pool of human capital-social, cultural and economic. In other words, every individual has an opportunity for fuller growth and development. It requires congenial climate of growth and development as well as an opportunity for the utilization of production capabilities of each individual. Obviously, the task is multifaceted and requires coordinated efforts from several sectors.

The present government is conscious of the fact that the country can enter the 21st century with a sense of confidence only if human resource development at a reasonable level of efficiency is ensured for all. The concern has been concretized in the constitution of the Ministry of Human Resource Development (MHRD) from birth through childhood to adulthood by way of providing education and care along with professional input have been integrated into this ministry. Early childhood care and education, general and technical education, sports and youth services, cultural development, etc., have been brought within its fold. Education of the disabled has yet to be fully integrated into this Ministry (MHRD).

REFERENCES

1. David T. Wasserman, Robert Samuel Wachbroit, Jerome Edmund Bickenbach *Quality of Life and Human Difference*, Cambridge University Press.

2. L.Govinda Rao, Jayanthi Narayan, M.N.G.Mani (2005), *Status of Education of Children with Disabilities*, NIMH, Secunderabad, AP.

3. Mani, M.N.G. (1985), *Source book for teachers of visually disabled children*, Bankok, UNESCO.

4. Summit of the Mind (2003) "All India Cross Disability Convention."

19

IMPORTANCE OF HUMAN RESOURCE PLANNING

*P. Subba Rao**

Introduction

Planning for Human Resource is more important than planning for any other resource as demand for the latter depends upon the size and structure of the former whether it is in a country or in an industry. Further, management of human resources hardly begins from human resource planning. In fact, it is the basis for most of the other functions.

Need of Human Resource Planning

The important objectives of manpower planning in an organization are:

1. To recruit and retain the human resource of required quantity and quality;
2. To foresee the employee turnover and make the arrangements for minimizing turnover and filling up of consequent vacancies;
3. To meet the needs of the programmes of expansion, diversification etc.;

---

* Assistant Professor, Department of Economics, M.R.P.G. College, Vizianagaram, A.P.

4. To foresee the impact of technology on work, existing employees and future human resource requirements;
5. To improve the standards, skill, Knowledge, ability, discipline etc.;
6. To assess the surplus or shortage of human resources and take measures accordingly;
7. To maintain congenial industrial relations by maintaining optimum level and structure of human resources;
8. To minimize imbalances caused due to non-availability of human resources of right kind, right number in right time and right place;
9. To make the best use of its human resources; and
10. To estimate the cost of human resources.

Definitions of Human Resource Planning

E.W.Vetter viewed Human Resource Planning as "a process by which an organization should move from its current manpower position to its desired manpower position. Though planning management strives to have the right number and right kind of people at the right places at the right time, doing things which result in both the organization and the individual receiving maximum long-run benefit".

According to Leon C. Megginson human resource planning is "an integrated approach to performing the planning aspects of the personnel function in order to have a sufficient supply of adequately developed and motivated people to perform the duties and tasks required to meet organizational objectives and satisfy the individual needs and goals of organizational members."

Human resource planning may be viewed as foreseeing the human resource requirements of an organization and the future supply of human resources and

a) Making necessary adjustments between these two and organizational plans; and
b) Foreseeing the possibility of developing the supply of human resources in order to match it with requirements

by introducing necessary changes in the functions of human resource management. In this definition, human resource means skill, Knowledge, values, ability, commitment, motivation etc, in addition to the number of employees.

Benefits and Importance of Human Resource Planning

Human Resource Planning (HRP) anticipates not only the required kind and number of employees but also determines the action plan for all the functions of personnel management.

The major benefits of Human resource planning are:

(i) It checks the corporate plan of the organization.

(ii) The Human Resources planning offsets uncertainties and changes to the maximum extent possible and enables the organization to have right men at right time and in right place.

(iii) It provides scope for advancement and development of employees through training, development etc.

(iv) It helps to anticipate the cost of salary enhancement, better benefits etc.

(v) It helps to anticipate the cost of salary, benefits and all the cost of human resources facilitating the formulation of budgets in an organization.

(vi) To foresee the need for redundancy and plan to check it or to provide alternative employment in consultation with trade unions, other organizations and government through remodeling organizational, industrial and economic plans.

(vii) To foresee the changes in values, aptitude and attitude of human resources and to change the technique of interpersonal, management, etc.

(viii) To plan for physical facilities, working conditions and the volume of fringe benefits like canteen, schools, hospitals, conveyance, child care centers, quarters, company stores etc.

(ix) It gives an idea of type of tests to be used and interview techniques in selection based on the level of skills, qualifications, intelligence, values etc of future human resource.

(x) It causes the development of various sources of human resources to meet the organizational needs.

(xi) It helps to take steps to improve human resource contributions in the form of increased productivity, sales, turnover etc.,

(xii) It facilitates the control of all the functions, operations, contribution and cost of human resources.

Factors Affecting Human Resource Plan

Several factors affect HRP. These factors can be classified in to external factors and internal factors.

External Factors

External factors are those factors which are outside the control of organization and organization has to follow these factors. These are given below.

(i) *Government Policies*: Policies of the government like labour policy, industrial relation policy, policy towards reserving certain jobs for different communities and sons- of the -soil etc. affect the HRP.

(ii) *Level of Economic development*: Level of economic development determines the level of HRD in the country and thereby the supply of human resources in the future in the country.

(iii) *Business Environment*: External business environmental factors influence the volume and mix of production and thereby the future demand for human resources.

(iv) *Level of technology*: level of technology determines the kind of human resources required.

(v) *International factors*: International Factors like the demand for the resources and supply of human resources in various countries.

Internal Factors

Internal factors are created in the organization due to company policies, Job Analysis, Trade Unions and company's production/ operation policy.

1).Company Policies and Strategies

Company's policies and strategies relating to expansion, diversification, alliances, etc, determines the human resource demand in terms of quality and quantity.

2) Job Analysis

Fundamentally, human resource plan is based on job analysis. Job description and job specification determines the kind of employees required.

3) Human Resource Policies

Human Resource policies of the company regarding quality of human resources, compensation level, quality of work life etc., and influences human resource plan.

4) Time Horizons

Companies with stable competitive environment can plan for the long run whereas the firms with unstable competitive environment can plan for only short-term range.

5) Type and Quality of Information

Any planning process needs qualitative and accurate information. This is more so with human resource plan, strategic, organizational and specific information.

6) Company's Production/Operations policy

Company's policy regarding how much to produce and how much to buy from out side to prepare and product influence the number and kind of people required.

7) Trade Unions

Influence of trade unions regarding numbers of working hours per week, recruitment sources etc., affect the Human resource planning.

Rationale of Manpower Planning

In the present days, trained manpower is perhaps the most fundamental resource for economic development. A nation with plans or aspirations for economic development cannot afford to ignore the ' preparation' of its human agents of production. The creation of a new steel plant, for example will serve no purpose unless arrangements are made in time for the scientists, engineers, managers, technicians, skilled workers etc, necessary to operate it. It takes a long time to produce manpower of the required 'Quantity' and 'Quality' to take up and implement the programmes of economic development. For instance, training of an engineer, scientist, management expert, doctors etc, requires five years or even more. Since it is the availability of the skilled and trained persons that will be the major determinant of economic advance in future, it is the future pattern of manpower requirements that must guide today's educational decisions. This is possible only if the educational system is well geared to the production requirements of the economy this requires careful manpower planning.

Ingredients of Manpower Planning

Human Resource production to meet the requirements of the economic system in future is the basic function of the educational system of a country. This requires forecasting the manpower requirements in the future. This is the basic objective of human resource planning. Also, since it takes considerable amount of time to train manpower in desired times, manpower forecasting for educational planning purposes must have medium to long terms horizons. Various models of manpower forecasting have been developed in recent decades in a bid to make as systematic a forecast as possible and in a bid to use as much evidence.

According to H.S.Parners, manpower forecasts that underlie educational planning are not unconditional forecasts. That is, they are not predictions of what will happen in the manpower field but indicate what must happen if certain targets for economic growth are to be realized. This brings us to a consideration of what is meant by ' man power requirements'. Parners makes a distinction between the term' manpower requirements' and the traditionally used term ' demand for labour'.

Process of Human Resource Planning

Process of Human Resources Planning consists of the following steps.

1) Analyzing organizational plans.
2) Demand Forecasting the overall human resource requirements in accordance with organizational plans.
3) Supply Forecasting: Obtaining the data and information about the present inventory of human resources and forecast the future changes in the human resource inventory.
4) Estimating the net human resource requirements.
5) In case of future surplus, plan for redeployment, retrenchment and lay-off.
6) In case of future deficit, forecast the future supply of human resources from all sources with reference to plans of other companies.
7) Plan for recruitment, development and internal mobility if future supply is more than or equal to net human resource requirements .
8) Plan to modify or adjust the organizational plan if future supply will be inadequate with reference to future net requirements.

Summary

Human resource planning is a vital sub-activity of employment function. In fact employment process begins with human resource planning. But it never ends with this function. It pervades through a number of activities after the process of human resource planning. Those activities include searching for prospective human resources, attracting them to the work and / or organization, finding out their suitability to the job and organizational requirements and finally taking steps to absorb those human resources as organs of the company.

REFERENCES

1. Sudhir Dawra, "Objectives of Human Resource Planning", *Human Resource Development* , Rajat Publications, New Delhi, 2003, pp. 57-71.

2. Misra, S.K. & Puri. V.K : " Population and Human Capital Formation in Economic Development" *Economics of Development and Planning*, Himalaya Publishing House, New Delhi, 2004, p. 327.

20

HUMAN DEVELOPMENT: ROLE OF ANGANWADI WORKER FOR CHILD DEVELOPMENT

Sujit Kumar Paul & Swatilekha Sanyal***

Introduction

The term 'development' has many connotations. In the usual sense of the word, development is gradual unfolding, or working out in full, like in natural growth or evolution. In a biological sense, development implies the complex process of natural growth and maturation that occurs in living organism. It also entails some deliberately designed effort towards improvement of human activity. Thus, the term 'development' derives its force from the attitude, desires and social phenomena. It has never been considered in isolation from prevalent human values. Human development cannot be easily defined because of its complex and dynamic character. Human development is a comprehensive economic, social, cultural and political process. Any development process involves active participation of the people. The question is, to which factor we should attribute development – the activities, freedom of participation, fair distribution of the benefits or

---

* Sr. Lecturer in Rural Development, Palli Charcha Kendra, Visva Bharati, Sriniketan, Birbhum, West Bengal.

** Research Scholar, Department of Social Studies and Rural Development, Palli Charcha Kendra, Visva-Bharati, Sriniketan, Birbhum, West Bengal, India.

enjoyment of these benefits? Development is determined by some extraneous physical or material factors – the availability of these constituting elements in upward movement of human development.

The human resources are vital from the point of view of economic welfare. Because human beings are not only instruments of production but also ends in themselves. The goal of Human Resource Development is to improve the performance of organizations by maximizing the efficiency and performance of our people.

Human development means all round development of human beings. Children are the pillars of a nation. So child development is essential for human development. The Integrated Child Development Services is one of the instruments and the Anganwadi Worker is the key person for the mental and physical development of a child.

The Integrated Child Development Services (ICDS) programme was launched on 2nd October, 1975 in 33 pilot projects. This project aimed at delivery of a package of services in an integrated manner to pre-school children, expectant and nursing mothers and women in the age group of 15-44 years. The main objective is to improve the nutritional and health status of children, reduce incidence of mortality, morbidity, malnutrition and school drop-outs, to lay foundation for proper psychological, physical and social development of the child. The major programme of ICDS seeks to lay a solid foundation for the development of national human resource by providing an integrated package. For this the main packages of this programme were:

1. Supplementary nutrition to child and pregnant and lactating mothers
2. Immunization for child and pregnant and lactating mothers
3. Health check-up
4. Referral services

5. Nutrition and health education to pregnant and lactating mothers

6. Non-formal education to children below six years.

The grass root level of ICDS, i.e. the Anganwadi Centres are situated in rural/tribal or slum areas. The Anganwadi is generally established in rural/tribal areas having a population of about 500-700. Each Anganwadi is looked after by an Anganwadi Worker assisted by a helper. A cluster of Anganwadi is supervised by supervision under the control of the Child Development Project Officer (CDPO) at the Block/ project level. All families in the area to be served by Anganwadi worker.

It has the following objectives: -

- To improve the nutritional and health status of children in the age group 0-6 years
- To lay foundations for proper psychological, physical and social development of the child
- To reduce the incidence of mortality, morbidity, malnutrition and school drop-out etc
- To achieve effective co-ordination of policy and implementation amongst the various departments to promote child development
- To enhance the capability of the mother to look after the normal health and nutritional needs of the children through proper nutrition and health education.

The Anganwadi Workers are only the key person for child development. Through this study, we have tried to find out the role of Anganwadi Worker for child levelopment. For better understanding of the objective, a study has been conducted in Nalhati-I Block of Birbhum District, West Bengal. The ICDS programme of this block is run by Non Governmental Organization viz. the Elmhirst Institute of Community Studies.

Status of Anganwadi Worker

The Anganwadi Workers are playing a vital role for

implementation of Integrated Child Development Services. They are the key person for child development. Therefore it is very relevant to know the status of Anganwadi Worker. In Nalhati-I Block, there are 263 Anganwadi Centres. There should be one Anganwadi Worker for each centre. At present there are 257 Anganwadi Workers working in 257 centres and the rest (6 No.) are vacant.

Educational Qualification of the Anganwadi Workers according to the Caste

Caste	*Educational Background*				
	VIII Passed	*Madhyamik Appeared*	*Madhyamik Passed*	*Higher Secondary*	*Total*
General	08 (5.88%)	10 (7.35%)	111 (81.62%)	07 (5.15%)	136
SC	10 (12.66%)	12 (15.19%)	54 (68.35%)	03 (3.80%)	79
ST	05 (31.25%)	01 (6.25%)	09 (56.25%)	01 (6.25%)	16
OBC	10 (38.46%)	02 (7.69%)	12 (46.15%)	02 (7.69%)	26
Total	33 (12.84%)	25 (9.73%)	186 (72.37%)	13 (5.06%)	257

The Anganwadi Workers must be female and the minimum qualification is Madhyamik pass. But from the above table it is seen that 12.84 percent workers are Class VIII pass and 9.73 percent workers are Madhyamik appeared. Initially, they were appointed as Anganwadi Helper and subsequently they got promotion from Anganwadi Helper to Worker. Rest of the workers have the desired qualifications.

The Anganwadi Workers get Rs 1000/- per month if their qualification is 10+ or above and get Rs 938/- per month if their qualification is VIII pass. This amount is given by the Central Govt. In addition to this the State Govt. is also giving Rs. 600/- per month both for 10+ or VIII passed workers. The increment is Rs. 31 after every five years.

Out of 257 Anganwadi workers in the study area, 64 workers are in the age group of 20-25. The maximum workers (83) are in the age group of 25-30. In the age group of 30-35 and 35+, there are 81 and 29 Anganwadi Workers are working respectively. We also see that 30 unmarried, 209 married, 10 widow and only 8 divorcee workers are working successfully in these centres.

Number of Training Received

Induction Training (6 days)	*Job Training (1 month)*	*Refresher Training (7 days)*
214	174	174

Training is very much needed for the worker for successful implementation of the programme. Out of 257 Angawadi Workers, 214 workers completed 6 days Induction training and only 174 workers completed 1 month Job training as well as 7 days Refresher training. It has been reported that all the Angawadi Workers will complete all the above mentioned training course, as it is a continuous process. Although the Induction training and job training occurs for 6days and 1 month respectively, the main contents are almost the same. These are mentioned below:

- Objectives of ICDS
- Role and responsibilities of Anganwadi Worker
- Relation with helper
- Pre-School education
- Maintenance of register
- Immunization
- Doses of Iron and Folic acid tablet.
- Nutrition and Communication

Role of Anganwadi Worker for Child Development

The ICDS is a unique child development programme in India and the biggest country wide multi-sectoral programme in the world which covers the main components of sustainable human development, viz. health, nutrition and education. In just two decades of its functioning the programme has been improving both pre-natal and post-natal environment of the children through reduction in the incidence of child health deficiencies, increase in child survival rate, improving its child health condition and providing nutrition and learning opportunities and other services in the rural and tribal areas and also in the urban slums. Besides maintaining the official formalities, the Anganwadi Workers have to perform all the above activities with the help of supporting staffs.

1. Provide Supplementary Nutrition to the Children

Supplementary nutrition is given to the children below six years of age. Special attention is paid to the delivery of supplementary nutrition to children below three years of age. It is given for 300 days in a year. The effort is to provide daily nutritional supplements to the extent of 300 calories and 10-15 gms of protein per child.

The type of food varies from state to state but usually consists of hot milk cooked at the Anganwadi containing varied combination of pulses, cereals, oils, vegetables and sugar. Some state provides ready-to-eat snacks containing the same basic ingredients. Some care is given to the children below the age of three years and parents and siblings are encouraged to bring them to the Anganwadi for feeding.

2. Facilitate/Organize Immunization Camp

Immunization against Diphtheria, Whooping Cough, Tetanus, Polinelitis and Tuberculosis of all infants is undertaken in the protected areas. Immunization against Measles is given if the local epidemiological situation warrants. Children of 5-6 years of age (school entry) receive Bocster dose for Diptheria and Tetanus (DT) and two doses of Typhoid Vaccination.

The immunizatic,ı of children upto six years of age is as follows

SL.NO.	AGE	VACCINE
01	Immediate after birth	B.C.G. Injection (Tuberculosis)+ Zero dose Polio (oral drops)
02	45 days	D.P.T. (Diphtheria) injection first dose + first dose polio
03	75 days	D.P.T. injection second dose + polio oral drop second dose
04	105 days	D.P.T. injection third dose + polio third dose oral drop
05	9 month	Measles (Hum) injection single dose
06	16 month	D.P.T. injection Booster + Polio oral drop
07	5-6 years	a. Booster DT (Diphtheria and Tetanus) and first dose of Typhoid monovalent or bivalent vaccine (injection)
		b. After an interval of 1-2 months give second dose of Typhoid vaccine (injection).

The minimum interval between doses of DPT and Polio vaccine should be one month. If infant have missed DPT and Polio vaccine by the first birthday should be given three doses of DPT and three doses of Polio by two years of age. The children over two years who have not received DPT should be given to doses of DT at an interval of one to two months. The immunization programme is done with the help of Health Worker. But the Anganwdi Workers have to continuously monitor the programme.

2. Provide Pre-School Education

Children of 3-6 years age have the benefit of non-formal pre-school education through the institution of Anganwadi set up in each village. It does not impart formal learning but develop in the child desirable attitudes; values and behavior pattern and aims at providing environmental awareness. The materials used in Anganwadi are of indigenous origin, made by the teachers or local artisans and are inexpensive. The Anganwadi establishes links with the elementary school so that the child moves from the Anganwadi to the school with necessary emotional and mental preparation.

3. Care of Children under Six Years of Age

The following activities are done:.

- Serial record of the height and weight of children with a view to keeping close watch over their nutrition status.
- Watch over other milestones in the growth and development of the child.
- Provide all the immunization according to the policy enunciated.
- Provide general check-up every three/ six months in order to detect diseases and other evidences of malnutrition or infection.
- Provide treatment for the widely prevalent diseases like diarrhea, dysentery, upper respiratory-tract infections, skin disease, eye disease like trachoma, conjunctivitis etc
- Deworm against the prevalent parasite infections, round-worm, hook-worm, thread-worm etc
- Provide prophylactic measures against diseases of nutritional origin like anemia, vitamin deficiencies, marasmus etc through distribution of drugs and diet supplements
- Refer serious cases to the appropriate hospital for specialized treatment.
- Provide first aid to the children wherever necessary and also provide iron tablet, vitamin tablet, cough syrup and paracitamoul tablets to the children. Health records of children should be maintained in cards. A card should be given to the mothers of children under six years of age.

4. Provide Referral Services

Children, with problems requiring specialized treatment will be referred to the upgraded PHC / Sub-division / District Head Quarters Hospital. The medical officer of PHC will refer such cases with a referral slip prescribed for the purpose. The hospital after completing the treatment will refer the child back to the primary health center with notes of treatment given and further treatment / advice to be followed.

Other Activities of Anganwadi Workers

In brief the other activities of the Anganwadi Workers are as follows:

- Conduct community survey, enlist participants and obtain data about the number of families, family members and family income.
- Maintain link with other institutions in the village like Panchayat, Mohila Mondals, school teachers etc.
- Conduct non-formal pre-school education of the children between three to six years of age.
- Assist health staff in immunization and health check-up.
- Provide primary health care and first aid.
- Organize supplementary nutrition of children aged 0-6 years and also of the pregnant and lactating mothers.
- Provide health and nutrition education to pregnant and lactating mothers as well as mothers of the children coming to Anganwadi.
- Refer cases of communicable disease, severely malnourished, under nourished, sick and 'at risk' children.
- Maintain records and registers of height and weight and child health card, supplementary nutrition records, Anganwadi attendance records etc.

Conclusion

The success of any programme depends, to a very extent, on the persons who are responsible for its working. The task of development worker is, therefore, not only to do the job himself/ herself but to guide the people among whom he/she is working towards a better and fuller life. The essential qualities of a development worker should zeal for public service, enthusiasm for raising the standard of village life, knowledge of local conditions, stamina for physical work, maturity for understanding and ability to convince the people of the usefulness of improved practices.

The authority is mostly engaging the Anganwadi Worker considering the above situation. They must be local female members with minimum educational background. The goal of Human Resource Development is to improve the performance of organizations by maximizing the efficiency and performance of our people. The task is to develop our knowledge and skills, our actions and standards, our motivation, incentives, attitudes and work environment. In our study, we found that the Anganwadi Workers who have already attained the job-training and refresher training course, successfully implement the programme in their field. The Anganwadi Workers are trying to develop our most crucial asset i.e. our children with the limited resource. More support to be provided to the Anganwadi Workers in all respect by the people and the authority.

REFERENCES

1. Berk, E. Laurate (1989), *Child Development*, Allyn and Bacon- Boston, London, Sydney, Toronto Publication, 1989.
2. Berns, M. Roberta (1993), Child, *Family, Community, Socialization and Support*, Harcourt Jovanovich College-Publication.
3. Chowdhury, Renuka (2006), "ICDS: India's response to Early Child Development" *Yojana*, Vol- 50, Nov, 2006.
4. Gilley, J.W. & Eggland, S.A. (1989), *Principles of Human Resource Development*, Addison - Wesley, NY.
5. Lakshman Nirmala (2006), "The Entitlement of Every Indian Child", *Yojana*, Vol-50, No .2006
6. Lidhoo Motilal (1988), *Child Rearing and Psycho- Social Development*, 1988, Ashish Publishing House, New Delhi
7. Rathan, Dr. Vijay (1997), *Integrated Child Development Services*, Vol-I&II, New Delhi, S. Chand & Co. 1997.
8. Sundaraman, T. (2006), "Universalisation of ICDS and Community Health Worker Programme", *Economic & Political Weekly*, Vol-XLI No-34, Aug, 26, 2006.
9. wcd.nic.in/ icds.htm
10. www.idianembassy.org

21

HEALTH EDUCATION AND HEALTH CARE IN INDIA

R.V.L.N. Ratnakara Rao & V. Krishna Murthy***

Introduction

Marquis de Vauvenargues says, "The greatest achievement of the human spirit is to live up to one's opportunities and make the most of one's resources". These resources could be social and financial resources, as the life moves around the human resources physically and around finances functionally. The development of the nations is measured in terms of human development taking parameters such as life expectancy, literacy and standard of living. Countries which are high on these three are also high in terms of human development index. However, countries like India, though developing at their optimum speed, have much to do to catch up with the so called advanced countries so that the level of development in India is appropriate to its history, traditions and resources as it is called Bharat - Bhagya-Vidhatha. India needs to do a lot more for education, especially secondary education (classes 5 to 10), health and undertake poverty eradication measures on a large scale so that life expectancy, literacy and standard of living will be improved to the possible extent, leading to over all improvement of human development. There are regional variations as we compare

* Dept. of Physical Education, Andhra University, Visakhapatnam

** Retd. Professor, Dept. of Education, Andhra University, Visakhapatnam

states like Kerala and Bihar, gender disparities between achievement of males and females and differences between rural and urban areas. Money properly utilized and schemes properly implemented and opportunities properly handled alone will improve the fate of millions of helpless persons suffering due to poverty, illiteracy and ill-health.

Two recent studies, by the World Bank and the Asian Development Bank, raised the poverty measures from a daily earning of $ 1 per person to $ 1.25 and $ 1.35 respectively. The World Bank benchmark is the estimated cost for buying food worth 2,100 calories deemed the minimum daily requirement for an adult. Judging by this India is home to one-third of the global poor.

An attempt to come up with a brand new template or "vulnerability atlas" to identify the urban poor is now being launched in India. The income criterion tenders to suppress figures for the urban poor. Proxy indicators such as social vulnerability and access to public services will be used to calculate income. The third indicator will be health.

Meaning of Health

The dictionary meaning of health is "freedom from disease, sound body and mind etc. that condition in which functions of body and mind are duly discharged". Health is the total outcome of the organic, nuero-muscular, interpretive and emotional development.

Health is basic to learning, to happiness, to success, to effective citizenship and to worthwhile living. In Ayurved 'Swasthya' (health) has been defined as a well balanced metabolism, a happy state of being, the senses and the mind. Swami Vivekananada said, "A weak person who has weak body or weak mind can never be master of a strong soul", Aristotle also stated that "a sound mind lives in a sound body".

Health is a state of physical, mental, emotional and social well being. J.W. Williams has appropriately summed up the concept as: "Health is that quality of life that enables an individual to live most and serve best". Health can be achieved, maintained and improved by supplying the basic physical, mental, emotional and social needs in proper proportion.

Definitions of Health

1. "Health means soundness of body or mind; that condition in which its functions are duly and efficiently discharged." - *Oxford English Dictionary.*
2. Health is "a state of complete physical, mental and social well being and not merely an absence of diseases or infirmity." This definition has been amplified and it has been added, "attainment of a level of health that will enable every individual to lead a socially and economically productive life." - *World Health Organisation.*
3. "Health is a condition or quality of the human organism expressing the adequate functioning of the organism in given conditions, genetic and environmental"- W.H.O Technical Report (1957).
4. "Health is that state in which the individual is able to mobilize all his resources - intellectual, emotional and physical, for optimum daily living"- *Encyclopaedia of Health.*
5. Health is "the condition of being sound in body, mind or spirit, especially freedom from physical disease or pain." - Webster.

Dimensions of Health

Authorities in the field of health have recognized three closely interwoven dimensions of health: (1) physical dimension, (2) Mental dimension and (3) Social dimension. However, it has been felt that a few more dimensions of health can be added: emotional, spiritual, vocational, educational, nutritional, environmental and curative & preventive.

Meaning of Health Education

Anything that educates anyone in the matter of health is health education (Thomas Wood). It is the education given for identifying the health needs and matching it with suitable adaptive

Dimensions of Health

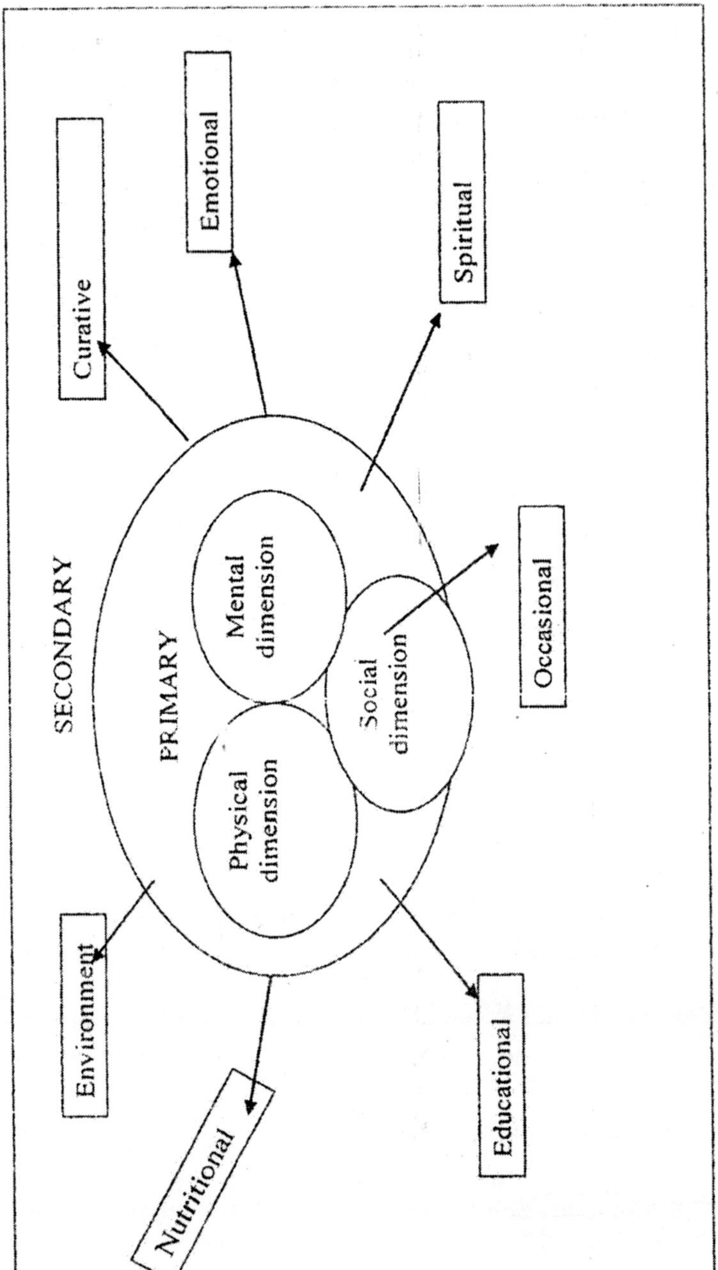

behavior. The entire process of involving people in learning about health and disease, making efforts for improving health and facilitating them to act appropriately for overcoming ailments and promoting a positive health is health education.

Defining of Health Education

1. "Health education, like general education, is concerned with changes in knowledge, feelings and behavior of people. In its most usual forms, it concentrates on developing such health practices as are believed to bring about the best possible state of well being". - W.H.O. Technical Report.
2. "Health education is a process that bridges the gap between health information and health practices. Health education motivates the person to take the information and something with it, to keep himself healthier, by avoiding actions that are harmful and practicing those that are beneficial" - Presidents' Committee on Health Education, New York (1973).
3. "Health education aims at creating such a quality of life as may enable an individual to live most and to serve best." - W.H.O. Expert Committee on Health Education.
4. "Health education is a process that informs, motivates and helps people to adopt andmaintain healthy practices and life styles, advocates environmental changes, as needed, to facilitate this goal, and conducts professional training and research to the same end." - Anne R. Somers.
5. Health education is "the translation of what is known about health into desirable individual and community behavior patterns by means of educational process." - Ruth E. Grout.

Objectives of Health Education

After analyzing the definition of health education as given by Somers and adopted by National Conference on Preventive Medicine (U.S.A), J.E. Park stated three main objectives of health education: (i) Informing people (ii) Motivating people (iii) Guiding into action.

Some authors/experts have also suggested similar objectives, however, naming the same differently, i.e. (i) development of health knowledge, (ii) development of desirable health attitude and (iii) development of desirable health practices.

Ruth E. Grout restated four objectives of health education.

1. optimum development of the individual with special reference to physical and emotional development,
2. betterment of human relationships, particularly from the stand point of health.
3. Application of health facts and principles in respect of economic efficiency in the production and consumption of goods and services.
4. Civic responsibility, especially in respect to health.

Components of Health Education

Health education recognizes three basic components, which are interdependent and constantly interact with each other

i) Unity of human beings in respect to their physical, mental and social aspect.

ii) The knowledge, attitudes and practices are important to influence health behavior.

iii) The focus of health education on the individual, family and community.

Scope of Health Education

Health education may be divided into three: (i) healthful living, (ii) health services and (iii) health instructions. All of them serve the general purpose of educating the individuals regarding health education.

Importance of Health Education

Knowledge of health education assumes great importance in India, where most of the people are ignorant about the basic principles of health and hygiene. Health education programmes are basically of preventive and promotive in nature, and such programmes are important in transmitting the knowledge, making the people aware of various diseases, occurrence of which could be easily avoided.

Maternal Health: MMR & IMR

Maternal deaths are one of the most obvious indicators of the widening gap between rich and poor. Keeping this in view, while training the Millennium Development Goals (MDGs) UN has given top priority for Maternal Health.

Table 1: Health Aspects

Health Aspects	*Period*	*Backward States (BWS)*	*Better off States (BOS)*	*15 Major States*	*India*
Infant Mortality Rate (IMR)	2005	70	43	54	58
Percentage of Children Undernourished	2002 04	52.5	12.5	17.9	19.2
Life Expectancy - Male	2001-06	61.6	66	64.3	63.9
Life Expectancy - Female	2001-06	61.7	69	66.1	66.9
Literacy - Person	2001	46.9	61.3	54.2	64.8
Female Literacy	2001	35.7	53.5	44.7	53.7

Sources: Weighted average of Backward, Better off and 15 Major States computed by Raja J. Chellaiah. K.R. Shanmugam (*Economic and Political Weekly*, August 25, 2007). Reproductive and Child Health Report (2002-04) for child nourishment data; *Economic Survey* 2006-07 for others.

Note: Bihar (combined Bihar i.e., Bihar and Jharkhand), Uttar Pradesh, Assam, Orissa,Madhya Pradesh and Rajasthan which had the six lowest ranks in per capitaincome in 1995-96 and 2004-05 are together referred to as backward states(BWS), and the others as better off states (BOS) by Raja J. Chelliah and K.R. Shanmugam (2007).

Reproduction and Child Health (RCH) scheme was given top priority and many new approaches were initiated by State and Central governments. National Rural Health Mission (NRHM) is one such initiated by Government of India. To strengthen this mission to encourage institutional deliveries Janani Suraksha Yojana (JSY) has been initiated with the aim to reduce MMR and IMR Rates, which in turn influences human development.

Reduction of Maternal Mortality Rate (MMR) to 100 and Infant Mortality Rate (IMR) to 10 by 2012 is the primary goals of Millennium Development Goals. The high MMR and IMR are most sensitive and disturbing factors which become stumbling blocks for Human Development in Third World Countries. The higher (407 per 1,00,000 live births) MMR in India is jeopardizing the entire Human Development and pushing India to the last rows in Human Development Index (HDI) ranking. Government of India has taken it (MMR) as a serious concern, and introduced several innovative measures to bring down MMR and IMR rates.

Major Trends in Health (India)

1. Four in every 10 Indian children malnourished, says a UN report.
2. India ranks a lowly 66 out of 88 countries in the Global Hunger Index 2008. The report says that India has more hungry people - more than 200 million - than any other country in the world.
3. One-third of the world's poor live in India, according to the latest poverty estimates from the World Bank.

   Based on its new threshold of poverty - $ 1.25 a day - the number of India's poor people has actually gone up from 421 million in 1981 to 456 million in 2005.
4. India ranks 128 out of 177 countries in the UN's Human Development Index. The Index goes beyond GDP and calculates human development by taking into account life expectancy, literacy and standard of living.

Life Expectancy

Life expectancy at birth has shown an impressive improvement from 50.3 years during 1970-75 to 62.3 years during 1995-2005 as per the census. The female life expectancy (2001-06) was only 58 years in Madhya Pradesh as against 75 years in Kerala. Control of disease and improvement in medical facilities contributed to improvements in survival rates.

a) Life Expectancy – Male

Weighted average of backward, better off and 15 major states computed by Raja J. Chellaiah and Shanmugam (2007) were formal to be 61.6, 66, and 64.3 while for India it was 63.9. The male life expectancy (2001-06) was only 59 years in Madhya Pradesh as against 71.7 years in Kerala.

b) Life Expectancy – Female

Similarly weighted average of backward, better off and 15 major states computed by Raja Chelliah and Shanmugam (2007) were 61.7, 69 and 66.1, while for India it was 66.9 indicating the impact of economic level of the states and life expectancy of the people. Better economic condition also has a positive effect on availing better educational, health and employment opportunities.

Education assists in improving the standards of life, better health facility, economic prosperity and better understanding towards the society. According to UNESCO, "40-60 per cent of the literacy rate is necessary for the development of a country. For a rapid development, it requires 60 and above percent".

1. UNDP Human Development Report 2003 clearly stated that the government in poor countries must rank health spending higher than other types of spending. But, government spending on health is very much less in India. Government of India contributes only 17 per cent on social economy, which is used for the country health care resources, whereas those of European markets' economy allocate 75 per cent.

2. In India, the government spending on health is meager and it is the 5th poorest in the world. Only Cambodia, Congo, Georgia and Sierra rank below India.

3. More than 70 per cent people live in rural areas; while provision of health care services and education are skewed towards urban areas.

4. Water borne and water related diseases like Typhoid, Malaria, Cholera, Hepatitis and Diarrhoea are basically targeting infants, children and old age people.

5. In the last 60 years, there has been an improvement on health facilities, and consequently there has been decline in birth rate, death rate and infant mortality rate.

6. Still, India is a land of largest number of illiterates (about 285 millions, or one-third of a total of 854 million illiterates in the World in 1999) and medically incurred people.

7. The government measures are quite disheartening both in terms of infrastructural as well as health expenditure.

Malnutrition as an Area of Darkness

One important health aspect that is of serious concern is the magnitude of malnutrition and its spread throughout the world and more so in India as shown below:

Table 2.: Malnutrition in Different Regions

Uttar Pradesh	*India*	*Least Developing Countries*	*South Asia Developing*	*Countries Average*	*World Average*
52%	43%	35%	42%	26%	25%

Source : The State of Children in Uttar Pradesh, Prepared by the States Planning Department and UNICEF (India Today, February, 2009).

Disability

The world's disabled population is estimated to be 650 million, making it in several ways, the world's largest minority. Recognition of the needs of the disabled began only in the last century and a half, when increased wars among nations and communities took a toll of human lives, and incapacitated large numbers.

Today, every country has enacted lav s and has some measures to guarantee equal living conditions for the disabled, including their health care and education. In December 2006, the UN General Assembly unanimously adopted a treaty on the rights of the disabled people. Signatories to the invention will have to get rid of legislation, customs and practices that discriminate against disabled people. But, Member Countries have different definitions of disability and negotiations were protracted because of varying cultural and social factors that decide disability. Moreover, prevalence rates of disability among countries vary widely, because of different methodologies for data collection at the national level. For instance, a study by the UN Economic and Social Commission for Asia and the Pacific reported that the disabled made up nearly 20 per cent of the Australian population in contrast to 2.13 per cent in India's case as 2.19 crores were enumerated as disabled in the Census of 2001. Independent and conservative estimates place the percentage of the disabled in India's population at a higher 5-6 per cent.

In India, which is yet to sign the UN convention, awareness of the rights of the disabled has been slow and what exists is only because of sustained campaign by involved organizations.

Concerns of the disabled in India have been addressed by three legislative enactments:

- The Persons with Disabilities Act, 1995;
- National Trust for Welfare of Persons with Autism, Cerebral Palsy, Mental retardation and Multiple Disability Act, 1999, and
- The Rehabilitation Council of India Act, 1992.

A new national policy on disability was approved by the Union cabinet in February, 2006. It promises new initiatives towards intervention and rehabilitation and in reaching out towards disabled women and children. It also states that 75 per cent of the disabled live in rural areas where infrastructure and other amenities are largely absent or primitive. While many of its initiatives look good on paper, implementation requires sustained initiative that appears hobbled by the presence of several nodal agencies and departments whose functions appear to overlap.

The provisions of the national policy have been criticized for:

- Having no defined time limit in place. It is at best only a directive to different governments and their agencies.
- The emphasis on self-employment, critics argue, also would lead to a greater isolation of the disabled.

It is only very recently too that steps have been taken with regard to the education of Children with Special Needs (CWSN). The Sarva Shiksha Abhiyan (SSA) programme has adopted a multi-option model of 'inclusive' education, but constrained largely by resources. The programme has found it difficult to reach out-of-school CWSN. CWSN identified is only 1.54 per cent of the total child population in the SSA, in comparison to the census figure of 2.1 per cent of the population having been found to have some disability.

To meet fully the rights and aspirations of the disabled in India, a sustained effort beginning with sound data collection measures, intervention and other health care initiatives, and the coordinated involvement of other non-government agencies is necessary. Till then, meeting the UN convention directives would remain a difficult proposition, perhaps possible only in a few urban centers. (Raja J. Chelliah and K.R. Shanmugam, 2007).

The UN General Assembly has called for eight MDGs by 2015.Heads of the State and delegates met on September 25, to review the MDGs, identify gaps and map out steps to remain on track. The event was the first summit level gathering on the MDGs since 2000, when world leaders committed to the goals laid out in the Millennium declaration to be achieved on 2015. UN secretary general BanKi-moon said "we face nothing less than a development emergency. Halfway to the target date of 20015, it is clear that we are not on track to meet the goals, especially in Africa and the new global challenges- an economic slowdown, high food and fuel prices, and climate change threaten to serve the progress we have made".

The United Nations in a report reviewing its Millennium Development Goals (MDGs) stated that an ambitious goal to eradicate extreme poverty in the world was thwarted by the recent upward trend in food prices. The recent sharp increase in food prices would mean that an estimated 1 billion people would go hungry while another 2 billion will be under nourished. Poverty and hunger worsened in Africa, while China, with a population of 1.3 billion was praised for pulling an estimated 400 million out of poverty. Mixed results were reported in achieving universal primary education, gender equality, reducing child and maternal mortality, stopping the spread of HIV/AIDS, and ensuring environmental sustainability. While the latest report issued in September 2008 cited story progress in some areas, it was not enough to meet the target date.

Release of the Report (September 10th, 2008): Need for Strong Institutions and Good Governance:

Lok Sabha Speaker Somanath Chatterjee, while releasing the report in the Capital on September 10th 2008 said: "India needs strong institutions and good Goverence to achieve the various MDGs laid down by the UN". Half way in to the period time line to achieve the Millennium Development goals (MDGs) suggested by the UN, to be achieved on 2015, India seems to be shipping on most of the eight goals.

A coalition of NGOs under the ban new of "Wada to Na To do Abhiyam'(Don't leave the promise) has calculated that India's failure to meet the target of millennium development goals (MDGs) will fail the world, because of its huge population but also because of its share in all the identified goals. On the eve of half-way period for the MDGs, the coalition urged Indian government to involve people in key anti-poverty programmes to make them effective.

1. The National mid-term check list revealed that 80% of the people living below $ 1 in south Asia are in India

2. The TB Prevalence rate in India (344 per 100,000 People) in comparable to that of some of the countries of sub-Saharan Africa.

3. The check list also says that despite the rapid studies in economic growth in the last decade, India accounts for the largest number of maternal deaths in the world, and maternal and infant mortality rates are ever worse than some countries in sub-Saharan Africa.

4. India is also home to world's highest number of under-nourished children (46 Million).

Table 3: State of Public Health in India

Sl. No.	Issues	Percentage
1.	Infant Mortality Rate:	58 for the country, with a low of 12 for Kerala and a high of 79 for Madhya Pradesh
2.	Maternal Mortality Rate:	301 for the country, with a low of 110 for Kerala and a high of 517 for UP and Uttaranchal in the 2001-03 period
3.	Non-Hospitalized Treatment from Government Sources:	22 per cent for the country, from a low of 5 per cent in Bihar to a high of 68 per cent in Himachal Pradesh
4.	Patient treated in Public Hospitals:	41.7 per cent for the country, from a low of 14.4 per cent in Bihar to a high of 91.3 per cent in Jammu and Kashmir
5.	Average Medical Expenditure per Hospitalization:	Rs. 3238 in Government Hospitals compared to Rs. 7408 in Private Hospitals in rural areas.
6.	Anaemia among Children and Women:	79.1 per cent of 6-35 month children are anaemic.56.1 per cent of married women aged 15-49 are anaemic.
7.	Immunisation:Malnourished Children's:	Only 43.5 per cent children are fully immunized.Four in every 10 Indian Children (40%) are malnourished (a UN report)
8.	Child Morbidity:	32 per cent children had fever21 per cent had diarrhea17 per cent had persistent cough11 per cent had extreme weakness 5

	per cent had skin rashes2 per cent had eye infections during the two weeks (Preceding the Survey)50 per cent children had one of the above problem
9. Status of Health Facilities:	The percentage of Primary Health Centre's (PHCs) having adequate staff (i.e., at least 60 per cent of the required) is more than 90 per cent in Tamil Nadu, Maharashtra and Kerala
10. Decline in Sex Ratio:	According to government reports 2 million fetuses are aborted each year for reason none other than that they happen to be females. Medical Termination of Pregnancy Act (MTP Act) was enacted in 1971. According to this, conditional abortion are allowed but within 20 weeks of pregnancy.

Note: *excludes Mao-Maram, Paomata and Purul sub-divisions of Senapati district of Manipur.

Table 4: Disabilities in India

Data on Disability (Census of India, 2001)*	*Persons*	*Males*	*Females*
	1,028,610,328	532,156,772	496,453,556
Total Disabled Population	21,906,769	12,605,635	9,301,134
Disabled Population (Per lakh)	2,130	2,369	1,874
Types of Disability			
In seeing	48.5%	45.5%	52.7%
In speech	7.5%	7.5%	7.5%
In hearing	5.8%	5.3%	6.3%
In movement	27.9%	31.0%	23.7%
Mental	10.3%	10.7%	9.8%

Note: *excludes Mao-Maram, Paomata and Purul sub-divisions of Senapati district of Manipur.

Discussion on Healthcare

Though there has been considerable improvement in the health status as measured by aspects like the increase in life span (33 to 62 years), fall in infant mortality and the crude death rate, statistics also show that such achievements have fallen far short of the nation's expectations. United Nations provided statistics reveal that in Sub-Saharan Africa and Asia, millions of people still die from communicable but preventable diseases like tuberculosis, malaria and schistosomiasis, besides the scores succumbing to newly emerging diseases such as Severe Acute Respiratory Syndrome (SARS), bird-flu, chickungunya and dengu. About one-third of the World's population is infected with TB with almost two-thirds of them living in Asia. In the developing world, 1.2 billion people lack access to safe water, adequate sanitation and poor housing, 800 million people lack access to health services. (All India People's Science Network, 2002).

Health Status among Social Groups in India – 1998-99

Attaining better health is both the ends and means of economic growth. Better health is facilitated by sufficient education, favorable work environment, and satisfactory income levels of a person so that we can have better access to health and medical care services.

a) Unfortunately, health and medical care services are not only inadequate (in terms of the population size), but also inequally distributed across different parts of the country eg. In different states, urban-oriented services etc.

b) Accessibility to health and medical care services is also not even across different sections of the society both in rural and urban areas.

The health status of social groups at the All India level is presented in terms of a few selected indicators capturing the level of reproductive and child health, malnutrition and undernutrition. Women and children suffering from anaemia, maternal and infant/child mortality rates for the year 1998-99 as per the National Family Health Survey (NFHS 1998-99).

The data presented in the table show that –

a) The proportion of women accessing the reproductive health care services such as family [planning, ante natal checkups etc is found to be quite lower in the case of STs (family planning 39.1%, ante natal checkup 56.5%), SCs (family planning 44.6%, ante natal checkup 61.1%), as compared to others (family planning 53.5%, ante natal checkup 71.3%).

b) The proportion of women suffering from nutritional deficiency; children undernourished and women and child with anaemia is too high in respect of STs and SCs as compared to others.

- Women with nutritional deficiency (SC 42.1%, ST 46.3%, Others 30.5%)
- Children under nourished (SC 53.5%, ST 55.9%, Others 41.1%)
- Women with anaemia (SC 56.0%, ST 64.9%, Others 47.6%)
- Child with anaemia (SC 78.0%, ST 79.0%, Others 72.0%)

c) The fertility rates are found to be quite high in the case of STs (3.06) and SCs (3.15) as against others (2.66) and hence the females belonging to STs and SCs are more likely to suffer from more health risks and several health problems as argued by Noble and Potts (1996), Sharma, Rajalakshmi, and Jeyaraj (2001).

d) It has also been found that the infant mortality rate (IMR) and child mortality rate (CMR) per thousand live births are quite significant in the case of SCs and STs as compared to others.

- Infant Mortality Rate (IMR) (SCs 83, STs 84.2, Others 61.8)
- Child Mortality Rate (CMR) (SCs 39.5, STs 46.3, Others 22.2)

This clearly shows that the health status of SCs and STs vis-à-vis others is far from satisfactory. This can partly be attributed to a greater incidence of poverty, working in unsafe occupations, and persistence of illiteracy among them. As health status among SCs and STs as compared to others is unsatisfactory, adequate and qualitative health, medical care services must be made freely available to SCs and STs up to a certain level and till equality in health status is achieved leading to the MDGs of health for all. At the same time, the on-going poverty alleviation programmes and educational programmes have to be effectively and comprehensively implemented with a special emphasis for SCs and STs.

Table 5: Health Status among Social Groups in India, 1998-99

Health Indicators	*SC*	*ST*	*Others*	*All*
Married women using any family planning method (%)	44.6	39.1	53.5	48.2
Any Antenatal checkups (%)	61.1	56.5	71.3	65.4
Women with nutritional deficiency (%)	42.1	46.3	30.5	35.8
Children (weight for age) under nourished (%)	53.5	55.9	41.1	47.0
Women with anaemia (%)	56.0	64.9	47.6	51.8
Child with anaemia (%)	78.0	79.0	72.0	76.0
Total fertility rate	3.15	3.06	2.66	2.85
Infant mortality rate (per thousand live births)	83.0	84.2	61.8	67.6
Child mortality rate (per thousand live births)	39.5	46.3	22.2	29.3

Source: National Family Health Survey (NFHS) 1998-99, Biradar (2008)

Healthcare Providers in India

That health services have been dismally poor and inaccessible for a large majority of the population in India has not been disputed. More than 70 per cent people live in rural area, while provision of health care services and education are skewed towards urban areas. Such observations have been adequately acknowledged even by Government of India health policy documents (GOI 2002, 2005). One of the arguments in health sector debates is that lack of adequate institutional health services leads to ill-health and continuing mortality and that superstition, irrationality, ignorance continue to haunt rural India and hence the high levels of ill-health and mortality.

The 'inaccessibility to primary health care', 'pathetic situation of community health centre's (CHCs)' and advanced stage of decay of health services system in the country' (Mukhopadhyay, 1997) have been explained by social scientists. Within the nationalist imagination, Gandhi said, his motto was 'self-reliance' (Swawalambana) which is possible only where there is self-health reliance (Swasthyawalambana). "To deepen modern (English or Western) medicine is to deepen our slavery" (Gandhi, 1993). However, it is paradoxical or an irony that despite nationalist leads such as Gandhi's advocating Swawalambana and Swasthyawalambana, the institutionalization of allopathic medicine has taken place without much debate.

In effect, there are three streams of health providers that have emerged in the post independent India: the qualified allopathic doctors, qualified doctors from the Indian systems of medicine (ayurvedic, unani, homeopathy) and unqualified health providers (UHPs) both the qualified allopathic doctors, both working in the public and private sectors, and the qualified doctors from the Indian systems of medicine relegated to a subordinate position in the plural medical system. Cater to the affordable group (20 - 25 per cent) which has turned out to be an expensive and unaffordable proposition for the vast majority of the poor. Hence, it is the third system i.e., UHPs who by default have become the main stay of health sciences for about 75 per cent of the population in India. The poor sick are not only deprived of basic health services but also other basic needs like proper food, drinking water, sanitation etc. (Prasad, 2007).

Medical Tourism

India has some of the best hospitals and treatment centres that are equipped with infrastructure and technology which are at par with those in US, the UK and Europe and providing treatment at a fraction of the cost. We need to leverage this more effectively in the coming years. According to financial advisory, audit and consulting firm Deloitte, in 2007, about 450,000 patients from abroad visited India for medical treantment. Experts say that the growth of the country's medical tourism would be 30-35 per cent in 2008-09.

Cost-cutting would be the main reason why more international patients would come to India, especially from the US, as medical costs are four to five times lesser in India. For example, a heart by pass surgery in the US costs between $ 75,000 and $ 100,000. The same surgery could cost around $ 8,000 - 9,000 in India. Similarly, a liver transplant in the US costs around Rs. 1.5 crore and in the UK around Rs. 80 lakh. However, in India, it costs only about Rs. 18-20 lakh for adult and Rs. 12-15 lakh for children. Even if we include airfare costs of a patient plus a companion, and accommodation costs in India, the cost of getting treated in India is significantly lower.

Unlike developed economies, India will continue to have more cosmetic surgeries and non-surgical cosmetic procedures in 2009. Anti-aging procedures such as neck lifts and face lifts, and lip suction procedures are some of the most sought-after cosmetic procedures in India and on an average, cost barely 25 per cent of what they cost in the UK. Thus, the concept of medical tourism in India is growing fast. More and more patients from countries like UK, USA, France, Switzerland, Germany and other affluent nation are being attracted toward India for healthcare facilities due to its cost effective health structure and modern facilities. According to our estimate over 1.5 lakh medical tourists visited India in 2007. Low cost treatment, language skills, no waiting period, best qualified professional, latest technology etc and some of the key reason of preference for India for medical care.

Conclusions

Promoters of public health advocate through 'health for all', 'health for the millions' etc while private healthcare through 'quality', 'efficacy', 'quick care' etc. People are compelled to look towards private hospitals; it has only created high opportunities for private sectors to earn. The Canadian healthcare model is often cited as a successful experiment, which can be replicated across the world. However, the specific trajectory of healthcare in each nation is either ignored or under missed in advocating such models to be replicated. Western medicine, English medicine, et are various terms used to denote the allopathic medical system that was introduced and practiced during colonial rule in India.

A strong plea for a rational approach to the evolution of an integrated system of medicine in India was made in 1948, soon after independence by the President of the Indian Science Congress. The hegemony of one system of knowledge on the other needs to be contested but within the democratic principles of working out an inclusive knowledge base and the institutional mechanisms. We have to introspect and argue why all the medical knowledge, traditional or modern, have not been democratized in order to ensure accessibility to the masses, poor-sick and the rural so that the UN MDGs can be achieved in the area of health education. It is high time for the planners and government authorities to move on the path to make education and health within the reach of the common man, the aam admi. The non-institutionalised medicine/UHPs, which is generally available to the poor-sick is of poor quality because of its general subordination and exclusion from the organsied system eg. folk, traditional and other indigenous forms of medicine.

REFERENCES

1. All India Peoples Science Network (2002), *Globalisation and the Indian People – Assault on Public Health*, Prajasakthi Book House, Hyderabad.

2. Biradar, R.R. (2008), "Multiple Facts of Social Exclusion in Rural India, Emerging Evidences", *South India Journal of Social Sciences*, Vol. VI, No. 2, December, pp. 18-35.

3. Bucher, Charles A. (1979), *Foundations of Physical Education*, 8th Ed. C.V. Mosby Co., St. Lowis.

4. Dandiya, P.C., Jafer, I.Y.K and Jafer Afifa (1998), *Health Education and Community Pharmacy*, 2nd Ed., Vallabh Prakashan, New Delhi, Reprint 1996.

5. Data on Disability, *Census of India 2001*, Office of the Registrar General, New Delhi, India.

6. Gandhi, M.K. (1993), *Nature Cure*, Navajivan Publishing House, Ahmedabad.

7. Kamalendra Kanwar (2009), "The Promise of Medical Tourism", *The Hindu Business Line*, February 20.

8. Mukhopadhyaya, Alok, ed. (1997), *Report of Independent Commission on Health in India*, Voluntary Health Association of India.

9. Noble, J. and M. Potts (1996), "The Fertility Transition in Cuba and the Federal Republic of Korea: The Imapct of Organised Family Planning", *Journal of Biosocial Science*, 28 (2).

10. Purendra Prasad, N. (2007), "Medicine, Power and Social Legitimacy", *Economic and Political Weekly*, August 25.

11. Ramachandriah, L & Dharma Lingam, T. (1997), *Health Education: A New Approach*, Vikas Publsihing House, New Delhi.

12. Sharma, R.S., M. Rajyalakshmi and D. Antony, Jeyaraj (2001): *Current Status of Fertility Methods in India*, Indian Academy of Sciences, 26 (4) pp. 391-405.

13. Williams, J.F., Brownell, C.L & Vennier, E.L., (1961): *The Adminsitration of Health Education and Physical Education*, 5th Ed., W.B. Samaders, London.

22

HUMAN RESOURCE DEVELOPMENT—A SPECIAL FOCUS ON INDIAN WOMEN

*D. Sujatha**

Introduction

The late 19th and early 20th centuries produced new educated women in India whose interests went beyond household activities. Women started organizing themselves into groups and formed associations. Gradually women distinguished themselves in different professional positions also. Therefore, their role as activists in uplifting the status of women in different professional fields cannot be disregarded.

The UNDP sixth human development report (1998) contains two gender aware measurements. The first is the gender related development index which disaggregates the three variables of the human development index (life expectancy, educational attainment and adjusted real income) by gender. The second is the gender empowerment measure which looks at women's representation in parliament, women's share of managerial and professional jobs and women's share of national income.

Human development index has been the first successful attempt to bring to the fore a number of other aspects of human life besides the national income (GDP or GNP, gross domestic product or gross national product) that indicates only the economic

* Asst. Professor, Dept. of Economics, Maharaja's Post Graduate College, Vizinagaram, Andhra Pradesh.

achievement of the country. The welfare of both women and men constitutes the human welfare. To understand the magnitude of deprivation of human rights and entitlements of women compared to men, it is important to look at the gender dimensions. There is a need to highlight the gender inequity in human development. As has been observed by some researchers in the field, "Women and men share many aspects of living together, collaborate with each other in complex and ubiquitous ways, and yet end up - often enough - with very different rewards and deprivations. From looking at the state of advantages and deprivations that women and men respectively have, there is an important need to look at the contrast between (*i*) the efforts and sacrifices made by each, and (*ii*) the rewards and benefits respectively enjoyed. This contrast is important for a better understanding of gender injustice in the contemporary world. The exacting nature of women's efforts and contributions, without commensurate rewards, is a particularly important subject,"1. Often there is a need for looking at the measurable indicators that show the evidence of inequity so that proper policies and programmes can be devised realising the importance.

A Special Focus on Indian Women

Key facts:-

- Women population in India constitutes 48.1% out of which 62% were literate.
- The labour force participation of women is 22.7%.
- The majority of women in both rural and urban areas of India are employed in the informal sector, which is characterized by low productivity, minimal incomes, and a lack of economic and social security. In rural areas, 87 per cent of women are employed in agriculture as labourers and cultivators. In urban areas, about 80 per cent of the women workers are employed in household industries, small trade and services, and building and construction.
- When livelihood resources are destroyed due to displacement, women are forced to look outside their

homes and villages for employment. This makes them more vulnerable to sexual and other forms of exploitation

- Women's working is getting harder and more time consuming due to ecological degradation and changing agricultural technologies and practices.
- Women have an active role extensive involvement in live stock production, forest resource use and fishery processing.
- Women contribute considerably to household incomes through farm and non farm activities as well as through work as landless agricultural labourers.
- There are high degrees of inter-state and intra-state variations in gender roles in agriculture, environment and rural production.

Employment

Employment Status	*Sex*	*India*		
		Total	*Rural*	*Urban*
Total Workers	P	402,234,724	309,956,070	92,278,654
	M	275,014,476	198,839,153	76,175,323
	F	127,220,248	111,116,917	16,103,331
Main Workers	P	313,004,983	229,186,552	83,818,431
	M	275,147,813	169,101,251	71,046,562
	F	72,857,170	60,085,301	12,771,869
Marginal Workers	P	89,229,741	80,769,518	8,460,223
	M	34,886,663	29,737,902	5,128,761
	F	54,363,078	51,031,616	3,331,462
Non -Workers	P	626,375,604	432,534,569	193,841,035
	M	257,142,296	182,763,521	74,378,775
	F	369,223,308	249,771,048	119,462,260

Source: India, Registrar General and Census Commissioner. (2004). Census of India 2001: Primary Census Abstract : Total Population. New Delhi, p. 1.

Organised Sector

Female employment in the organized sector in 1997 was only 16.4%, a gain of 0.6 percent from 1995. Employment of women as also growth of female employment is highest in Southern region, followed by Western region. Northern and Eastern regions not only reflect low female employment but also recorded a negative growth. Distribution of female employment reveals concentration in community, social and personal services - whereas lowest female employment has been recorded in electricity, gas and water sectors. Women workers constitute 52 per cent of plantation workers, 6 percent in mine and 12 per cent in factories.

Women's share in the organised work-force has also shown an increasing trend, from 2.8 million (12.2 per cent) in 1981 to 4.8 million (17.2 per cent) in 1999 (Table 2.11.13). Between 1991 and 1999, rise in the percentage points of women was 3.1. In contrast, the share of men has been declining. However, women's participation in the organized sector is still very low, as compared to men. Similarly, women's employment in the public sector has also recorded an increase from 1.5 million (9.7 per cent) in 1981 to 2.8 million (14.5 per cent) in 1999 (Table 2.11.14). However, it is still much lower than that of men.

Women in the Organised Sector (1981-99)

(Figures in million)

Year	*Women*	*Men*	*Total*
(1)	(2)	(3)	(4)
1981	2.8(12.2)	20.1	22.9
1991	3.8(14.1)	23.0	26.7
1999	4.8(17.2)	23.3	28.1

Note: Figures within parentheses indicate percentage to total.

Source: Director-General of Employment and Training, Ministry of Labour, Government of India, New Delhi.

Women in the Public Sector (1981 – 99)

(Figures in million)

Year	*Women*	*Men*	*Total*
(1)	(2)	(3)	(4)
1981	1.5(9.7)	14.0	15.5
1991	2.4(12.3)	16.7	19.1
1999	2.8(14.5)	16.6	19.4

Note: Figures within parentheses indicate percentage to total.

Source: Director-General of Employment and Training, Ministry of Labour, Government of India, New Delhi.

Women in the Government (1981-97)

(Figures in million)

Year	*Women*	*Men*	*Total*
(1)	(2)	(3)	(4)
1981	1.2(11.0)	9.7	10.9
1997	1.6(14.6)	9.1	10.7

Note: Figures within parentheses indicate percentage to total.

Source: Director-General of Employment and Training, Ministry of Labour, Government of India, New Delhi.

Just as in the case of women in Public Sector, they also hold a low-key with only 14.6 per cent of the total 10.7 million employees in Government in 1997. No doubt, there has been an increasing trend in the representation of women in Government, as it rose from 11 to 14.6 per cent between 1981 and 1997, but at the same time, their representation can be rated as very low, when compared to the number of educated women. Women's employment in the public and private organized sector was as given below:

Women's Employment in the Organized Sector, 2001

Sector	*Employment (in thousands) as on 31st March*		*Percentage change*
	2000	*2001*	
1	*2*	*3*	*4*
Public	2857.0	2859.2	0.08
Private	2065.8	2090.1	1.18
Total	4922.8	4949.3	0.54

Source: India, Ministry of Labour, Directorate General of Employment and Training, (2003). Employment Review January-March 2001: Employment marketinformation programme, New Delhi. P. 13.

Unorganised/Informal Sector

Women in the Informal Sector will receive special attention during the Tenth Plan as they account for more than 90 per cent and are still conti uing to struggle in the most precarious working conditions without any legislative safe-guards. To start with, efforts will be made to ensure both minimum and equal wages for women on par with men, towards fulfilling the Constitutional commitment of 'equal pay for equal work'. To this effect, the Tenth Plan will also endeavor to extend the important labour legislations to the Informal Sector, especially those legislations where the employers have a mandatory binding for providing basic minimum working conditions along with necessary welfare services for women workers. While formulating necessary policies and programmes for the betterment of women in the Informal Sector, the findings/results of the Fourth Economic Census (2001) as well as the un-attended recommendations of the National Commission on Self-Employed Women and Women in the Informal Sector (Shram Shakti), will be taken into consideration.

Women Empowerment

After the World War I three major national women's organisations were founded. The Women's Indian Association, The National Council of Women in India and The All India

Women's Conference emerged between 1917 and 1927. In recent times, many political parties have established their women's organizations to work for and represent women's issues. On the other hand there are autonomous groups such as National Council for Women, *Samata Manch, Stree Sangharsh Samiti, Stree Mukti Sangathan,* Feminist Network Collective, *Stree Shakti Sangathan and Purogami Sangathan,* etc. Issue based activism has also brought women to the forefront. The Self Employed Women's Association (SEWA) has emerged as a forceful effort of working women under the guidance of Ela Ramesh Bhatt, a Magasaysay award winner. Mrinal Gore was known as the "Paniwali Bai' in Mumbai for her activities to solve the water problem which plagues women's lives. Medha Patkar has been fighting relentlessly for the cause of environment. The Chipko Movement was also one of the major achievements of women to save the environment and the forests. Women academics and activists such as Dr. Phulrenu Guha, Dr. Vina Mazumdar, Dr. Neera Desai, Dr. Leela Dube, Dr. Lotika Sarkar are also playing their part in fighting for the cause of women through their own platforms such as the Centre for Women's Development Studies and SNDT Women's University. All these efforts of several women's groups are playing an important role in changing the status of women in India.

Decision-Making

Women's equality in power sharing and active participation in decision-making, including decision making in political process at all levels will be ensured for the achievement of the goals of empowerment. All measures will be taken to guarantee women equal access to and full participation in decision making bodies at every level, including the legislative, executive, judicial, corporate, statutory bodies, as also the advisory Commissions, Committees, Boards, Trusts etc. Aff rmative action such as reservations/quotas, including in higher legislative bodies, will be considered whenever necessary on a time bound basis. Women-friendly personnel policies will also be drawn up to encourage women to participate effectively in the developmental process.

Policies & Schemes

Judicial Legal Systems

Legal-judicial system will be made more responsive and gender sensitive to women's needs, especially in cases of domestic violence and personal assault. New laws will be enacted and existing laws reviewed to ensure that justice is quick and the punishment meted out to the culprits is commensurate with the severity of the offence.

At the initiative of and with the full participation of all stakeholders including community and religious leaders, the Policy would aim to encourage changes in personal laws such as those related to marriage, divorce, maintenance and guardianship so as to eliminate discrimination against women.

The evolution of property rights in a patriarchal system has contributed to the subordinate status of women. The Policy would aim to encourage changes in laws relating to ownership of property and inheritance by evolving consensus in order to make them gender just.

Mainstreaming a Gender Perspective in the Development Process

Policies, programmes and systems will be established to ensure mainstreaming of women's perspectives in all developmental processes, as catalysts, participants and recipients. Wherever there are gaps in policies and programmes, women specific interventions would be undertaken to bridge these. Coordinating and monitoring mechanisms will also be devised to assess from time to time the progress of such mainstreaming mechanisms. Women's issues and concerns as a result will specially be addressed and reflected in all concerned laws, sectoral policies, plans and programmes of action.

National Policy for the Empowerment of Women

Goal and Objectives

The goal of this Policy is to bring about the advancement, development and empowerment of women. The Policy will be widely disseminated so as to encourage active participation of all stakeholders for achieving its goals. Specifically, the objectives of this Policy include equal access to women to health care, quality education at all levels, career and vocational guidance, employment, equal remuneration, occupational health and safety, social security and public office etc.

Economic Empowerment of Women

Poverty Eradication

Since women comprise the majority of the population below the poverty line and are very often in situations of extreme poverty, given the harsh realities of intra-household and social discrimination, macro economic policies and poverty eradication programmes will specifically address the needs and problems of such women. There will be improved implementation of programmes which are already women oriented with special targets for women. Steps will be taken for mobilization of poor women and convergence of services, by offering them a range of economic and social options, along with necessary support measures to enhance their capabilities.

Micro Credit

In order to enhance women's access to credit for consumption and production, the establishment of new, and strengthening of existing micro-credit mechanisms and micro-finance institution will be undertaken so that the outreach of credit is enhanced. Other supportive measures would be taken to ensure adequate flow of credit through extant financial institutions and banks, so that all women below poverty line have easy access to credit.

Women and Economy

Women's perspectives will be included in designing and implementing macro-economic and social policies by institutionalizing their participation in such processes. Their contribution to socio-economic development as producers and workers will be recognized in the formal and informal sectors (including home based workers) and appropriate policies relating to employment and to her working conditions will be drawn up.

Women and Agriculture

In view of the critical role of women in the agriculture and allied sectors, as producers, concentrated efforts will be made to ensure that benefits of training, extension and various programmes will reach them in proportion to their numbers. The programmes for training women in soil conservation, social forestry, dairy development and other occupations allied to agriculture like horticulture, livestock including small animal husbandry, poultry, fisheries etc. will be expanded to benefit women workers in the agriculture sector.

Women and Industry

The important role played by women in electronics, information technology and food processing and agro industry and textiles has been crucial to the development of these sectors. They would be given comprehensive support in terms of labour legislation, social security and other support services to participate in various industrial sectors. Women at present cannot work in night shift in factories even if they wish to. Suitable measures will be taken to enable women to work on the night shift in factories. This will be accompanied with support services for security, transportation etc.

Support Services

The provision of support services for women, like child care facilities, including crèches at work places and educational institutions, homes for the aged and the disabled will be expanded and improved to create an enabling environment and to ensure their full cooperation in social, political and economic life. Women-friendly personnel policies will also be drawn up to encourage women to participate effectively in the developmental process.

Social Empowerment of Women

Education

Equal access to education for women and girls will be ensured. Special measures will be taken to eliminate discrimination, universalize education, eradicate illiteracy, create a gender-sensitive educational system, increase enrolment and retention rates of girls and improve the quality of education to facilitate life-long learning as well as development of occupation/vocation/technical skills by women. Reducing the gender gap in secondary and higher education would be a focus area. Sectoral time targets in existing policies will be achieved, with a special focus on girls and women, particularly those belonging to weaker sections including the Scheduled Castes/Scheduled Tribes/Other Backward Classes/Minorities. Gender sensitive curricula would be developed at all levels of educational system in order to address sex stereotyping as one of the causes of gender discrimination.

Health

A holistic approach to women's health which includes both nutrition and health services will be adopted and special attention will be given to the needs of women and the girl at all stages of the life cycle. The reduction of infant mortality and maternal mortality, which are sensitive indicators of human development, is a priority concern. This policy reiterates the national demographic goals for Infant Mortality Rate (IMR), Maternal Mortality Rate (MMR) set out in the National Population Policy 2000. Women should have access to comprehensive, affordable and quality health care. Measures will be adopted that take into account the reproductive rights of women to enable them to exercise informed choices, their vulnerability to sexual and health problems together with endemic, infectious and communicable diseases such as malaria, TB, and water borne diseases as well as hypertension and cardio-pulmonary diseases. The social, developmental and health consequences of HIV/AIDS and other sexually transmitted diseases will be tackled from a gender perspective.

To effectively meet problems of infant and maternal mortality, and early marriage the availability of good and accurate data at micro level on deaths, birth and marriages is required. Strict implementation of registration of births and deaths would be ensured and registration of marriages would be made compulsory. In accordance with the commitment of the National Population Policy (2000) to population stabilization, this Policy recognizes the critical need of men and women to have access to safe, effective and affordable methods of family planning of their choice and the need to suitably address the issues of early marriages and spacing of children. Interventions such as spread of education, compulsory registration of marriage and special programmes like BSY should impact on delaying the age of marriage so that by 2010 child marriages are eliminated.

Women's traditional knowledge about health care and nutrition will be recognized through proper documentation and its use will be encouraged. The use of Indian and alternative systems of medicine will be enhanced within the framework of overall health infrastructure available for women.

Nutrition

In view of the high risk of malnutrition and disease that women face at all the three critical stages viz., infancy and childhood, adolescent and reproductive phase, focussed attention would be paid to meeting the nutritional needs of women at all stages of the life cycle. This is also important in view of the critical link between the health of adolescent girls, pregnant and lactating women with the health of infant and young children. Special efforts will be made to tackle the problem of macro and micro nutrient deficiencies especially amongst pregnant and lactating women as it leads to various diseases and disabilities.

Intra-household discrimination in nutritional matters vis-à-vis girls and women will be sought to be ended through appropriate strategies. Widespread use of nutrition education would be made to address the issues of intra-household imbalances in nutrition and the special needs of pregnant and lactating women. Women's participation will also be ensured in the planning, superintendence and delivery of the system.

Drinking Water and Sanitation

Special attention will be given to the needs of women in the provision of safe drinking water, sewage disposal, toilet facilities and sanitation within accessible reach of households, especially in rural areas and urban slums. Women's participation will be ensured in the planning, delivery and maintenance of such services.

Housing and Shelter

Women's perspectives will be included in housing policies, planning of housing colonies and provision of shelter both in rural and urban areas. Special attention will be given for providing adequate and safe housing and accommodation for women including single women, heads of households, working women, students, apprentices and trainees.

Environment

Women will be involved and their perspectives reflected in the policies and programmes for environment, conservation and restoration. Considering the impact of environmental factors on their livelihoods, women's participation will be ensured in the conservation of the environment and control of environmental degradation. The vast majority of rural women still depend on the locally available non-commercial sources of energy such as animal dung, crop waste and fuel wood. In order to ensure the efficient use of these energy resources in an environmental friendly manner, the Policy will aim at promoting the programmes of non-conventional energy resources. Women will be involved in spreading the use of solar energy, biogas, smokeless chulahs and other rural application so as to have a visible impact of these measures in influencing eco system and in changing the life styles of rural women.

Gender Sensitization

Training of personnel of executive, legislative and judicial wings of the State, with a special focus on policy and programme framers, implementation and development agencies, law enforcement machinery and the judiciary, as well as non-governmental organizations will be undertaken. Other measures will include:

a) Promoting societal awareness to gender issues and women's human rights.

b) Review of curriculum and educational materials to include gender education and human rights issues

c) Removal of all references derogatory to the dignity of women from all public documents and legal instruments.

d) Use of different forms of mass media to communicate social messages relating to women's equality and empowerment.

Partnership with the Voluntary Sector Organizations

The involvement of voluntary organizations, associations, federations, trade unions, non-governmental organizations, women's organizations, as well as institutions dealing with education, training and research will be ensured in the formulation, implementation, monitoring and review of all policies and programmes affecting women. Towards this end, they will be provided with appropriate support related to resources and capacity building and facilitated to participate actively in the process of the empowerment of women.

Women Empowerment Project (WEP) in collaboration with Indira Gandhi National Open University

Self Help Groups (SHGs) of women in India have been recognized as an effective strategy for the empowerment of women in rural as well as urban areas : bringing women together from all spheres of life to fight for their rights or a cause. Since the overall empowerment of women is crucially dependent on economic empowerment, women through these SHGs work on a range of issues such as health, nutrition, agriculture, forestry, etc. besides income generation activities and seeking micro credit. Therefore, the main purpose of the Women Empowerment Project (WEP) is to organize women into effective Self Help Groups and through the medium of IGNOU's training Certificate Programme "Empowering Women through Self Help Groups" prepare a cadre/network of master trainers for the sustainability of these SHGs.

For the purpose, the WEP has also established 150 Programme Centres all over the country with the satellite Direct Receiving System (DRS) to enable the women learners, at these Programme Centres, to interact directly through teleconferencing sessions with the experts at IGNOU headquarters. These teleconferencing sessions will be available to the learners on the Doordarshan Educational Channel 'Gyan Darshan' on the first and fourth Friday of every month from 3.00 - 5.00 p.m. (i.e. for two hours each time). On all the other Fridays, we will show programmes relevant to the course from 3.00 - 4.00 p.m. (i.e. one hour each time). Regular face-to-face counselling will also be provided at the Programme centres and interactive radio counselling over Akashvani's 'Gyan Vani'. The learners can also benefit from the other educational programmes telecast regularly over 'Gyan Darshan', which functions for 19 hours each day (5.00 a.m. to 12.00 p.m.). Details of all these programmes will be sent to our learners every month in the form of a booklet.

Thrust on Employment and Training for Women

In line with the Eighth Plan strategy, the nodal Department of Women and Child Development has reset its priorities to accord special emphasis on employment and income generation activities for women. The ultimate objective in all these efforts is to make women economcally independent and self-reliant.

Support to Training and Employment Projects (STEP)

The programme of STEP, launched in 1987, aims to upgrade the skills of poor women, mobilise, concretise and provide employment on a sustainable basis to women in traditional sectors such as - agriculture, dairying, fisheries, sericulture, handlooms and handicrafts. In addition to training and employment support, the three special features which this programme includes are - 'gender sensitization', 'women in development (WID) inputs' and provision of 'support services'.

Training-cum-Employment-cum-Production Centres (NORAD)

The second major programme of 'Training-cum-Employment-cum-Production Centres' which is commonly known as 'NORAD assisted Training Programmes for Women' extends financial assistance to public sector undertakings/corporations/autonomous bodies/voluntary organisation to train women in non-traditional trades and provide employment on a sustainable basis. Priority is given on training in areas like electronics, electricals, watch assembly and manufacturing, computer programming, printing and binding, handlooms, garment making, weaving and spinning, hotel management, fashion technology and tourism. Since the inception of the programme in 1983, more than 50,000 women and girls have benefitted from training as well as employment opportunities provided under this scheme.

Socio-economic Programme

The third major programme of employment and training for women is the Socio-Economic Programme (SEP)implemented by the Central Social Welfare Board (CSWB). SEP provides 'work and wage' to needy women such as destitutes, widows, economically backward and the handicapped. Since the inception of the programme, 154,000 literate and illiterate women have been given 'wage and work' in the traditional as well as agro-based and non-traditional industries.

Condensed Courses of Education and Vocational Training for Adult Women (CCE & VT).

The scheme of condensed courses of education and vocational training for adult women was started in 1958 and was recast and redefined by the CSWB in 1975. This scheme aims to provide new vistas of employment through continuing education and vocational training for women and girls who are school drop-outs. Since the inception of this programme, about 800,000 adult women and young girls have undergone vocational training.

Institutional Mechanisms

1. Institutional mechanisms, to promote the advancement of women, which exist at the Central and State levels, will be strengthened. These will be through interventions as may be appropriate and will relate to, among others, provision of adequate resources, training and advocacy skills to effectively influence macro-policies, legislation, programmes etc. to achieve the empowerment of women.

2. National and State Councils will be formed to oversee the operationalisation of the Policy on a regular basis. The National Council will be headed by the Prime Minister and the State Councils by the Chief Ministers and be broad in composition having representatives from the concerned Departments/ Ministries, National and State Commissions for Women, Social Welfare Boards, representatives of Non-Government Organizations, Women's Organisations, Corporate Sector, Trade Unions, financing institutions, academics, experts and social activists etc. These bodies will review the progress made in implementing the Policy twice a year. The National Development Council will also be informed of the progress of the programme undertaken under the policy from time to time for advice and comments.

3. National and State Resource Centres on women will be established with mandates for collection and dissemination of information, undertaking research work, conducting surveys, implementing training and awareness generation programmes, etc. These Centers will link up with Women's Studies Centres and other research and academic institutions through suitable information networking systems.

While institutions at the district level will be strengthened, at the grass-roots, women will be helped by Government through its programmes to organize and strengthen into Self-Help Groups (SHGs) at the Anganwadi/Village/Town level. The women's groups will be helped to institutionalize themselves into registered societies and to federate at the Panchyat/Municipal level. These societies will bring about synergistic implementation of all the social and economic development programmes by drawing resources made available through Government and Non-Government channels, including banks and financial institutions and by establishing a close Interface with the Panchayats/ Municipalities.

Conclusion

The process of development, in any society, should ideally be viewed and assessed in terms of what it does for an average individual. It has to be seen in terms of the benefits and opportunities that it generates for people and how these are eventually distributed – between men and women, the well off and deprived and across regions. Experience shows that, often, there is no direct correspondence between economic attainments of a society and the quality of life. Regions and nations with high levels of income and economic growth need not necessarily have similar social attainments that are desirable not only in themselves but also because of their role in supporting better opportunities for people. It becomes necessary, therefore, to have a framework and evolve development strategies that forge and strengthen the link between the two, and encourage the most effective and efficient use of available resources for furthering the well-being of the people.

The human development approach can not be limited to just building relevant indicators and indices. It is not always possible to assign a number to an attainment or a state of deprivation, nor is it always possible to quantify the processes that mediate between the inputs, on one hand, and the development outcomes, on the other. Human development has to reflect and address the social concerns and the processes that underlie the various outcomes.

It is of critical importance that we establish new benchmarks of efficiency in public management of available resources and direct them for achieving the collective goals of the nation most effectively. A country like ours can hardly afford mismanagement and poor governance. Sayeeda Hamid a member of Planning Commission, which is responsible for resettlement programs responded to women's position at present day, acknowledges that there is a big gap between policies and there implementation. Over all, the government's responses had the requisite language and jargon but felt short on commitments. By placing the onus of women's empowerment on an active judiciary, SHGS, Micro-credit and a slew of government schemes, the government delegation did seem to convey the impression that it was interested in a qualitative change in the lives of women in the country.

REFERENCES

1. Government of India, Planning Commission. *The State of Human Development, National Human Development Report2001*. New Delhi: Planning Commission 2001. Available from: *http// planningcommission.nic.in.*

2. Sustainable Development Department (SD), Food and Agriculture Organization of the UN(FAO).

23

CONTINUING EDUCATION FOR HUMAN RESOURCE DEVELOPMENT

E. Mahadeva Reddy, D. Uma Devi** & P. Audinarayana Reddy****

The rapid progress in Science and Technology has led to the industrialization of the country. The new industries require competent manpower to man the new technology to produce quality products at reduced rates. This has created demand for the skilled manpower at various levels. The new development has created a lot of impact on the system of education and in the employment sector. The impact of this new industrialization is reflected both in terms of lay off the existing outdated manpower and created more job opportunities for the competent and suitable manpower. The half suite of this development is reflected in establishment of more technical colleges with innovative combinations of the subjects. Of course, the manpower generated out of these institutions is found to be world ranking and occupying the covert positions in the industrial establishment of the world.

In order to run the modern industry which is producing specialized items requires production of different components and to assemble them or procure the components produced at various auxiliary industries and assembled them. The majority of the manpower used at the auxiliary units are found to be mostly physical and requires lower levels of competencies and

---

* Research Scholar, ** Research Associate and ***Director, Department of Adult and Continuing Education, S.V. University, Tirupati, Andhra Pradesh.

education. Even in this case also, the change in the manufacturing process has made the industries to recruit new manpower or to retrain its employees to suite the needs.

On the other hand, the rapid industrialization has also lead to the urbanization and migration of labour in search of better employment opportunities. The better employment opportunities generated through the industrialization has also created an impact on the living standards of the people. The increase in living standards was also responsible for the increase in the domestic expenditure on food and other facilities leading to the acquisition of more and more domestic appliances. The usage of these domestic appliances in day-to-day life also requires to learn new skills and abilities.

Human Resource Development

The human resource development is a process of developing competencies such as knowledge, information, attitudes, values and skills required to perform various tasks / functions associated with their present or future expected roles. Further, it is intended to develop their enabling capabilities as individuals to discover and utilize their own inner potential for their own or organizational development purposes. In order to realize the above the industries should take care of in training the new entrance and through in-service training programmes for those who are already employed.

The human development index of the population of the country clearly demonstrates that a large section of the population are illiterate or low educated, but, participating in the process of development of the country. The pace of the development of the country can be accelerated by promoting these human resources through development of newer skills and abilities. No doubt, there is lot of avenues created for this section to improve their skills and abilities and to change their occupation from traditional to non-traditional not only to improve the quantity of the product but also quality of the product.

Continuing Education

There is a need to upgrade the competencies of the manpower for accelerating the pace of production and national development. Keeping this in view, the country has created a number of avenues and opportunities for the people to improve their competencies by participating in the skill improvement programmes in the form of continuing education programmes. It is a form of Adult Education, where in need based skill development or skill promotion activities were organised in sequential manner to enhance the competency of the person in a given profession. In addition to the profession development activities, life-enrichment content will also form an integral part of the curriculum of this programme. These programmes may be of long-term dura ion and short-term duration, Traditional or non-traditional or distance mode. Keeping in view of the vast potentialities of the masses and to make them as partners of the development, the Government of India has launched a special programme of continuing education intended to cover the low educated population.

Objectives of Continuing Education Programme

1. Provision of facilities for retention of literacy skills and continuing education to enable the learners to continue their learning beyond basic literacy.
2. Creating scope for application of functional literacy for improvement of living conditions and quality of life.
3. Dissemination of information on development programmes and widening and improving participation of traditionally deprived sections of the society.
4. Creation of awareness about national concerns such as national integration, conservation and improvement of the environment, women's equality, observance of small family norm etc., and sharing of common problems of the community.
5. Improvement of economic conditions and general well-being as well as improvement of productivity by organising short-duration training programmes, orientation of courses for

providing vocational skills and by taking up linkage activities for establishing direct lineage between continuing education and development activities.

6. Provision of facilities for library and reading room for creating conducive environment for literacy efforts and a learning society.

In order to operationalize the above objectives a continuing education centre was established at the village level to cover 2,000 to 2,500 population or 500 literates. The basic functions of the continuing education centre is as follows:

1. An Evening Class

For upgradation of literacy and numeracy to be organise for 3-4 hours once in a week, the learners would have the option to come for an hour or so, at time of their convenience on that day.

2. A Library and Reading Room

For which books would be purchased from the non-recurring and recurring provisions; copies of old journals will be maintained and useful booklets relating to development programmes will be published by concerned agencies. Wallpapers and newspapers, appropriate for adult learners, informative and entertainment journals, developmental literature, etc would also be available.

3. A Charcha Mandal (Discussion Group)

Simple and short duration relating to such subjects as health and family welfare, new developments in agricultural and animal husbandry, conservation of energy, improved stove etc

4. Income generating programmes

Continuing Education Centres may also help the local youth to benefit from various vocational training programmes. Income generation programme which helps participants to acquire or upgrade vocational skills and enable them to conduct income generating activities should be made available in structured packages.

5. Sports and Adventurous Activities

The stress being on indigenous sports, walking, excursions, cycling, trips in groups etc. If savings are available, visit by bus to development projects could also be arranged.

6. Recreational and Cultural Activities

Particularly traditional and folk forms of art, rural theater, puppetry etc.

7. An Information Window

For securing information on various developmental programmes, information and material suitable for neo-literate may be procured from the concerned development agencies.

8. A Communication Centre

Where community radio, audio-cassette player-cum-recorder may be provided in the Nodal continuing education centre.

Types of Continuing Education Programmes

The types of continuing education programmes which may sought to be promoted for achievement of its objectives may vary in different regions depending on literacy levels, strength and spread of formal and non-formal education systems and the socioeconomic conditions prevailing in the region. In the present scheme of continuing education, the endeavor would be to draw upon the experience of the previous programmes, take into account the varied socio-economic conditions in different parts of the country and to try synthesis the nature, characteristics and scope of the country and to try to synthesize the nature, characteristics and scope of continuing education programme could be classified into four types. They are:

1. Equivalency Programmes (EPs)
2. Income Generating Programmes (IGPs)
3. Quality of Life Improvement Programmes (QLIPs) and
4. Individual Interest Promotion Programmes (IIPPs)

1. Equivalency Programmes (EPs)

Equivalency programme can provide an opportunity to adults and out-of-school children who have acquired basic literacy skills or who have completed primary education and willing to continue their education for acquisition of competencies. The programme is meant for mobilization of all possible alternative systems of education-formal, non-formal, open schooling and distance education etc., to create opportunities for wider access to all the major target groups especially for women, SC, ST and other disadvantaged groups.

Unlike the formal education system, the equivalency programmes can have several variants to provide an integrated general and vocational education. Though, the content areas of equivalency programmes may broadly be the same as in the formal education, the content may be written in the form of modules or do-it yourself learning materials with option to choose one vocational skill for a living, out of a series of skill booklets or courses may be made available. EPs developed as non-formal alternatives can also draw upon all three types of delivery systems simultaneously i.e., learning centres, self-paced learning, distance education and open learning systems. Implementation of EPs will be collaborative efforts between ZSSs, SRCs, national and open school.

2. Income Generating Programmes

Income generating programme are the vocational and technical education programmes which will help the neo-literates to acquire or upgrade their vocational-skills so as to enable them to increase their income generating activities. Designing of Income Generating Programmes as a component of continuing education involves development of a variety of innovative, locally relevant, employment oriented vocational courses which may be delivered in multiple non-formal modes comprising of direct contact sessions, demonstrations, study visits, self-learning modules, on-site training, apprenticeship training, distance learning or a combination of the above.

The major components of Income Generating Programmes includes (a) a bridge course to upgrade literacy and to promote social and technological awareness; (b) skill development programmes covering commonly required basic skills, trade skills, on-site training and relative trade theory to provide scientific understanding; and (c) entrepreneurial skills including book-keeping, marketing and money saving skills. IGPs may also take the form of supplementing the existing arrangements under schemes such as TRYSEM, DWCRA, JRY, IRDP, Krishi Vignan Kendras, Farmers Training Center etc., with part time vocational course or short duration training programmes.

3. Quality of Life Improvement Programmes (QLIPs)

QLIPs are especially designed with an aim to equip learners and the community with essential knowledge, attitudes, values and skills to enable them to improve quality of life individuals and as members of the community. The role of QLIPs is to facilitate positive societal change with respect to the indicators, viz., biological, social, economic, humanistic environment through education.

QLIPs should be capable of delivery through multi-sectoral approach because many sectors of the Governement may be concerned with development programmes covering different elements of quality of life such as family welfare, health, nutrition, drinking water, sanitation, population education, environment, social services, communal harmony, transportation, etc. The methods of delivery may include structured courses conducted through learning centres, distance education technics, public education campaigns, information dissemination through mass-media, self-learning, printed material, etc.

4. Individual Interest Promotion Programmes (IIPPs)

These Continuing Education Programmes aim to provide opportunity for individuals to participate and learn about their chosen social, cultural, spiritual, health, physical and aesthetic interests. The major objective of IIPPs is to provide learning experience to promote and improve individual interests of all adults, but especially people such as youth, women and the elderly people in rural areas. The courses developed may include a wide variety of learning programmes which encourage people to constructively utilize their leisure time and also simultaneously facilitate self-actualization.

These programmes may include leisure time interests such as sports or hobbies, cultural interests such as art, painting, drawing, traditional music, dance, drama etc., interest catering to promote self-reliance and vocational skills such as dress designing, sewing, knitting, healthy cooking, repair of agricultural machinery and electrical appliances, first-aid, self-defence for women etc., and personal development and self-actualisation interests such as mediation, creative writing, speed reading, leadership skills etc. The IIPPs may be delivered by any of the methods such as contact sessions at learning centres, individual self-paced learning, and distance education or by a combination of the above.

1. All these programmes revolves around the Human Resource Development components, viz. promoting positive attitude, values, skills, competencies, knowledge and finally the positive competitiveness. It takes care of the Adults with low literacy or illiterates and provides an opportunities to promote their level of literacy and to practicing the newly learned skills in their day-to-day life. In addition, they were provided with latest know how in their occupation and the information on the developmental programmes, so as to make them as partners of the development. They were organised as self-help groups so as to protect themselves from the external exploitation and built themselves as a strong driving force in the society.
2. *Out of school youth*: The continuing education centre also covers the out of school youth and provide further educational opportunities through equivalency programmes, individual interest promotion programmes and through income generating activities. They were equipped with the employable skills so as to enable them to secure the wage employment or self-employment. It also exposes and involves them in the demonetarization of the institutions.

3. *Women:* The continuing education programmes takes adequate care of the women with different levels of literacy, facilitate to organise them as self-help groups, empower them to discharge their rightful roles and also promote their participation in all developmental spheres and in domestic decision making process. A special discussion group was also organised to create self-confidence among them in communication and involvement in democratic process of identification of problems and solving them by themselves.

4. *Youth:* The youth are prime group of the society who requires special attention, not only in grooming them but also keep them in the right track. They are the key both for the production and re-productive spears of the society. Hence they should be oriented and equipped with required skills. The continuing education centre organise sports and games involves the youth, to channelise their energies and to promote integration among different sections of the population and paves way for their involvement in the social institutions.

The above clearly indicates that the continuing education programmes is one of the important programmes organised at the grass root level involving all sections of the population and empowering them with required skills and competencies to promote their productivity and converting them as the assets of the society through the process of human resource development.

24

HUMAN RESOURCE DEVELOPMENT IN VOLUNTARY ORGANISATIONS

V. Hari Babu & M. Mary***

Voluntary Organizations (Non-Governmental Organizations) have been playing a significant role in several areas of the development of India. The role of these organizations in rural India is quite remarkable. These organizations have been functioning on the principle of Voluntary Service. A voluntary organization is an organization, which motivates people, creates demand for the service, takes up follow up action, research evaluation and even rehabilitation. They may also conduct parallel programmes and redefine the scope, identify new approaches and methods and experiment with new ideas. Voluntary action in India is not a new phenomenon. There are, as many as 2000 Non-Governmental Organizations (NGOs) or groups in India working for rural development. Voluntary Organizations may be of different types depending on their objectives and membership. They may be International (Rotary Club, I.P.P.F., Y.M.C.A.). National (B.G.M.S., A.I.W.S). State Level and purely local. International voluntary Organisations have some common programmes and some are taken up at National or Local levels within the framework. Local Organizations crop up according to local needs or of its

* Research Associate, UGC-Academic Staff College, Andhra University, Visakhapatnam, A.P.

** Research Scholar, Department of Politics & Public Administration, Andhra University, Visakhapatnam. A.P.

members and are free to frame their Constitution and take up any activity they deem proper. Workers in these organizations may be classified as (a) active volunteers (b) members (c) salaried staff. Active volunteers usually are the pioneers who start the activity and slowly enroll members for raising funds as well as enlarging the area of activity. Though the rural development programmes have been started in the first five .year plan period, due recognition has been given only in the Sixth Plan (1980 - 85). The official statistics indicates that at the national level, the targets for sixth plan under Integrated Rural Development Programme (IRDP) have been achieved in respect of quantitative parameters set out in the programme guidelines. (Performance has been uneven between States). During the plan period 165.62 lakh beneficiaries with a total expenditure of Rs. 1,661.17 crores have been covered as against the target of 150 lakh beneficiaries with a total allocation of Rs. 1,500 crores. The role of NGOs in various rural development programmes has been defined in the Seventh Plan documents. A plan expenditure of about Rs. 100 and Rs. 150 crores in the Central and State sectors has been proposed on specific programmes for use in active collaboration with Voluntary Agencies. Several NGOs have been associated with rural development and upliftment of the poor. Some of them are:

(a) Tagore's Sriniketan (West Bengal)
(b) YMCAs Organization at Marthandam (Tamilnadu)
(c) Friends Society at Rssulia (M. P.)
(d) Vadchhi Movement (Gujarat)
(e) Sulabh Shauchalaya Samsthan (Patna)
(f) Sarva Seva Farm (Madurai)
(g) Gandhi Peace Centre.

Review of Literature

Research studies on Voluntary Organizations were very scant in India. The Human Resource Development components of NGSs were not studied in detail. Sahay and Malik attempted to study the issues relating to voluntary funding for Rural Development. The role of voluntary organizations in Rural

Development with reference to some voluntary organizations in Visakhapatnam was studied by Ananda Rao and Satya Sundaram. Krishna Murthy V. studies these uses relating to Aid to voluntary organizations. H.R.D. Activities peoples participation and voluntary action were reviewed by Rajasekharan. Rural Sanitation Programme and the role of Non- Governmental Organizations were examined by an other author. The difficulties of voluntary organizations ad the land development through voluntary action were analyzed by Krishna Murthy and Natarajan Mamata Lakshmamma studies the various types of voluntary organizations in population control. The role of voluntary organizations was reviewed by another author.

Need for the Study

The review of research and literature on voluntary organizations reveal that micro level studies on Human Resource Development in voluntary Organizations were limited in India. The Voluntary Organizations have been functioning with multifaceted objectives to uplift the rural and urban poor. The rural poor needs special attention because most of them are illiterates and ignorant of the government enactments. The voluntary organizations also deserve special treatment from the government to serve the region better and contribute their best to fulfill the national objectives. Some voluntary organizations in India are functioning well with the predetermined goals or objectives. Bhagavathula Charitable Trust (BCT) is one among them. It has been rendering yeoman services to the people of Visakhapatnam District. It has encouraged several sister organizations also to function on the similar lines. The area under the BCT has benefited a lot from different perspectives. The organization has become a model organization to several other organizations in India. I t has conducted several training programmes to several needy and deserving rural folk in and around Yelamanchili in Visakhapatnam District. The present study is intended to cover the HRD activities of BCT because there is no study conducted so far on this subject. Moreover, it is highly useful to other similar organizations to follow some important measures. With this in view, the present study is expected to bridge the gap in the existing literature.

Objectives

The following are the main objectives of the study with reference to B.C.T.

a) To examine the HRD activities.

b) To study the development profile of women in the region.

c) To present the profile of various beneficiaries.

The ultimate objective of the study is to offer some suggestions for the effective implementation of various HRD activities in the organization.

Methodology of the Study

The study was conducted on the basis of primary and secondary sources of data. Primary data was collected with a small questionnaire to understand the profile of various beneficiaries. Random sampling method was adopted to select 50 women beneficiaries and all of them were interviewed as per their convenience. They also cooperated well in answering the questions. Thus, the impact of HRD activities was studied. Secondary data was based on the publications of the government of India, the literature available from the books, journals and newspapers and also the records and reports of the voluntary organizations.

Main Findings

In India, several Voluntary Organizations have been functioning at different places to uplift the rural and urban poor. Some organizations focusing on education, health and nutrition, sanitation, environmental protection, etc. In Andhra. Pradesh also the role of voluntary organizations is quite significant. Gandhi Peace Centre has been encouraging and assisting several such organizations. Bhagavathula Charitable Trust (BCT) is one among the successful voluntary organizations in Andhra Pradesh. It was started by a mineral scientist Dr. B. Parameswara Rao, who had a vast knowledge on the Management of Voluntary Organisations. He had high level of commitment, dedication and devotion. The BCT is laying stress on leadership generation with a view to improving the capability of the villagers to handle the programmes by themselves and for themselves. The BCT is training every year village animators who possess commitment, understanding, dedication. These youngsters proved to be coordinators of the village activities, being formulated by youth clubs, Mahila Mandalas and other groups. They are also helping in the health activities as well as in village front for the poorer sections as well as for women. The BCT has started the community health project in 1979 with 11 health workers on the lines worked out in the programme and putting them to training. Out of the 11 women trained, only 9 were retained finally as village level health workers for a cluster of seven villages. According to the surveys conducted by the health workers, the majority of the diseases were either due to malnutrition or poor sanitary conditions. The village health workers were supplied with medical kits and medicines for curing minor ailments. The community health organizer supervised their work and conducted weekly reviews of their performance and monitored the feedback. There were regular orientation courses for health workers every year, up to July 1982. Due to paucity of funds, the BCT could not maintain health workers for a long time. The village animators and community workers have been receiving training in basic nutrition and healthcare. The BCT has developed a demonstration farm at Panchadarla. A cattle cross breeding farm was also started there. A silvipastoral (scheme) was launched with the financial assistance from PADI. The educational background of the beneficiaries revealed that about 70 per cent had no formal education. About 10 per cent studied Intermediate and also 5th standard. The total percentage of beneficiaries above matriculation were only 20 per cent. It shows the low level of education in the region. The training programme conducted by the organization were need based. Several programmes were conducted on the activities of toy-making, etc., 18 per cent of the beneficiaries attended the programmes on nursery followed by add a leaf making (16 per cent), dairy (16 per cent), para veterinary (16 per cent), nursing (12 per cent) and tailoring (12 per cent). The training programmes were more effective and helped for increasing the incomes of the various participants. About 50 per cent of the beneficiaries had an income increase of Rs.5,000 to Rs.10,000. About 48 per cent beneficiaries had an income of Rs.500 to Rs.5,000. All the respondents were asked to respond on the impact of training programmes in the village. It is heartening to note that there was a remarkable positive change in the village as a result of the activities of the voluntary organization. All the respondents felt that the BCT changed the profile of the village and the status of several individuals. The respondents were free to express the required facilities to them in the area. They did not have social security benefits. Therefore, the aged respondents gave preference for the old age benefits. About 40 per cent of them were interested to expand their activities. Therefore, they were in need of additional loans from the banks or financial institutions. About 24 per cent felt that employment and welfare facilities were to be considered priority. 20 per cent of the respondents started that medical and educational facilities were provided to them.

Conclusion

In order to develop rural areas, several measures are to be undertaken in India. NGOs are to be encouraged to take up certain activities with the required managerial and financial support. The officials of the Government Organizations are to be posted compulsorily to work with the Voluntary Organizations for some period so that they can serve better. The youth studying in colleges and universities are to be encouraged to work in rural voluntary organizations to understand the real problems of the people and organize them for improving their economic position. The involvement of NGOs should be encouraged for the development of social sectors for cost effective implementation of various programmes and also higher level of people participation in various programme.

REFERENCES

1. Mamata Lakshmanna (1983) Voluntary Organization Population Control, *Yojana* 26th January, p. 23.

2. Rajasekharan, M.V., (1982) People Participation and Voluntary action, *Kurukshetra*, Vol.XXX, No.1, p. 21.

3. Satya Sundara (1986), Voluntary Agencies and Rural Development, *Kurukshetra*, Vol.XXX, pp. 4-7.

4. Krishnamurthy, V. (1982) Voluntary Agencies and Rural Development, *Kurukshetra*, Vol.XXX, 18th June, p. 47.

5. Ananda Rao R. (1981) Integrated Rural Development and the Role of Voluntary Agencies, Ph.D Thesis Andhra University, Visakhapatnam.

25

TRENDS IN HUMAN DEVELOPMENT SPENDING IN THE STATES OF INDIA

K. Dasaratha Ramaih & K. Thulasi Naik***

Introduction

Despite substantive gains in human development over the years, India's standing among the nations of the world remains low and much remains to be done to improve its performance. India placed at the lower end of the middle level performing countries regarding its Human Development Index. The problem is much more serious than these figures indicate for, in some of the heavily populated Central and Northern States of Bihar, Jharkhand, Madhya Pradesh, Orissa, Rajasthan and Uttar Pradesh, human development situation is alarming.

It is in this context that the Millennium Development Goals and the more ambitious targets set for the 10th Five Year Plan gain significance. These include reduction in the headcount measure of poverty by five percentage points, improving high quality employment, universal enrolment by 2003 and universal completion of five years schooling by 2007, improving the literacy rates, reducing gender gaps in literacy and wage rates, reducing the population growth rate, reducing infant and maternal mortality, improving the forest cover, ensuring potable drinking water for all and cleaning of all major polluted rivers. The Common

* Professor, ** Associate Professor, Dept. of Economics & Applied Economics, S.K. University, Anantapur, Andhra Pradesh.

Minimum Programme (CMP) too has emphasised the need to significantly augment investment to 6 percent of GDP in the case of education and 2-3 percent of GDP in the case of healthcare in a phased manner.

By any reckoning, achieving these targets would require significant augmentation of investments by the Central and State Governments as well as reforms in the design and implementation of policies and delivery mechanisms. Thus, both augmenting investments for human development and improving the productivity of these investments by improving delivery systems and achieving greater synergy through public private partnerships are essential to achieve the objectives of human development in the country.

Pressure on the States from declining transfers from the Centre on the one hand, and virtually stagnant revenues from own sources on the other, have constrained the availability of resources for investment in human capital. Declining revenues combined with competing claims on expenditures particularly, to meet large increases in pay, pensions and interest payments has crowded out spending on productive sectors such as basic education, healthcare, water supply and sanitation and poverty alleviation.

The large losses in the finances of the power and irrigation sectors have only added to the fiscal problems of States. It must be noted that much of the public investments in human capital - over 85 per cent in both primary education and healthcare are incurred at the State level and deterioration in States' finances has adversely affected allocation to these sectors.

The Constitution of India assigns the State governments a predominant role in human development. Almost 85-90 per cent of the spending on education and healthcare is carried out at the State level. Over the years, fiscal pressure has resulted in the compression of spending on social sectors from States' own resources and Central sector and centrally sponsored schemes have increased in importance. Nevertheless, the role of the States in both financing and implementing human development is predominant.

The fiscal developments at the State level have had adverse impact on investment in human capital both due to lower resources allocated and due to higher cost of providing them. Thus, declining overall resources combined with the lack of prioritisation in favour of social sectors, have reduced investments in human capital as seen from the declining social sector allocations and social priority allocations.

Simultaneously, sharp increase in expenditures due to pay and pension revisions of government employees including those in the health sector has escalated the unit cost of providing public services significantly. Thus, even as per capita expenditures on education and health sectors have shown a marginal increase over the years, the real increase after taking account the increase in the unit cost of providing these services has been negligible.

The problem should be seen not merely in aggregate terms but also in terms of the capacity of different States to make investments in human development. Notably, the poorer States with lower means are in much greater fiscal mess than more affluent States. In fact, these are the States with much lower achievements in human development. It is imperative that they catch up with the achievements in more affluent States not merely to improve the wellbeing of the large mass of population residing in these States but also to ensure the very stability of federalism and integrity of the country. Channelling larger volume of financial resources to these States for investment in human capital and enhancing the productivity through policy and institutional changes in them are difficult challenges.

Major Issues in Financing Human Development

There is considerable analysis of human development in India and India's position in achieving human development vis-à-vis Millennium Development Goals. The Human Development Reports of the various states have helped to identify the shortcomings in the human development achievements up to the district level and help to focus interventions on the lagging regions and sub-regions. The analysis so far has helped to identify important issues and raised a number of testable hypotheses pertaining to financing human development in different States in India.

The level of government expenditures on social services in India are considerably lower than (a) those in countries with comparable level of development (b) the expenditures incurred by the fast growing East Asian Economies during their period of transition; (c) the UNDP norms and (d) the level of expenditures incurred by the States in the 1980s. There is considerable lag in achieving the MDGs and the Tenth Plan targets in several States in India.

Considerable amount of additional public spending on social sector and poverty alleviation is required to achieve these targets. There are wide inter-State differences in social sector expenditures as well as human development achievements. The per capita expenditures or expenditure per beneficiary individual is higher in more affluent States though the expenditure – GSDP ratio is inversely related to per capita GSDP. The studies have shown that spending on education and health sectors are important determinants of levels of achievements in education and health in the States.

Therefore, differences in per capita expenditures among States tend to increase disparities over time. Given that the human development achievements are significantly lower in poorer States and less affluent districts within the States, the prevailing pattern of expenditures is not well targeted to achieve the human development goals. Within the social sectors, in many States the proportion of public spending on those that are in the nature of investments in human capital are declining and those of consumption nature are on the increase.

In poorer States, within education and health expenditures, wages and salaries constitute predominant proportions and this leaves very little for non-wage items such as textbooks in the case of education and medicines in the case of health sectors. This tends to reduce productivity of spending on social sectors in poorer States. This aspect needs to be examined in the context of individual States. An important development in the 1990s

Table 1: Human Development Targets

Focus	*Tenth Plan Target*	*Millennium Development Goal*
Poverty	Reduction of poverty ratio by 5 percentage points by 2007 and 15 percentage points by 2012	Between 1990 and 2015, the proportion of people whose income is less than one dollar a day should be reduced by one-half
		The proportion of people suffering from hunger should be reduced by one-half.
Education	All children in school by 2003 and all children to complete 5 years of schooling by 2007	Ensure that by 2015, children everywhere, boys and girls alike will be able to complete a full course of primary schooling
	Increase in literacy rates to 75 percent within the Tenth Plan period (2002-07)	
Gender Gap	Reduction in gender gaps in literacy by at least 50 per cent by 2007	Eliminate gender disparity in primary and secondary education preferably by 2005 and in all of education by 2015
Infant/child Mortality Rate	Reduction of IMR to 45 per 1000 live births by 2007 and to 28 in 2012 mortality rate	Reduce by two-thirds, between 1990 and 2015, the under-five
Maternal Health	Reduction of MMR to 2 per thousand live births by 2007 and 1 by 2012.	Reduce by three quarters, between 1990 and 2015, the Maternal Mortality Ratio
Drinking Water	Access to potable drinking water in all villages in the plan period	Have by 2015, the proportion of people without sustainable access to safe drinking water and basic sanitation

HIV/AIDS	80 % coverage of high risk groups through targeted interventions, 90% coverage of schools and colleges through education programmes, 80% awareness among the general population in rural areas, reducing transmission through blood to less than one percent, establishing at least one voluntary testing and counselling centre in every district, scaling up of mother -to-child transmission activities up to the district level, achieving zero level increase of HIV/AIDS prevalue by 2007	Have halted by 2015 and begun to reverse the spread of HIV/AIDS
Malaria Targets	Annual Blood Examination Rate (ABER) over 10 %, Annual Parasite Incidence (API) 1.3 or less, 25 % reduction in morbidity and Mortality due to Malaria by 2007 and 50 % by 2010 (NHP 2002)	Have halted by 2015 and begun to reverse the incidence of Malaria and other major diseases

is the increase in Central financing of expenditures on social sectors. While the proportion of central financing in social sectors has shown an increase in recent years, there have been attempts to decentralise the delivery of these services.

In many States, subsequent to the 73rd Constitutional amendment, the responsibility of delivering elementary education and basic healthcare in rural areas has been assigned to district and taluk/block level panchayats. However, with little flexibility and autonomy in determining the services levels, decentralisation has not led to incentives to improve service delivery nor has it led to increase in accountability.

The Table-1, shows the Human Development targets on various social services during the tenth plan and Millennium Development goals.

Trends in Human Development Spending in the States

The human development expenditures by the State governments include expenditures on social services and rural development. According to budgetary classification, social services include education, health and family welfare, water supply and sanitation, nutrition, social welfare, other social services. Expenditure on rural development is mainly on rural poverty alleviation. The expenditure includes all those shown in the State government budgets. This implies that the expenditures incurred through Central sector and Centrally sponsored schemes that do not pass through the State budgets are not included. These are the grants given directly by the centre to the District Rural Development Agency (DRDA) for rural poverty alleviation.

Also grants given by the Central government for Sarva Shiksha Abhiyan is not included in the analysis. Information in these will have to be collected separately and included in the total expenditures on human development. Thus, this analysis presents only the broad trends.

The spending on each of the items under human development in per capita terms and as a percentage of GSDP is presented in the Tables 2 and 3 along with the two measures of fiscal stress in the States, the revenue deficit and fiscal deficit. The composition of each of the expenditure items under human development is presented in Table 4.

Interestingly, fiscal stress as indicated by the ratio of revenue deficit to GSDP is not systematically related to per capita GSDP. In fact, the average revenue deficit for high income States at 3.8 per cent of GSDP in 2001-02 was higher than both middle income (3.2 per cent) and low income States (3.6 per cent).

In fact, Gujarat and Punjab, the two high income States had their revenue deficits higher than five percent of GSDP. It may be noted that only West Bengal among the middle income States and Orissa among low income States had their revenue deficit-GSDP ratios higher than five per cent. At the same time, the ratio of fiscal deficit to GSDP was positively correlated with the level of per capita GSDP.

The high income States on an average had the fiscal deficit at 4.8 per cent of GSDP whereas it was higher at 5.2 per cent for middle income States and still higher at 5.8 per cent for low income States. Thus, in high income States although the fiscal deficit was lower, the largest proportion of this was due to revenue deficits and the ratios of capital expenditures to GSDP were lower in them.

Interestingly, in special category States, the revenue deficits were low at 1.3 per cent of GSDP whereas fiscal deficit was high at about 6.4 per cent of GSDP. This is explained by the fact that the loan component of plan assistance is low (10 per cent) and yet, much of the capital investments in physical infrastructure has to be financed by borrowing.

An interesting feature is that in non-special category States the ratio of human development expenditures in GSDP shows an inverse relationship with per capita GSDP in the States. In other words, as ratio of GSDP, richer States spend less on human development than poorer States. However, per capita expenditures in richer States are substantially higher than in poorer States.

It is also seen that in per capita terms, human development

Table 2: Per Capita Expenditures in States (2001-02)

(in Rupees)

State	Revenue Deficit	Fiscal Deficit	Human Development Expenditure								Per capita GSDP
			Education	Health & Family Welfare	Water Supply & Sanitation	Nutrition	Social Welfare	Other Social Services	Rural Development	Total	
General States	-618	-919	558	149	70	22	131	134	128	1194	17500
High income States	-1018	-1300	826	183	81	31	137	270	62	1589	27020
Goa	-1685	-3044	1823	655	883	12	327	181	146	4027	57309
Gujarat	-1313	-1270	637	142	64	25	111	697	79	1756	24810
Haryana	-493	-1280	691	150	202	15	228	99	63	1449	28139
Maharashtra	-837	-1114	960	188	54	45	141	104	57	1548	27160
Punjab	-1540	-202	747	252	75	0	86	193	41	1394	28434
Middle Income States	**-669**	**-1065**	**615**	**192**	68	**39**	**167**	**141**	**156**	1378	20682
Andhra Pradesh	-379	-885	510	180	63	73	206	136	218	1385	19927
Karnataka	-617	-1104	659	204	70	20	190	160	107	1410	19863
Kerala	-815	-1023	779	237	41	1	145	111	218	1531	22632
Tamil Nadu	-439	-759	689	195	109	74	205	111	85	1469	22994
West Bengal	-1096	-1461	564	175	50	8	94	170	160	1221	19373

Low Income States	**-411**	**-657**	**405**	**107**	**67**	**8**	**105**	**71**	**138**	**901**	**11278**
Bihar	-278	-476	365	86	25	4	41	23	141	686	6026
Madhya Pradesh	-518	-597	348	113	73	13	181	107	126	960	13763
Orissa	-765	-1072	475	122	68	13	135	164	121	1097	11470
Rajasthan	-662	-1993	603	174	203	24	64	178	108	1353	15423
Uttar Pradesh	-367	-588	362	82	34	0	73	16	118	685	11211
Chhattisgarh	-257	-507	333	117	70	19	325	113	174	1151	14105
Jharkhand	37	-603	471	141	104	4	208	94	346	1369	11205
Spl. Category States	-201	-989	963	271	227	16	133	161	212	1985	15390
Arunachal Pradesh	254	-2493	1662	614	595	104	274	327	579	4155	16667
Assam	-328	0539	697	134	59	14	67	52	145	1168	12241
Himachal Pradesh	-1404	02465	1499	453	560	16	160	291	132	3111	24377
Jammu and Kashmir	720	-732	917	430	319	2	115	271	274	2328	15547
Manipur	-664	-1402	1197	297	204	15	243	100	214	2272	13220
Meghalaya	-144	-944	1069	395	399	29	93	199	274	2459	17009
Mizoram	-2887	-4682	2371	801	841	93	756	675	602	6139	21332
Nagaland	219	-1786	1088	406	399	34	211	344	252	2734	20180
Sikkim	2589	-1211	2763	750	660	105	288	876	304	5744	20639
Tripura	170	-1683	1437	289	198	43	425	311	485	3188	18961
Uttaranchal	-116	-496	815	171	197	0	100	64	186	1533	15209
All States	**-591**	**-923**	**584**	**157**	**80**	**22**	**131**	**136**	**134**	**1244**	**17367**

Source (Basic Data):1. Reserve Bank of India, 2004, Finances of State Governments, Government of India, Mumbai,

2. Website www.mospi.nic.in. of Central Statistical Organisation, Ministry of Statistics and Programme Implementation, Government of India,

Table 3: Financing of Human Development in Different States

(Percent to GSDP)

State	Revenue Deficit	Fiscal Deficit	Human Development Expenditure							
			Education	Health & family Welfare	Water Supply and Sanitation	Nutrition	Social Welfare	Other Social Services	Rural Development	Total
General States	-3.53	-5.25	3.19	0.85	0.40	0.13	0.75	0.77	0.73	6.82
High income States	-3.77	-4.81	3.06	0.68	0.30	0.11	0.51	1.00	0.23	5.88
Goa	-2.94	-5.31	3.18	1.14	1.54	0.02	0.57	0.32	0.26	7.03
Gujarat	-5.29	-5.12	2.57	0.57	0.26	0.10	0.45	2.81	0.32	7.08
Haryana	-1.75	-4.55	2.46	0.53	0.72	0.05	0.81	0.35	0.22	5.15
Maharashtra	-3.08	-4.10	3.53	0.69	0.20	0.17	0.52	0.38	0.21	5.70
Punjab	-5.42	-7.10	2.63	0.89	0.26	0.00	0.30	0.68	0.14	4.90
Middle Income States	-3.24	-5.15	2.97	0.93	0.33	0.19	0.81	0.68	0.75	6.67
Andhra Pradesh	-1.90	-4.44	2.56	0.90	0.32	0.37	1.03	0.68	1.09	6.95
Karnataka	-3.11	-5.56	3.32	1.03	0.35	0.10	0.95	0.80	0.54	7.10
Kerala	-3.60	-4.52	3.44	1.05	0.18	0.00	0.64	0.49	0.96	6.77
Tamil Nadu	-1.91	-3.30	3.00	0.85	0.47	0.32	0.89	0.48	0.37	6.39
West Bengal	-5.66	-7.54	2.91	0.90	0.26	0.04	0.49	0.88	0.83	6.30
Low Income States	-3.65	-5.83	3.59	0.95	0.60	0.07	0.93	0.63	1.23	7.99
Bihar	-4.61	-7.90	6.06	1.43	0.42	0.07	0.68	0.37	2.34	11.38
Madhya Pradesh	-3.77	-4.34	2.53	0.82	0.53	0.09	1.31	0.78	0.91	6.98

Orissa	-6.67	-9.35	4.14	1.06	0.59	0.11	1.18	1.43	1.06	9.56
Rajasthan	-4.29	-6.50	3.91	1.13	1.32	0.15	0.41	1.15	0.70	8.77
Uttar Pradesh	-3.28	-5.25	3.23	0.73	0.30	0.00	0.65	0.15	1.05	6.11
Chhattisgarh	-1.82	-3.59	2.36	0.83	0.50	0.13	2.31	0.80	1.24	8.16
Jharkhand	0.33	-5.38	4.21	1.26	0.93	0.03	1.86	0.84	3.09	12.22
Spl. Category States	-1.30	-6.43	6.26	1.76	1.48	0.11	0.86	1.05	1.38	12.90
Arunachal Pradesh	1.53	-14.96	9.97	3.68	3.57	0.62	1.64	1.96	3.47	24.93
Assam	-2.68	-4.41	5.70	1.10	0.49	0.11	0.55	0.42	1.18	9.54
Himachal Pradesh	-5.76	-10.11	6.15	1.86	2.30	0.07	0.66	1.19	0.54	12.76
Jammu and Kashmir	4.63	-4.71	5.90	2.77	2.05	0.01	0.74	1.74	1.76	14.97
Manipur	-5.02	-10.61	9.06	2.25	1.54	0.12	1.84	0.76	1.62	17.18
Meghalaya	-0.84	-5.55	6.29	2.32	2.35	0.17	0.55	1.17	1.61	14.46
Mizoram	-13.53	-21.95	11.12	3.76	3.94	0.43	3.55	3.16	2.82	28.78
Nagaland	1.09	-8.85	5.39	2.01	1.98	0.17	1.05	1.70	1.25	13.55
Sikkim	12.55	-5.87	13.38	3.63	3.20	0.51	1.39	4.25	1.47	27.83
Tripura	0.90	-8.88	7.58	1.52	1.05	0.23	2.24	1.64	2.56	16.82
Uttaranchal	-0.77	-3.26	5.36	1.12	1.30	0.00	0.66	0.42	1.22	10.08
All States	**-3.41**	**-5.32**	**3.36**	**0.90**	**0.46**	**0.13**	**0.76**	**0.78**	**0.77**	**7.16**

Source (Basic Data):1. Reserve Bank of India, 2004, Finances of State Governments, Government of India, Mumbai,

2. Website www.mospi.nic.in. of Central Statistical Organisation, Ministry of Statistics and Programme Implementation, Government of India

Table 4: Composition of Human Development Expenditure 2001-02

(Percent to Total)

State	*Human Development Expenditure*							
	Education	*Health and Family Welfare*	*Water Supply and Sanitation*	*Nutrition*	*Social Welfare*	*Other Social Services ment*	*Rural Deve- lop-*	*Total*
General States	46.74	12.52	5.90	1.88	10.99	11.24	10.74	100
High income States	**51.94**	**11.51**	**5.10**	**1.94**	**8.63**	**16.98**	**3.90**	**100**
Goa	45.28	16.27	21.93	0.29	8.11	4.49	3.63	100
Gujarat	36.25	8.10	3.67	1.45	6.34	39.70	1.48	100
Haryana	47.72	10.38	13.91	1.02	15.77	6.83	4.37	100
Maharashtra	62.01	12.12	3.46	2.92	9.10	6.71	3.68	100
Punjab	53.57	18.07	5.40	0.00	6.19	13.82	2.96	100
Middle Income States	**44.62**	**13.93**	**4.94**	**2.84**	**12.10**	**10.26**	**11.31**	**100**
Andhra Pradesh	36.80	12.99	4.58	5.27	14.85	9.80	15.71	100
Karnataka	46.75	14.48	4.97	1.44	13.45	11.34	7.57	100
Kerala	50.86	15.44	2.69	0.04	9.46	7.25	14.26	100
Tamil Nadu	46.89	13.30	7.43	5.05	13.95	7.58	5.80	100
West Bengal	46.15	14.33	4.12	0.63	7.73	13.91	13.13	100
Low Income States	**44.95**	**11.84**	**7.48**	**0.84**	**11.64**	**7.88**	**15.36**	**100**
Bihar	53.22	12.58	3.68	0.64	6.01	3.29	20.59	100
Madhya Pradesh	36.25	11.73	7.58	1.35	18.81	11.19	13.09	100
Orissa	43.29	11.09	6.20	1.15	12.29	14.93	11.05	100
Rajasthan	44.55	12.86	14.99	1.75	4.71	13.15	7.99	100
Uttar Pradesh	52.84	11.95	4.99	0.00	10.63	2.38	17.21	100
Chhattisgarh	28.93	10.13	6.09	1.62	28.26	9.82	15.16	100

Jharkhand	34.42	10.34	7.62	0.27	15.20	6.89	25.26	100
Spl Category States	**48.53**	**13.67**	**11.46**	**0.82**	**6.70**	**8.11**	**10.70**	**100**
Arunachal Pradesh	40.01	14.78	14.33	2.50	6.58	7.87	13.93	100
Assam	59.68	11.48	5.08	1.17	5.74	4.44	12.40	100
Himachal Pradesh	48.18	14.57	18.01	0.51	5.15	9.34	4.23	100
Jammu and Kashmir	39.39	18.48	13.69	0.08	4.94	11.65	11.76	100
Manipur	52.71	13.10	8.98	0.67	10.70	4.40	9.44	100
Meghalaya	43.48	16.06	16.23	1.19	3.80	8.11	11.15	100
Mizoram	38.62	13.05	13.70	1.51	12.32	11.00	9.80	100
Nagaland	39.78	14.84	14.60	1.23	7.73	12.58	9.23	100
Sikkim	48.08	13.05	11.48	1.82	5.01	15.26	5.30	100
Tripura	45.06	9.07	6.23	1.35	13.33	9.77	15.20	100
Uttaranchal	53.13	11.15	12.86	0.00	6.55	4.19	12.12	100
All States	**46.92**	**12.63**	**6.46**	**1.77**	**10.56**	**10.92**	**10.74**	**100**

Source (Basic Data):1. Reserve Bank of India, 2004, Finances of State Governments, Government of India, Mumbai,

2. Website www.mospi.nic.in. of Central Statistical Organisation, Ministry of Statistics and Programme Implementation, Government of India,

in these States varied from Rs. 686, in Bihar, the State with the lowest per capita GSDP to Rs. 4027 in Goa, the State with the highest per capita GSDP. In special category States, however, both as a proportion of GSDP and in per capita terms, human development expenditures are higher in States with higher per capita GSDP.

This implies that in these States, human development expenditures seem to be a priority as with greater resource availability with higher per capita GSDP, these States tend to allocate more resources to human development expenditures both as a proportion of GSDP and in per capita terms. Interestingly, on an average, per capita human development expenditure in special category States at Rs. 1985 was higher than the general category (Rs. 1194) States by 66 per cent and in Sikkim and Mizoram, the expenditures on human development were Rs. 5744 and Rs. 6139 respectively.

The pattern of expenditures in different states according to their fiscal stress as measured by fiscal deficit can be seen from the Table 3. In the case of non-special category States, while the expenditures as a ratio of GSDP were higher in States with higher fiscal deficits, this is because, the overall expenditure-GSDP ratio in these States were higher. In fact, there seems to be a deliberate attempt to compress expenditures on human development when there is fiscal stress as indicated by the share of human development expenditures in total.

In the case of special category States too, the expenditure-GSDP ratio was higher in States with higher fiscal stress as measured by the fiscal deficit-GSDP ratio. It is also seen that the per capita expenditures were also higher in States with higher fiscal deficit-GSDP ratios.

In table 5, we present some broad indicators of financing human development during two time periods. Average Social Allocation ratio which is share of expenditure on social services in total expenditures has declined from 34 per cent during 1988-91 to 32 percent during 1999-2002.

Major decline can be seen in most of the states like AP, Punjab and Haryana etc. Another measure of financing of human development is Social priority expenditures which basically include Elementary education, Rural Health, water supply, sanitation and Nutrition. Social priority expenditures as percent of GSDP are stable between these periods though in some States it has declined sharply. Even if one includes expenditure on rural development as part of human developmental expenditure, there has been sharp decline in majority of the States.

Table 5
Financing of Human Development in Major States: Some Indicators Social Allocation Ratio, Social Priority Ratio, Social Priority Expenditure as % of GSDP, Human Developmental Expenditure as % of GSDP

	1988-89 to 1990-91	*1999-00 to 2001-02*	*1988-89 to 90-91*	*1999-00 to 01-02*	*1988-89 to 90-91*	*1999-00 to 01-02*	*1988-89 to 90-91*	*1999-00 to 01-02*
Major States	34.367	32.683	44.48	44.52	2.74	2.70	7.05	6.72
Andhra Pradesh	35.792	32.511	34.32	42.25	2.26	2.59	7.84	7.10
Bihar	35.215	31.779	54.30	59.26	3.84	4.28	8.75	8.85
Goa	40.639	25.694	35.94	40.56	3.96	2.67	11.40	6.76
Gujarat	32.728	34.024	46.46	38.29	2.64	2.75	6.47	7.69
Haryana	31.297	29.132	34.87	43.93	1.77	2.14	5.58	5.08
Karnataka	33.714	34.216	40.16	40.58	2.59	2.60	7.28	6.85
Kerala	42.267	34.064	44.40	38.13	3.57	2.39	8.68	7.42
Madhya Pradesh	35.477	34.842	46.83	45.15	2.71	2.43	6.77	6.08
Maharashtra	30.901	34.007	39.75	43.16	2.00	2.35	5.36	5.65
Orissa	33.068	34.366	46.93	45.92	3.42	4.12	8.65	10.12
Punjab	32.202	23.033	30.81	30.94	1.74	1.41	5.84	4.64
Rajasthan	37.769	39.427	55.69	54.34	3.81	4.36	7.89	8.57
Tamil Nadu	40.142	36.385	45.69	43.57	3.28	2.69	7.92	6.64
Uttar Pradesh	31.582	27.193	49.79	50.03	2.84	2.61	7.00	6.26
West Bengal	40.209	34.555	32.08	28.31	1.85	1.72	6.66	6.66
Smaller States	34.055	32.664	46.47	50.77	5.56	5.46	12.99	11.72
All States	34.335	32.681	44.68	45.26	2.89	2.90	7.38	7.07

Conclusions

The analysis highlights that there is considerable catching up to do in order to meet the targets set for the Tenth Plan. It is also seen that among the non-special category States, the richer States tend to allocate less resources as a percentage of GSDP to human development and they are content to ensure that the per capita expenditures in them are higher. In other words, they allocate proportionately more to other sectors. In contrast, the special category States tend to allocate more to social sectors even as a ratio of GSDP as their per capita GSDP increases. This indicates that they assign high priority to human development expenditures.

Another interesting finding from our analysis is that in more fiscally stressed non-special category States, although the share of human development expenditures in GSDP is higher, they seem to try and contain the share of human development expenditures in the total.

In special category States, however, fiscal stress, to a considerable extent, seems to be due to high priority assigned to human development expenditures. The share of human development expenditure both in GSDP and in total expenditures are higher in more fi cally stressed special category States.

REFERENCES

1. Deolalikar, Anil (2005), *Attaining the Millennium Development Goals in India*, New Delhi: Oxford University Press for the World Bank.
2. Deaton, Angus, and Jean Dreze (2002), "Poverty and Inequality in India: A Re-examination," *Economic and Political Weekly*, September 7.
3. Dutta, Bhaskar, Manoj Panda and William Wadhwa (1997), Human development in India, in S. Subramanian (ed) *Measurement of Inequality and Poverty*, New Delhi: Oxford University Press.
4. Government of India (2001), National Human Development Report, Planning Commission, Government of India, Planning Commission.
5. Himanshu (2004), "Estimates of School Attendence based on unit level data from 55th Round of Employment – Unemployment Survey",

Mimeo, Centre for Economic Studies and Planning, Jawaharlal Nehru University, New Delhi.

6. Prabhu, Seetha(2001), *Economic Reform and Social Sector Development*, New Delhi: Sage Publications.

7. Rao, M. Govinda (1997), *Accommodation Public Expenditure Policies in Fast Growing Asian Economies*, World Development.

8. Sen, Abhijit and Himanshu (2004), "Poverty and Inequality in India-I", *Economic and Political Weekly*, September 18.

9. Sen, Amartya (2004), "Women Agency and Social Change" in *Development as Freedom*, Oxford University Press.

10. Shariff, Abusaleh, Prabir Ghosh and S. K. Mondal (2002), State Adjusted Public Expenditure on Social Sector and Poverty Alleviation Programmes, *Economic and Political Weekly*, Vol. XXXVII, No. 8 February 23. pp. 767-786.

26

NEED OF KNOWLEDGE MANAGEMENT SERVICES FOR HUMAN DEVELOPMENT

*M. Satyanarayana**

Introduction

The expression "Knowledge" is often used synonymously with information. But knowledge is more than that. It is the key issue in the natural growth of human society. Some Authors are able to make differ.nce between these two terms. Farrandane makes difference between these two terms, information is physical surrogate of knowledge (i.e. language) used for communication. While knowledge is memorable records of a process in the brain, something available in the mind; production of consciousness in the mind is at present quite unexplained.

Knowledge is a body of information, principles, and experience to actively guided task execution and management, decision-making, and problem solving. Knowledge Management is the Management of knowledge resources and embodied knowledge. The knowledge is embodied in the objects, processes and phenomena of nature including sentiment intelligent and conscious human beings.

Information Management Services in the society are not sufficient to face the new challenges emerging in the present

* Associate Professor, Library and Information Science, Andhra University, Visakhapatnam.

Information era. The computers and satellites have radically changed the entire character of retrieval process of information and knowledge. In this new age of the ICT (Information and Communication Technology), it would be possible for a person anywhere in the world to have an immediate access to the knowledge and information available anywhere in the world. The ICT has a worldwide networking or what is called World Wide Web. This new information revolution has doubtlessly created a new concept of Knowledge Management Services for Human development. The time has come for the existing information centers to redefine the concept and their role. Now they need to change their role as knowledge Management services with ICT for Human Development.

Knowledge and Types of Knowledge

Knowledge is the totality of all existing information that is known, every piece of information that is recorded in logical and systematic manner creates knowledge. Denham Gray stated that "Knowledge is the full utilization of information and data, coupled with the potential of people's skills, competencies, ideas, intuition, commitments and motivations".

Beckman defines Knowledge is reasoning about information and data to actively enable performance, problem solving, decision making, learning and teaching. According to New Webster's World Dictionary & Thesaurus "Knowledge is defined as acquaintance with facts, range of information, awareness or understanding or Knowledge is all that has been perceived or grasped by mind; learning; enlightenment.

Knowledge applies to anybody of facts gathered by study, observation etc., and to the ideas inferred from these facts, and connotes an understanding of what is known (Man's knowledge of the universe).

There are two distinct types of knowledge, which are Explicit Knowledge and Tacit Knowledge. Explicit Knowledge is that which is written down or expressed in some tangible form. This is verbal, theoretical and objective. Tacit Knowledge is communicable through mechanism like observations, conservation on-the -job learning and so on. It is very intangible and makes its management a challenge.

Concept and Definitions of Knowledge Management

It was in 1989 that the phrase "Knowledge Management" was first introduced and later many Management Journals have started featuring articles on the subject.

Knowledge Management is the ability to manage 'Knowledge". It refers to the basic elements include accessing, evaluation, managing, organizing, filtering and distributing information in a manner that is useful to the End Users. It includes the identification and analysis of available and required knowledge, its planning and control to fulfill organizational objectives.

Hibbard writes "Knowledge Management is the process of capturing a company's collective expertise wherever it resides.- in data bases, on paper or in people's heads- and distributing in to wherever it can help produce the biggest pay off"

Peter Drucker and James Quinn defined "Knowledge Management is a process of a question of proper vision, organization networks, educated decisions and the best use of lessons learned as the key of organization learning"

Nonaka states "Knowledge Management is a form of application of sound management practices to human resources as whole which are the carrying vectors of knowledge. "Knowledge Management in a sense is the management of the organization towards the continuous renewal of the organizational structures, facilitation of organizational members putting information technology instruments with emphasis on teamwork and diffusion of knowledge into place.

Knowledge Management may be defined as the set of processes that create and share knowledge across an organization to optimize the use of judgment in the attainment of mission and goals. Knowledge Management is an audit of intellectual assets that highlights unique sources, critical functions and potential bottle necks which hinder knowledge flow to the point of use. O'Dell explained "Knowledge Management applies systematic approaches to find, understand and use knowledge to create value".

Principles of Knowledge Management

Thomas H Daven Port, one of the well-known experts in Knowledge Management concepts, framed the following principles for Knowledge Management

1. Knowledge Management is expensive.
2. Effective Management of Knowledge requires hybrid solutions of people and technology.
3. Knowledge Management is highly political- Knowledge Managers have to acknowledge and cultivate politics. They will act as brokers between those who have knowledge and those who may use it.
4. Knowledge Management requires Knowledge Managers.
5. Knowledge Management benefits more from maps than models, more from markets than from hierarchies.
6. Sharing and using Knowledge are often unnatural acts.
7. Knowledge Management means improving knowledge work process.
8. Knowledge Management Access is only the beginning.
9. Knowledge Management never ends.
10. Knowledge Management requires a knowledge contract.

It is observed on the basis of the principles that the Knowledge Management is an extension of Information Management. The function of Information management is collection and the function of Knowledge Management is creation.

Information Management and Knowledge Management

We often use information and knowledge interchangeably and more so because we are unable to clearly distinguish between the two as they are very much related. However, while trying to manage them, the distinction would be fairly clear in the sense that Knowledge Management involves not only all activities of Information Management. But some more specialized activities centered on creation and recording of new knowledge and sharing it.

Information Management basically deals with Information present in the documents while Knowledge Management deals not only with the Information in the documents but also with the Knowledge present in the Human brain. Also in Information Management, coded information becomes knowledge for the future use, but in Knowledge Management, coded Knowledge (Explicit Knowledge) becomes information for future Knowledge base. Information Management and Knowledge Management have different challenges to meet. For Information Management, the Challenge lies in valuing separate Information items and demonstrates the power of Information Management in context of profit margins, increased organizational efficiency etc. As far as Knowledge Management is concerned, the challenges lie in tapping the Tacit Knowledge (Knowledge which cannot be easily codified) and create an environment that would facilitate creation of new Knowledge and sharing it for Organization development.

Knowledge Management Services in Society

Knowledge is the key factor in the development of Human Society. Owing to its importance, Human Society is in need of knowledge for its applicability, creation and transferability. Under these circumstances, Knowledge Management Services have pivotal role in the society to access the available knowledge for Human Development.

The basic character of Knowledge is that it can't be controlled. However, the Knowledge Management Service Centers can navigate knowledge in multi-domain. For Example, the Data and Information, linked with other Data and Information leads to Knowledge. Knowledge domain when put for action, may be research, in social context it will become the assumptions/ theories and finally the philosophy of the subject. When the perspective values are established the Knowledge becomes Wisdom that encompasses totality or universal concept. Thus the Knowledge Management Services can play a role in each of the domains that leads to another and thus contribute to Knowledge creation by sources.

In the present Digital environment, the knowledge in the digital form is available from Data bases, Text bases, and World-Web etc. It is possible to tap the Knowledge in this Digital environment through Information and Communication Technologies. The Knowledge Management Services are not only to provide needed information but also on the knowledge about related resources, skills, and technologies involved to retrieve the information from the available sources in this Digital era. Knowledge Management Services make the persons in the society to have knowledge on technology for getting needed information in right time for their socio-economic development. The Management Services are able to encourage the use of information needed for increasing the knowledge for Human Development.

Conclusion

Knowledge is organized information available to problem solving for Human Development. Knowledge is stored in the individual's brain or encoded in organizational process, documents, products, services, facilities, and systems.

Knowledge Management is management of Knowledge. The Knowledge Management Services enhance the ability and capacity of persons for their development in all spheres. The Information Management Services are designed for providing information needed by the people. The entry of Information and Communication Technologies paved the way in the Information Management Services to create digital collections for improving the services in order to satisfy the changing information needs. The entire activities are concentrated on managing information for providing the needed information to the persons leaving the other information not required by the people. This information is not sufficient to improve the ability and capacity for their developmental activities. The information to create knowledge relating to the skills and technology for retrieval of needed information is as important as the needed information for any development. The existing Information Management Services are to be redesigned with the available Information and Communication Technologies as Knowledge Management Services for Human Development.

REFERENCES

1. Anjali Gulati, (1999), Knowledge Management: an Information Technology prospective. *DESIDOC Bulletin of Information Technology*. Vol.19, No.6, pp. 3-7.

2. Bansal, Alka, (2000), Knowledge Management: a review. *DESIDOC Bulletin* of Information Technology. Vol. 20, No. 4, pp. 3-9.

3. Binwal, J C. (2001), Knowledge Management. *IASLIC Bulletin*. Vol. 46, No. 2, pp. 65-78.

4. Neelameghan, A. (2000), *Knowledge: its economics and management. Information Studies*. Vol. 6, No. 3, pp. 141-142.

5. Neelameghan, A. (2000), *Knowledge resources management. Information Studies*. Vol. 6, No. 4, pp. 203-204.

6. Sangeetha, M A. and Ravichandra Rao, T K. Evolution of Knowledge Management. *SRELS Journal of Information Management*. Vol.37, No.1. 2000, pp. 17-32.

7. Satyanarayana, M. and Venkateswara Rao, L. (2001), Knowledge Management vs Academic Libraries. Proceedings of the National Conference on Recent Advances in Information Technology (READIT-2001), September 18-19, pp. 276-279.

8. Siva Subramanian, V. (2001), Knowledge Management: task a head for library professional. Proceedings of the National Conference on Recent Advances in Information Technology (READIT-2001), September 18-19 pp. 269-275.

9. Sudharma Haridasan (1998), Knowledge Management: A new challenge for LibraryProfessionals. *IASLIC Bulletin*. Vo. 43, No. 4, pp. 145-147.

27

TRICKLE DOWN EFFECT - A KEY TO RURAL AND HUMAN DEVELOPMENT

*K. Mouurlin**

"India lives in its villages," — *Mahatma Gandhi*

Introduction

The Indian economy has witnessed a growth rate in gross domestic product of over 8 per cent in last three years. However, an average rate of 2.5 per cent during 1997-98 to 2006-07 in the agriculture and allied sector has been well blown the growth of 7.9 per cent in the non-agriculture sector, indicating that Indian agriculture has entangled in a low growth equilibrium trap. The economic survey 2007-08 pronounces a similar performance of Indian agriculture at only 2.6 per cent in 2007-08. Since more than two-thirds of the total country's population live on agriculture and allied activities and stay in rural areas, the government's aim has been directed towards ensuring an inclusive economic growth where benefits of economic growth are to percolate to the poor and underprivileged.

In this context, Rural Development can play an important role to bridge the gap as well as bring desired change in the lives of the rural people. To ensure that rural India develops as the country grows, several rural development programmes in

* Xavier Institute of Development Studies and Actions (XIDAS), Jabalpur, Madhya Pradesh.

areas like Education, Health care, employment, etc are taken up by the government of India to promote sustainable livelihoods for the rural mass.

Hence rural development is a metamorphic necessity. It can contribute to both the economic betterment of people as well as greater social transformation. Increased participation of people in the rural development process, decentralization of planning, better enforcement of land reforms and greater access to credit and inputs go a long way in providing the rural people with better prospects for economic development. Improvements in health, education, drinking water, and energy supply, sanitation and housing coupled with attitudinal changes also facilitate their social development.

The prime goal of rural development is to improve the quality of life of the rural people by alleviating poverty through the instrument of self-employment and wage employment programmes, by providing community infrastructure facilities such rural as drinking water, electricity, road connectivity, health facilities, housing and education and promoting decentralization of powers to strengthen the Panchayat raj institutions.

Although there has been significant economic development and generation of wealth since the 90s after the economic liberalization policies were implemented, most of it has remained concentrated among the middle classes and the much hoped for "trickle down" effect has not really happened in as large a scale as was hoped for.

In this paper, an attempt has been made to explain how rural development strategies and programmes could promote sustainable livelihood for rural people by reducing poverty and unemployment and increase their income status. Outline of the research paper (Section wise) is described below: The Abstract describes about the summary of the research paper. This is dealing with introduction, how the research paper has been sectioned.

The first section is about the introduction of the research paper and it helps to have an over all view of the paper. It also explains the basic elements of rural development.

The second section deals with methodology of the research study. It deals also with the relevance of Rural Development Programmes and its pitfalls. It also shows the comparative analysis of existing programmes.

The third section presents a need for alternative model, which could be a shift from bureaucratic approach to Participatory approach. The main focus is to develop a comprehensive model of development.

The fourth section provides a strategic formalization, which includes operational strategies like establishing JLGs, WADI project and other gross root level interventions.

The fifth section describes about the conclusion.

Elements of Rural and Human Development

Whatever the geographical location, culture and historical stage of development of a society, there are at least three basic elements which are considered to constitute the "true meaning of rural development".

Basic Necessities of Life: People have certain basic needs, without which it would be impossible (or very difficult) for them to survive. The basic necessities include food, clothes, shelter, basic literacy, primary health care and security of life and property. In this sense, we may claim that economic growth (increased per capita availability of basic necessities) is a necessary condition for improvement of the "quality of life" of rural people, which is rural development.

Self-respect: Every person and every nation seeks some sort of self-respect, dignity, or honor. Absence or denial of self-respect indicates lack of development.

Freedom: In this context, freedom refers to political or ideological freedom, economic freedom and freedom from social servitude (Katar Singh, 1999).

Section II – Rural Development Programmes: An Overview

Relevance of Rural Development Programmes

The earlier attempt towards rural development channelised the efforts of the Government more intensively after independence. All those experiments like Sevagram and Gurgaon experiments had moral and spiritual base and largely depended on cooperation of the villagers and the village institutions. However their objective was to reconstruct and bring new life in the rural people.

It is clear that while the economic reform did bring in prosperity to the country, the benefits are not evenly distributed and some are even deprived of the benefits. It is also pertinent that some of them are unable to be part of the economic reform and do not have the capacity to participate in the economic development process. Such groups need government intervention to ensure that they are not left behind in the development process and deprived of the benefits because they do not have the capacity to be part of global economy.

Accordingly, the Government put top priorities for rural reconstruction activities, which help changing the life of rural population. Therefore. Central and State Governments launched countrywide programmes. These programmes have been classified into self-employment programmes, wage employment programmes, food safety programmes and social security programmes.

Self-Employment Programmes

This programme was started in 1970s in rural areas of the country in the name of Integrated Rural Development Programme (IRDP) to increase the source of income of small farmers and landless labourers. The beneficiaries were given subsidized credit, training, and infrastructure, so that they could find new sources of earning. In this scheme, agricultural labourers and small farmers received new skills to involve in vocations other than cultivating land. They included fishery, animal husbandry, and forestry. In the 1980s, this scheme was extended to schedule castes and tribes, women and rural artisans.

Drawbacks of IRDP

IRDP suffered from certain shortfalls. One important factor is the attempt to develop an entrepreneur out of the unskilled landless labourer, who has no experience in managing an enterprise. Therefore, unviable projects were undertaken and sub-critical investments were made leading to collapse of these micro-enterprises. Banks were also indifferent to provide credits to the poor. It did not make a good banking sense to provide a loan to individual poor farmer and landless labourer, who did not have any experience in entrepreneurship. Targeting of the Poor was another problem, where many non-poor managed to get the benefits.

Wage Employment Programmes

The main purpose of the wage employment programmes is to provide a livelihood during the lean agricultural season as well as during drought and floods. Under these programmes, villagers worked to improve the village infrastructure such as deepening the village ponds, constructing village schools and improving the rural roads. Thus the programmes not only provided employment to the villagers but also improved village infrastructure and created village public assets.

A positive fall out of this programme is that it created higher demand for village labour, thereby pushing up the wage of the labourer in the villages. Wage employment programmes were first started during the Sixth and Seventh Plan in the form of National Rural Employment Programme (NREP) and Rural Landless Employment Guarantee programmes (RLEGP). These two programmes were later merged in 1989 into more well known *Jawahar Rozgar Yojana* or JRY. The JRY was supposed to produce employment for the unemployed and the underemployed and to improve the village infrastructure and assets.

Drawbacks of Wage Employment Programme

The wage employment programmes suffered from various problems leading to poor implementation of schemes. First, it was difficult to understand the nuances of the programme for the rural poor. As a result, they were cheated and false muster rolls were prepared to siphon off the money. Second, the schemes suffered from the bureaucratic muddles. It is a centrally sponsored programme with rigid guidelines, which may not fit into local conditions. By the time it reached the poor, it passed through the central government, State government, *Panchayat* and the beneficiary.

At every level, there is red tapism and delays leading to underutilization of funds. Adding to all these, the government started reducing the allocation to the wage employment programme from the Ninth Plan.

Food Security Programme

Meeting the very basic need of access to food is a major challenge to the government in the post-economic reform era. Those who are below poverty line are faced with the problem of meeting this very basic need. Starvation and hunger have been reported in different parts of the country, even in economically advanced States like Maharashtra. There is malnutrition in all age groups, especially among children. Problem of low birth weight due to under nutrition of mother during pregnancy and underweight of children are rampant in the country. The purchasing power of certain section of the society is so low that they cannot access food at the market price. They need the safety net of food subsidy.

In this context, public distribution system or PDS assumes importance. The PDS was originally a universal public distribution system or UPDS. The original UPDS was not conceived as an anti-poverty programme. The main objective was to create a demand for food grains thereby farmers benefiting from their produce. It was meant for price stabilization of foodgrains by giving price support.

In the post-economic reform era, the PDS became a very significant poverty alleviation programme of the government. The central government initiated a new PDS programme in June 1997 and called it targeted public distribution system or TPDS. Under this scheme, the States are to identify households below poverty line and provide them 10 kg of food grains at highly subsidized price and this amount was raised to 20 kg in April 2000.

Drawbacks of Food Security Programme

This programme suffered from several problems during the implementation. Due to the centralized procurement system, it incurred very high administrative cost. Further, there were problems of wastage and pilferage at every stage of its operation. Then there are problems at the consumer level in terms of buying a large quantity of food grains at a time from the fair price shops. Finally, the problem of targeting was a major issue, where non-poor are included and many BPL groups like migrants and pavement dwellers are left out of PDS. All these problems led to much lesser benefits reaching the poor. While the PDS has very high potential to protect the poor from starvation and hunger, problems of its implementation have reduced its actual potential to a great extent.

Social Security Programmes

Social Security Programmes are meant for those who are at the bottom of the BPL facing destitution and desertion. The central government has launched the National Social Assistance Programme or NSAP in August 1995. Under NSAP, there are three schemes. The first one is the National Old Age Pension Scheme or NOAPS. A pension amount of Rs. 75 per month is given to those who are above the age of 65 yr and are destitute without any regular source of income or support from any family members or relatives. The second scheme under NSAP is National Family Benefit Scheme or NFBS. Under this scheme, a lump sum of Rs. 10,000 is paid to a family, where the breadwinner of the family died of natural or accidental causes. The total amount is given to a member of the deceased family who has assumed the role of head of family. This scheme is available to BPL families only.

Another scheme under NSAP is National Maternity Benefit Scheme or NMBS. Under this scheme, a lump sum of Rs. 500 is given to pregnant women belonging to the BPL households.

The pregnant woman should be 19 year or above and the sum is given 8 to 12 wk before delivery. The purpose of the scheme is to enhance the nutritional intake of these pregnant women during pregnancy to safe guard the life and health of the mother and the infant though there are large number of persons needing protection under NSAP, these social security schemes are small and their out reach is limited.

Development Programmes – A Comparative Analysis

Contrasting Effects of Development Programmes

In this section, a comparison between the self-employment programmes and wage employment programmes is made to bring out input-output relationships. This also shows about the transition of early passive beneficiaries to new beneficiaries with active role in demanding their rights.

Indicators	Self-employment Programmes Wage employment Programmes
1) Growth & Scope	Improved over the period by adopting SHG approach. It was declined over a period of time even after merging different programmes as one.
2) Participative	It was highly participative in nature. Implemented by the Government.
3) Management	Managed by SHGs and Government played supportive role. Management by Government.
4) Cost and accountability	Due to supportive role of the Govt, reduction in administrative costs and less corruption and increase in beneficiaries. Administrative costs were high and the scope of corruption was remarkable and lack of transparency was prevailing.

A Paradigm Shift from Survival to Right to Work

The primary objective of almost all the plans so far has been to alleviate rural poverty, which is inextricably linked with low rural productivity, unemployment and under-employment, and to bring about improvement in the living standards of the rural population. Accordingly, the policies and programmes have been designed for the economic betterment of the people as well as for promoting grater social transformation. It is good to compare

Indicators	*IRDP*	*NREGA*
1.	Aim	To promote livel·hood Securities T o promote Sustainable Livelihoods and asset creation in the locale
2.	Objective	The basic Objective of IRDP was to improve the economic and social conditions of the poorest sections of the rural society. The objective of NREGA is to provic e 100 days of employment to every Rural household, and the creation of durable assets and livelihood resources for the poor through the works.
3. Benefits		SC/STs- 50% coverageDisabled- 3% coverageWomen- 40% coverage S C : 27.42%, STs: 29.35%, Women: 42.59% Others: 43.23%
4. Drawback		Corruption at all levels of district, Block and Panchayat, Manipulating the beneficiaries, Attitudinal aberrations amongst beneficiaries. Qualitative failure of the scheme Corruption at all levels of district. Block and Panchayat, Lack of awareness on the part of the Panchayat sevak, Absence of worksites facilities, Presence of contractors, Wage Discrepancy and other Problems
5. Special feature		Nil It provides Legal right of employment to rural population.Social Audit to ensure transparency and accountability.Gram Sabha has the power of social audit.

NREGA with other development programmes, such as, IRDP, Indira Awaas Yojana (IAY) and others. Although the existing programmes contribute to alleviate poverty and unemployment, yet they have fallen short of the objectives of the programmes due to leakage, corruption, administrative failure and inefficiency at the local level.

Missing Link in Rural Development Programmes

Although above measures have been successful (to some extent) in curbing poverty, these approaches have a very basic flaw. Under these approaches resources are transferred from urban economy to rural economy just for short-term political motives. This is affecting both areas, not letting rural economy develop on its own and hampering growth and investments in urban economy. Although lot of money was spent on these schemes, the results obtained are not up to the mark and employment promotion has been satisfactory.

According to Rural Development Report, NIRD (1994) states that only 58.88 per cent of persons trained have been including self-employment and wage employed. While the percentage of people self-employed is less than 50 per cent of the trained. The progress achieved through these programmes is not satisfactory and the important reason for this is that the programmes are not properly integrated with IRDP. The difficulties experienced in implementing TRYSEM schemes have been pointed out as (1) the programme is not provided for an integrated system of supply of raw materials and marketing of products through Government sponsored agencies or corporations. (2) The Programmes are not adjusted in a way that will enable them to get employed in village industries and artisan pursuit after necessary training instead of expecting them to set up industries, business and services ventures on their own.

Quest for Participatory Human Development Model

Economic upliftment alone cannot alleviate poverty but it must lead to social upliftment in terms of access to services, empowerment and independence. Therefore, the current poverty alleviation programmes and initiatives in the country should broaden their focus and goal in addition to increasing income to achieve the target of removing poverty from the country. Since the development programmes had a bureaucratic influence, it has led the beneficiaries to be passive recipient than plan their activities.

Involvement of the local communities is the key to the success of poverty alleviation programmes. In the absence of community involvement, the programmes are plagued with bureaucratic muddle and corruption at every level. Therefore there is an urgent need for community participation to bring the development programmes sustainable. To increase the community participation, micro planning is essential. The micro planning needs to be vertically integrated with national plans and horizontally integrated with inter-sectoral coordination between different sectors–agriculture, industry, and services–within a specific spatial framework.

Participatory approaches can also challenge perceptions, leading to a change in attitude and agendas. They can also provide new and sometimes surprising insights. The participative approach goes along with Gandhian Philosophy. Gandhi recognized the need for rural development, which he called as village reconstruction. He laid so much importance on rural development that he made it an integral part of his philosophy of improvement of rural areas by calling it as "Grama Sudhara Programme."

The main tenet of participative approaches to development is that the community and stakeholders are collaborators in a project at every stage of project development. Thus, participative methods are meant to generate a sense of ownership of decisions and actions. This is in contrast to the alternative model of development where people external to the community who are characterised as "experts" impose project conceptualization, objectives and design on the community.

Basis for Participatory Human Development

Since rural development is primarily initiated to alleviate rural poverty, it must be carefully, designed and developed to increase production per unit. There are a few requisites to remember when we go for participatory development approach.

Targeted Group Approach

Effective rural development work can be undertaken only by identifying targeted groups among the rural poor for whom special measures to raise production of agriculture and other enterprises along with the income increased can be designed and in whose case the benefits resulting, direct and indirect, can also be identified and measured.

Technology Transfer

Technology Transfer therefore becomes an important and rather a central concern of a successful rural development programme for attacking rural poverty. Where technology is available, it is available, it is often not made use of because of development educational services, support services, like credit and input supply, transport, storage, marketing, facilities are not adequate.

People's Participation

The important feature of rural development is that it cannot be delivered to a passive group. Where the programmes sought are in the field of agriculture, health, education, public works or any other, the active participation and assistance of rural poor must be solicited if the expected changes are to be effective, widespread and of a permanent nature. In particular, participatory approaches allow a community to:

- Express and analyze the realities of their lives;
- Plan themselves what action to take to change the situation;
- Monitor and evaluate the results themselves.

Social Mobilization

Social mobilization lies at the root of genuine development. It gives impetus to the necessary changes that must occur before development-whether social, political or economic can be realized. Social Mobilization is the process of dialogue, negotiation and consensus building for action by people, communities and organizations to identify, address and solve a common problem. It can be an effective strategy to create the kind of supportive environment necessary to create sustained behavioral change that will bring about community participation for sustainability and self-reliance.

Strategic Formulation

Formation of Joint Liability Groups (JLG)

In India SHGS is the most popular concept of providing Microfinance services. It has brought unpredictable solutions to the problems. Though there are many advantages, still there is a problem of multiplying the saving. Since the groups are homogenous with female thrust, the risk bearing ability is less as compared to men. The successful SHGs are the ones who have total recovery of the loan are 100%. Yet the multiply effect is less.

Therefore establishing Joint Liability Groups (JLG) would help the villagers to plan and execute the plans for the development of the village in a desired manner. The purpose of these JLGs is to develop an integrated development of the village. These groups could be a heterogeneous group and a mixture of both men and women or may be a family unit (husband and wife). The advantage of including men in the groups has greater advantage. When the loan is taken as a joint loan (family unit), both can decide and take right decisions to begin a business, which would be feasible technologically, ecologically sustainable and economically viable.

Promoting Innovative livelihood through WADI

Another innovative solution to rural problems is to create permanent assets through orchard development. The "WADI" in Gujarati means a "small orchard" covering one or two acres. The WADI referred as an effective tool for socio-economic development. The poor families participating in this programme popularly known as *Wadi* (Orchard Development), establish drought tolerant fruit crops such as mango, cashew, Indian gooseberry, tamarind, custard apple, ber, etc. on their marginal or wastelands covering 0.4 to 1.0 ha. The interspaces are used for cultivating arable crops, which they have been growing earlier and the field bunds and borders are used to establish hardy shrubs and trees useful for fodder, fuel, timber and herbal medicines.

The is programme has been highly successful in Gujarat and other places. Over 0.1 million poor tribal families, who participated in this programme are now earning Rs. 25000-30000 (USD 600) per annum to lead a sustainable livelihood. This programme has ensured women empowerment, food security, healthcare, education for children and prevented migration.

Establishment of Thrift Cooperative (TC)

At the village level, thrift cooperatives would be established to supply local credit facilities for the local people. This main purpose of this cooperative is to help the group members to save and get benefit out of it. It is a voluntary association of individuals who come together to meet their savings, credit and insurance needs. If they were linked with MFIs or Government Banks, these organizations would provide them savings, credit and insurance services through various schemes on the basis of self-help and mutual-aid and on terms and conditions decided by members themselves. The successive story is narrated below.

Impact of participative approach at the grass root level

The above case studies show that participation of the people in development works would earn more results. The participatory approach at the grass root level creates awareness among community inhabitants, about structures and processes, which influence their living situation negatively. This also brings changes in some of the laws and policies, rules and regulations that form part of the root causes of injustice, deprivation, exploitation and marginalization. It strengthens people's ability to analyze their problems and possible solutions and augment their individual and collective skills to undertake work for improving their living situations.

Participation of the people would try to build local organizations for development action, encompassing only, or promote participation of disadvantaged or inactive people in existing organizations. It promotes people's confidence and mobilizes their own and other under-utilized or not utilized resources to generate employment. Working with people establishes links between community organizations and outside institutions for various kinds of support from outside.

It tries to sensitize policy-makers to the realities and the needs of the local people. It provides improved access to a huge variety of information, training, research and educational resources that are usually unavailable in the local areas due to costs associated with assessing printed materials and book. The Skill Development Initiatives (SDI) is basically aimed at persons in rural areas looking for wage employment or livelihood opportunities both through group or individual activities.

Conclusion

The participatory development model is designed to realize a vision that will attain socially cohesive an stable rural communities with viable institutions, sustainable economies and universal access to social amenities, able to attract and retain skilled and knowledgeable people, who equipped to contribute to growth and development.

The key to participatory development fulfills the potential of people by enlarging their capabilities, and this necessarily implies empowerment of people, enabling them to participate actively in their own development. In order to fulfill their potential, people, especially those who are vulnerable and disadvantaged, must participate actively in establishing and maintaining independent organizations representing their interests, within each country's constitutional framework.

Instead of planning from the top and implement with inefficient functionaries who lack vision and mission is major drawback of almost all the Rural development programmes, the planning from below should be encouraged. Thus the policy shift towards integrated rural development reflects the complex linkages and interaction within the system of overall rural development. Putting too much emphasis on agriculture and ignoring its linkages to the rest of the economy could result in analytical bias.

Finally, Rural development is one the pillars on which the future of economy stands. Most of the Rural development programmes undertaken thus far have lacked focus and seem to be misdirected, though some of the programmes have yielded exceptionally high economic and social return.

However it is my firm belief that focused infrastructure development and people's participation combined with gainful, sustained employment, Industrialization and effective fiscal decentralization can pave way to a much resilient economy and lead to achievement of our lofty targets in future.

REFERENCES

1. Riley John, M. *Stakeholders in Rural Development,* Sage Publication, New Delhi, 2002, pp. 153-165.
2. Verma, S.B. *Rural-Based Development Strategies* Deep and Deep Publications Pvt.Ltd New Delhi, 2006, pp.7-40 & 93-100.
3. Srivastava, S.P. *The Development Debate: Critical Perspectives,* Rawat Publications, New Delhi, 1998, pp. 19-39 & 303-313.
4. Singh.K.K., *Rural Development Strategies in Developing Countries,* Sarup & Sons, New Delhi, pp. 260-280.
5. C.A.K. Yesudian, *Poverty alleviation programmes in India: A social audit.* Indian Journal of Medical Research 126, 2007, pp.364-373.
6. Singh, K, *Rural Development -Principles, Polices and Management,* Sage Publication, New Delhi, 1999, pp-15-26.
7. Poverty alleviation programmes India, Planning Commission, 6May 2007, <http://planningcommission.nic.in/plans/annualplan/ap2021pdf/ap2021ch4-1.pdf>
8. Action Aid India: International development agency that strives for a world without poverty, 6 May 2007, <http://www.actionaidindia.org>
9. Poverty in India, Online Resource Center, 8 May 2007, http://nposonline.net/art_craft.shtml

28

GROWTH, POVERTY AND HUMAN RESOURCE DEVELOPMENT IN INDIA

A.V. Naga Varma, Y. Rama Krishna** & J. Chandra Prasad****

The Concept of human development is complex and of multi dimensions. It is however certain that HD is much more than mere poverty eradication. It requires a situation where people can freely identify and select their choices. In this paper I confined to the concept of Human Development (HD) form the vantage point of policy makers and planners who believe in intervention of the state and civil society for better social order for development of all. The present concept of HD has gained currency with the efforts of the United Nations Development Project (UNDP). Mahbub ul Haq, one of the architects of UNDP, spells out the concept in the following manner:

Poverty

Statistically speaking, proportion of people living below poverty line has declined in all South Asian countries. In India it has done down from around 54 per cent in the early 1950s

* Senior Faculty in Economics, P.G. Courses & Research Centre, D.N.R. College, Bhimavaram - 534 202, West Godavari Dist., Andhra Pradesh.

** Reader, P.G. Courses & Research Centre, D.N.R. College, Bhimavaram-534 202, West Godavari Dist. Andhra Pradesh.

*** Associate Professor in Commerce and former Director, P.G. Courses and Research Centre, D.N.R. College, Bhimavaram- 534 202, West Godavari Dist., Andhra Pradesh.

to 33 per cent in 2000 and 25 per cent in 2004. It is 25 per cent in Sri Lanka and 34 per cent in Pakistan and Bangladesh in 2000. There is however no significant decline in the absolute number. In India around 300 million persons live below poverty line. It is argued by several economists and planners that downward trend in poverty is steep during the late 1990s after the following the path of structural adjustment programme. Liberalisation has accelerated economic growth and hence overall prosperity leading to the poor to escape poverty. Hence, growth is good for the poor (Dollar and Kraay 2002).

Many contest these statistical evidences. Some economists question the methodology of computation and interpretation of official data (Sen 2000; Mehta and Venkatraman 2000). According to some, the trend is opposite (Patnaik 2004). Intricacy of methodology is beyond my competence therefore I will not deal with that aspect. But on the basis of my field work in Gujarat I will go by the observation of those social scientists - economists, sociologists, anthropologists etc-who themselves personally are involved into micro level studies. According to them there is, at any rate, no obvious pattern of 'acceleration' or 'slowdown' in the rate of poverty the 1990s (Deaton and Dreze 2002). Moreover, contribution of poverty alleviation programmes though somewhat slow downed, cannot be ignored (Thamarajkshi 2003).

The downswing in the rate of poverty in the 1990s however does not reflect in the availability of food and nutrition intake of the people. According to the economic Survey there has been a slow decline in the availability of per capita food-grains per day from 485 grams in 191-92 to 427 grams per day in 2002-2003. "Thus, by 2000-01 the average Indian family of four members was absorbing 93 kg less food-grains, compared to a mere three years earlier - a massive and unprecedented drop, entailing a fall in average daily intake by 64 grams per head, or a fall in calorie intake by 256 calories from food-grains (which accounts for 65 to 70 per cent of the food budget of the poor) (Patnaik 2004)".

Potable Water

According to a national survey 25 per cent of the households reported breakdown of taps/hand-pumps once in three months. Sometimes it takes several weeks to get them repaired. Only 27 per cent households were fully satisfied with quality of water and 20 per cent were satisfied with adequacy of water (Paul et al. 2004).

Newspapers' reports on the incidents of contamination of water are frequent. Interestingly, those who clam of providing safe drinking piped water do not have faith in their own system that they use 'mineral bottled water' for their personal use. (It is also observed that mineral water is also unsafe but that is a different story). In several areas industries overuse ground water for their manufacturing plants depriving source of water to the local residents. Not only that but also many chemical industries pollute river and ground water making drinking water more unsafe for the poor residents. Pollution of Ganga near Lucknow and Kanpur in UP, Tapi in Gujarat, Godavari in Andhra Pradesh are examples. In Goa five star hotels store water for the customers that deprive the villagers of their close vicinity. The plants for beverages and so-called mineral water grab common resources of steam and ground water at the cost of common residents. Just take a case of Coca Cola Company in Kerala, established in 1998-99. The Coca Cola factory is located very close to some of the bigger water storage systems in this area. It has constructed two big wells within its compound, close to the main canal from the Moolatara barrage. They also dug about 60 tube-wells within the 40 acres of the factory premises and sucked canal and pond water.

Health and Health Care System

Infant mortality has gone down significantly in all the South Asian countries. In the case of India it has declined from 146 in 1951 to 110 in 1980 and reduced further to 90 in 1990. But then it had remained more or less the same level in the 1990s. There is a striking variance, more than twice, of IMR between the upper and lower strata. In 1998-99 IMR among the poor was 88.8 per 1000 births; whereas it was 42.7 among the rich. One finds the same pattern in the anaemic condition of women across the strata. 60 per cent of lower strata of society suffer from anaemia, as against 41 per cent women of the upper strata. Incidents of Tuberculosis, Malaria, and respiratory infections over a period are increasing. Diarrhoea and gastro/hepatitis continue to remain endemic both among the urban and rural poor. Simultaneously, the cases of HIV/AIDS are rising. Nearly 42 per cent of the deaths in1998 were due to different communicable diseases such as dengue, cholera, kala-azar, hepatitis, malaria etc.

Private, charitable/voluntary and public health care system existed, though in a small scale and largely in urban centers before independence. In the fifties the government made concentrated efforts to develop public health system with the emphasis on primary health care system. Besides starting primary health centers (PHCs) and sub-centres public hospitals began to grow both in number and facilities. However from the 1970s onwards the government spending on health care has remained more or less stagnant. The country spends only 0.9 per cent of GDP on health care which is below the average of low-income countries (Misra et al. 2003) and private heatlh sector has gradually over taken the voluntary and public health care system. 19 per cent of the hospitals were the private in 1974.

Education

Over the five decades literacy rate has gone up from 18.33 per cent in1951 to 65 per cent in 2001. The rate in the female literacy has also been faster during the 1990s. It has reduced the difference in male-female literacy rate from 24.84 in 1991 to 21.7 in 2001. According to the Sixth All-India Education Survey 1999 71.18 per cent villages have primary schools. And 94 per cent of rural population has access to primary schools within a distance of one km. The enrolment ratio of children in the age group of 6-11 years has reached to 95 per cent. However, enrolment does not necessarily retain students at least for five years. Dropout rate from class I to V has not significantly declined. It was 40-67 per cent in 2000-2001; and was 42.6 per cent in 1990-91. Moreover, infrastructure facilities - building, drinking water, blackboard, class room etc. - are not evenly available in all schools. According to a survey one fourth of the teachers in primary schools do not regularly attend the schools (World Bank 2004). In rural areas, sixty to seventy per cent of the children belonging to different classes sit in one dilapidated room and being taught many subjects simultaneously by a single teacher (Shiv Kumar 2003). Only less than 20 per cent of the households have satisfaction with the teachers and quality of facilities in the school (Paul et al 2004).

Growth and Social Insecurity

India's economic growth in terms of Gross National Product (GNP) has been on an average above 3 per cent year since 1951. It has increased in the 1990s with an average above 5 per cent. Several economists, policy makers and political leaders call that India is 'shining'. But like all south Asian countries and elsewhere, economic growth is not geared to generation of employment. To measure employment in the 'under developed' countries is ticklish as none can survive without some kind of work - be it collection of small peaces of wood, cow and buffalo dung, wild beetroots, leaves and grass from roadsides in rural areas, and refuse, rage and / or rotten leftover food from garbage in urban areas.

According to the 2001 census there are 406.05 million in workforce. Of which 28.11 million (6.38 per cent) are in organized sector; and 412.79 million (93 per cent are in unorganized sector. With 'flexibilisation' labour policy under liberalization informal sector gets more and more importance in production process (World Bank 1995, Breman 1995).

In formal sector is one that employs more than ten workers and registered under the factory Act. Under the act the industry is supported to provide 'social security' to the workers. The provisions include weekly paid holiday, leave, medical care, pension/provident fund etc. Under the provisions Rules for hire and fire are stringent providing security of job to the workers. However all the workers in the organized sector do not get this benefit as many of the private manufacturing companies particularly of the small scale flout rules under one or another pretext. They employ many workers on temporary or on contract basis who do not get benefits of various provisions of the social security. More than ninety-two per cent of the units of SSI have not registered under Factories Act. Social security in different forms is available only to less than five per cent of the labour force. Number of beneficiaries of the Employees State Insurance Scheme (ESIS) has not increased corresponding with the rise in number of factories in the 1990s. The government of India has not yet ratified the ILO Convention No. 102, which aimed at providing comprehensive social security to workers (Prabhu 2001).

With liberalization, labour laws are increasingly relaxed in favour of the employers. Workers' right to strike has been attacked. It is now easier for the employers to 'fire' the workers at will. The companies having one thousand workers do not require government's permission for laying anyone off. Many big companies have reduced their labour force. For example, Tata Engineering and Locomotive has reduced its staff by 10,000 (29 per cent) between 1996 and 2000. Similarly Mahindra and Mahindra, Bajaj Auto, and Associated Cement Companies to name a few have believes that work must rightfully be given to Maharashtrians before the immigrants. Even the original inhabitants of Mumbai, the koli fisherfolk, have begun an aggressive movement against the "outsiders" who are ruining their business.

Growth and Human Development

It is true that economic growth has to some extent contributed in reduction of destitution. Over the last five decades more and more poor people, in comparison to the past, have gained some access to certain public services such as food, education, modern health services and 'safe' drinking water. IMR and longevity have improved. Statistically speaking HD index of all the south Asian countries have improved. In the case of India it has moved 0.174 points, from 0.416 in 1975 to 0.590 in 2001. Sri Lanka, which is already very high in the scale, has gained only 121 points. Bangladesh and Pakistan have also improved their position. But all of them are far behind to catch up with the developed countries. With the present rate of growth and other things remain constant, India would require at least next sixty years to attain high position in HD index. Assumption is that growth and HD are not only related but they have linear direction. But the fact remains that many of the Scandinavian countries attained the present level of HD just not by economic growth. Sri Lanka and Kerala, the state within India in also have better HD than high growth regions.

The countries, which already have high HD, are also in the race for high economic growth. Policy makers in these countries emphasize that "work is more important than income". Finance Minister of the Netherlands asserted that that if the country wanted to successfully resolve the problem of aging they should "learn a lot from the Americans... USA has a higher rate of economic growth because the people work longer there... "At the same time unemployment is increasing and wage freeze is being introduced. Health and education are increasingly being privatized. There is also more cut every year on social security provisions such as unemployment benefits and health care costs.

As we have seen in the case of India the economic growth has not generated employment. It is a jobless growth. The present development of high technology reduces a requirement for human-labour.

REFERENCES

1. Bagchi and U.B.Roy Choudhury, (1989) 'Poverty Measures as an index of Backwardness and their Relevance to Tax Devolution,' *Economic and Political Weekly*, 15 April, 1989.
2. Bhat, Ramesh (1993). Private/Public Mix in Health Care in India. *Health Policy and Planning* 8(1).
3. Gopalan C., (1983). "Development and Deprivation, Indian Experience", *Economic and Political Weekly*, 28(51).
4. Iyer Krishna V.R. (2003). "Ban on Strikes: A judicial Excess?" *Hindu October* 2.
5. Jhabvala Renana (2003). "Liberalization and Women", Seminar 531. November.
6. Kumar Arun (1999). *The Black Economy in India*, New Delhi, Penguin.

7. Naronha, E and R.N. Sharma (1999) 'Displaced workers and withering welfare state', *Economic and political Weekly*, 34 (23).

8. NSS. (2001) Employment and Unemployment in India 1999-2000. Key Results NSS Report No. 455. New Delhi: National Sample Survey.

9. Prabhu Seeta K (2001). Socio-economic Security in the Context of Pervasive Poverty: *A Case Study of India*. Geneva, International Labour Organization.

10. Shah Ghanshyam, Kannan K.P., Bose Pradeepkumar and Hargopal G. (1993). *Migration in India*. New Delhi: National Commission of Rural Labour, Government of India.

11. Shiv Kumar A.K. (2003). "Common School System: End Apartheid in Education," *The Times of India*, November 22.

29

HEALTH EXPENDITURE AND SHIFTS IN HUMAN DEVELOPMENT IN ANDHRA PRADESH

K. Rani Gopal & B. Sailaja Kumari***

Health status is a crucial factor in the context of the Development of the economy and Human Development Health Status is an important component of human capital, as it impinges significantly on one's capacity to learn and work, productivity and overall performance. On the other hand, illhealth leads to absenteeism which can result in loss of income, production and productivity. Human Development Reports and several recent studies stressed the qualitative dimension of the population. The issue of human development has become the major concern of all countries.

India is now facing the dilemma that economic reforms and accelerated growth lead to, seem to be of little help in triggering broad based human development and elimination of poverty. India finds itself consistently into lowest one third of about 180 countries ranked by HDI in the annual reports on human development prepared by the UN. This is the dark shadow cast by poverty on India's development record. HDI is slowly gaining acceptability as an indicator of poverty status of the country.[1]

---

* Professor, Dept. of Economics, Andhra University, Visakhapatnam.

** Reader, Dept. of Economics, Mrs. A.V.N. College, Visakhapatnam.

The Central vision of the Eleventh Plan is to build on our strength to trigger a development process, which ensures broad based improvement in the quality of life of the people, especially the poor, SC's / STs, other backward castes, Minorities and Women. The broad vision of eleventh plan includes several inter-related components : rapid growth that reduces poverty and created employment opportunities, access to essential services, in heath and education, especially for the poor, equality of opportunity, empowerment through education and skill development, employment opportunities under pinned by the National rural employment guarantee environmental sustainability, recognition of women's agency and good governance. The strategy in the eleventh plan aims at achieving a particular type of growth process which will meet the objectives of inclusiveness and sustainability. India has entered the Eleventh Plan Period with an impressive record of Economic growth. In the 9th plan GDP grew at nly 5:5.% per annum, but in the tenth plan period the average growth rate was 7.7% the highest in any plan period so far. There was acceleration even within the tenth plan period and the growth rate in the last four years of the plan averaged 8.7% making India one of the fastest growing economies in the World.[2]

Investment in health is a major determinant of health status of the people. Differences in health conditions are often explained in terms of expenditure on health mainly by the Government. UNDP Human Development Report, 2003 clearly stated that the Government in poor countries must rank health spending higher than other types of spending[3]. In this context an attempt is made to analyse the growth pattern of public expenditure on social sector in general and in particular Expenditure on medical and public health and family welfare in Andhra Pradesh during 1980-81 to 2000-2001.

The study has removed the influence of price change (price effect) on the growth of public expenditure and on the Net State Domestic Product (NSDP) by deflating the available data in terms of changes in the while sale price index of all commodities in India. Entire data is converted into real terms at 1993-94 prices. The study also removed population effect on public expenditure by presenting per capita expenditure.

Table 1
Public Expenditure on Social Services, Per Capita Social Services Expenditure, Proportion of Total Expenditure on Social Services and NSDP at Constant Prices in Andhra Pradesh

Year	*Expenditure on social Services (Rs. in crores)*	*Per Capita Social Services Expenditure (in Rupees)*	*Expenditure on Social Services as a per cent of Total Public Expenditure*	*Expenditure on Social Services as per cent of NSDP.*
1980-80	1358	257	34.97	6.38
1981-82	1454	272	34.82	6.07
1982-83	1598	290	37.91	6.54
1983-84	2292	407	43.29	8.70
1984-85	2377	413	40.52	8.97
1985-86	2331	396	37.31	8.20
1986-87	2682	446	38.31	9.31
1987-88	2583	420	37.54	8.13
1988-89	2630	419	33.56	7.01
1989-90	2929	457	36.49	11.81
1990-91	2884	440	34.18	6.79
1991-92	2839	424	32.62	6.22
1992-93	2979	437	32.31	6.61
1993-94	2999	432	29.74	5.81
1994-95	3096	439	31.28	5.64
1995-96	3879	541	38.37	6.57
1996-97	4159	573	37.77	6.49
1997-98	4180	570	34.12	6.47
1998-99	5103	687	35.96	6.91
1999-2000	5283	690	34.58	6.67
2000-2001	5342	705	31.06	6.58

Source : RBI Bulletins of various years, Economic Survey of Andhra Pradesh and Report on Currency and Finance, Government of India, various issues.

Table 1 shows trends in the Total Public Expenditure and Per Capita Expenditure on Social Services, Percentage expenditure on social services in total Public Expenditure and Net State Domestic product in constant prices during 1980-81 to 2000-2001. the Per Capita expenditure on Social Services increased from Rs.257 in 1980-81 to Rs.705 in 2000-2001. Its proportion in total Public Expenditure varied from 29 per cent to 43 per cent and its proportion in Net State Domestic Product increased slightly from 6.38 in 1980-81 to 6.58 in 2000-2001. This maybe due to growing realization of the importance of human development, as revealed by UNDP reports from 1990 onwards.

Table 2 shows trends in total public expenditure on medical and public health and family welfare per capital expenditure, as a percentage in expenditure on social services, total public expenditure and Net State Domestic Product at constant prices in Andhra Pradesh during 1980-81 to 2000-2001.

The public expenditure on medical & public health and family welfare shows an increasing trend, Rs.321 crores in 1980-81 to Rs.857 crores in 2000-2001. The per capita expenditure also shows an increasing trend from Rs.61 in 1980-81 to Rs.113 in 2000-2001. In fact, this increasing trend is due to the increase in the allocations of family welfare, but not on the health sector. Its proportion in social services varied between 12 per cent to 23 per cent during the period under consideration. Its proportion in total public expenditure shows a declining trend from 8 per cent in 1980-81 to 5 per cent in 2000-2001. Its proportion in Net State Domestic Product shows that there is not much variation over the period and it is staggering around 1 per cent.

With regard to the proportion of Net State Domestic Product it has declined even below 1 per cent in post-reform period. However, these ratios have deteriorated by the mid 1990's recovered by 1990-2000. The overall decline in the share and the percentage stagnation in the share of the medical & public health and family welfare are due to the decline in the budgetary allocation.

Despite the fact that human development is at the core of our planning and reforms, yet the allocations made to the social

Table 2
Public Expenditure on Medical & Public Health and Family Welfare, Per Capita Expenditure, Proportion of Expenditure in Social Services, Total Expenditure and Net State Domestic Product at Constant Prices in Andhra Pradesh

Year	*Expenditure on Medical Public Health and Family Welfare (Rs. in Crores)*	*Per Capita Expenditure on Medical & Public Health and Family Welfare (in Rs.)*	*Expenditure on Medical & Public Health and Family Welfare as percent of Social Services*	*Expenditure on Medical & Public Health and Health and Welfare as a per cent of total expenditure*	*Expenditure on Medical & Public Health and Family Welfare as a per cent of NSDP*
1980-80	321	61	23.60	8.25	1.51
1981-82	337	63	23.17	8.07	1.41
1982-83	366	66	22.91	8.69	1.50
1983-84	451	80	19.67	8.52	1.71
1984-85	462	80	19.45	7.88	1.74
1985-86	369	63	15.82	5.90	1.30
1986-87	353	59	13.16	5.04	1.23
1987-88	409	67	15.85	5.95	1.29
1988-89	445	71	16.91	5.68	1.19
1989-90	447	70	15.26	5.57	1.80
1990-91	441	67	15.28	5.22	1.04
1991-92	444	66	15.63	5.10	0.97
1992-93	451	66	15.14	4.89	1.00
1993-94	519	75	17.31	5.15	1.00
1994-95	500	71	16.15	5.05	0.91
1995-96	499	70	12.85	4.93	0.84
1996-97	605	83	14.55	5.50	0.94
1997-98	641	87	15.33	5.23	0.99
1998-99	739	99	14.49	5.21	1.00
1999-2000	797	106	15.37	5.32	1.02
2000-2001	857	113	16.04	4.98	1.06

Source: RBI Bulletins of various years.

sector as a whole and particularly to health during 1991-2001 are inadequate relative to our requirements. Keeping in view of the indispensable role played by the social sector and health sector in the context of the welfare of the people, public expenditure on health and social services has to be increased in AP. More resources should be spent on Preventive Care as the poor benefit more from this.

Table 3 reveals the selected indicators of the Human Development in Andhra Pradesh during 1981-2001. Literacy rates and Life Expectancy at birth have increased from 1981 to 2001. IMR declined from 86 in 1981 to 66 in 2001. Human Development index increased during 1981-91 but remained same during 1991-2001.

Table 3
Selected Indicators of HD in Andhra Pradesh during 1981-2001

Year	*Literacy (percentage)*	*Life Expectancy at birth (Years)*	*IMR per 1000*	*HDI*
1981	35.66	58.5	86	0.298(9)
1991	44.19	61.2	73	0.416(9)
2001	61.11	63.5	66	0.416(10)

Source: Economic Surveys of various years.

Empirical results of the study revealed that the per capita expenditure on social services increased. Allocation to social services by the Government has been increasing through out the period and more in 1991-2001. Coming to the total public expenditure on Medical and Public Health and Family Welfare, it has shown an increase i.e., from Rs.321 crores in 1980-81 to Rs.857 crores in 2000-2001. The per capita expenditure also showed an increasing trend from Rs.61 in 1980-81 to Rs.67 in 1991 and to Rs.113 in 2000-2001. This increasing trend is actually due to the increase in the allocation of family welfare, but not due to expenditure on the health sector. Its proportion in Total Public Expenditure shows a declining trend from 8% in 1980-

81, to 5.22 in 1990-91 and 5% in 2000-201. Its proportion in NSDP shows that there is not much variation over the period and it is staggering around 1 per cent. The overall decline in the share and the percentage stagnation are due to the decline in the budgetary allocations.

The need for importance of health expenditure by the Government can be visualized by the shifts in HDI. At the state level, i.e., in A.P., HDI has improved from 0.298 in 1981 with 9th rank to 0.416 in 1991 with 9th rank. But the value of HDI Index remained same in 2001 and the rank slipped to 10th rank. These figures clearly indicated similar shifts in health expenditure and Human Development Index during the period of study.

The development of human resources contributes to sustained growth and productive employment. Healthy educated and skilled workforce can contribute more significantly to the development of a country and promotion of the welfare of the people. In spite of some improvement in the provision of health care over the years, there are wide disparities. The Eleventh Plan aims at inclusive growth. In this connection, besides raising the public expenditure on health, there is a great need for the introduction of a comprehensive scheme of health insurance, where the contribution of the Government decreases as we go up to the higher levels of income and it will be maximum at the lowest level. Significant improvement in HDI will enable us to achieve the goal of development with a human face.

REFERENCES

1. *Indian Economic Journal*, 2007.

2. *Eleventh Five Year Plan*, Govt. of India, 2007-2012

3. UNDP Human Development Report, 2003.

4. *RBI Bulletins*, Economic Surveys.

5 V.M.Rao, "The emerging Poverty Scenario, Alternative development paradigm for poverty elimination", *The Indian Economic Journal*, Vol.55, No.3, October-December 2007, p.148-151.

5 Planning Commission, *Eleventh Five Yar Plan 2007-2012*, Govt. of India, Inclusive Growth, Vol.I, p.2,5,1,

7 UNDP Human Development Report, 2003.

30

HUMAN RESOURCES DEVELOPMENT IN INDIA: AN OVERVIEW

P.S. Ravindra & P. Rajya Lakshmi***

Introduction

The success of any organization in the long run depends very much on the quali'y of its human resources. Human resources comprise the aggregate of employee attributes including knowledge, skill, experience and health, which are presently and potentially available to an organization for the achievement of its goal. In other-words human resources consist of the value of the productive capacity of the firm's human organization. Of all the prime resources of an organization - men, materials, money and machine, the human resource is recognized as the most vital and the most valuable resource.

Human Resource Development (HRD) is mainly concerned with providing learning experiences for the people associated with an organization through a behavioral approach adopting various processes. Learning experiences for the people associated with an organization through a behavioral approach adopting various processes. "The individual is provided with learning experiences not in isolation but he shares others learning experiences also. Such learning experience are provided with

* Assistant Professor, Vignan's Institute of Information Technology, Visakhapatnam, A.P.

** Research Scholar, Department of Law, Andhra University, Visakhapatnam, A.P.

the main objective of developing human beings for their advantage and harnessing their physical, mental and intellectual endowments and abilities for the growth of the organization".

In the changing competitive business environment, industry has recognized the need for the productivity, innovation and customer orientation. It is commonly felt that these are the functions of technology i.e. new machines, new processes. But man is behind all of these who uses the technology and implement new system. Today modernization is called not only for necessary equipment and processes but also for human minds; its way of thinking and way of doing the things.

The nature of job is constantly changing due to changes in the environment, organizational goals, priorities, strategies, technology etc. Such a change in the nature of jobs requires continuous development of employee competencies to perform the job well. HRD aims at constantly assessing the competency requirement for different individuals to effectively perform the assigned jobs and provide opportunities for development of these competencies. The organizational effectiveness can be increased by systematically melding HR practices with the selected competitive strategy. The underlying emphasis for HRD would be to look for the appropriate 'fit' between work and man from time to time.

Significance of HRD

Fundamental changes in the business environment have created a sudden shift in focus of HR function. HRD is basically concerned with organizational effectiveness through the development of its HR. HRD is a continuous process to ensure the development of employee dynamism, effectiveness, competencies and motivation in a systematic and planned manner. Employees need to have a variety of competencies to perform different tasks. HRD aims to identify competency gaps for employees and train them to perform present role effectively and create conditions to help employees to bridge these gaps through development. In fact human resource issues are the business related issues as they influence the essence of business.

Most of the companies are beginning to recognize the importance of people to the success of their business.

HRD Perspective

Human Resource Development in the organization context refers to the process where by the employees are continuously helped in a planned way to:

(a) Acquire or sharpen capabilities required to perform various tasks and functions associated with their present or future expected roles;

(b) Improve their general enabling capabilities as individuals so that they are able to discover and exploit their own inner potential for their own and/or organizational development purposes; and

(c) Develop an organizational culture where superior-subordinate relationships, Teamwork, and collaboration among different sub-units are strong and contribute to the professional well-being, motivation and pride of employees.

HRD from the organizational point of view is a process in which the employees of an organization are helped / motivated to acquire and develop technical, managerial and behavioral knowledge, skills and abilities and mould the values, beliefs and attitudes necessary to perform present and future roles by realizing the highest human potential with a view to contribute positively to the organizational, group, individual and social goals.

Recent economic liberalizations announced by the Government of India tend towards market economy and started creating more dynamic environment of India than ever before. HRD plays a significant and crucial role in market economies under dynamic environments. Human Resources Development (HRD) should be effective and efficient. HRD cannot be effective for the candidates who do not possess potentials to perform present and future roles in organizations with dynamic environment. HRD to be effective should essentially have a strong base of human resources planning, recruitment and selection based on effective HRD requirements.

The outcomes of HRD are four-fold, viz. to the organization, to the individuals, to the groups and to the society. HRD benefits the organization by developing the employees and make them ready to accept responsibilities, welcome change, adapt to change, enables the implementation of the programmes of total quality management, maintenance of sound human relations, and increase in productivity and profitability. HRD also benefits individuals in achieving of potentials, increase in performance, fulfilling their needs and enhancing social and psychological status.

The HRD helps the groups in the form of increase in-cooperation, increase in collaboration and team effectiveness. Further, it helps the society in the form of developing human resources and increased contribution of human resources to the society. Labour welfare, social security measures, retirement/ terminal benefits are all parts of the same scheme to provide for the employees present and future needs, to the extent possible, for he solely depends on his employee for satisfaction of his and his family's current and future requirements. Labour welfare will not be complete if social security measures are not considered an integral part of it. Hence, social security has to provide protection to members of the community by collective action against undue hardship and privation.

Retrial benefits are part of social security. At present the benefits of provident fund, Gratuity and Pension are available, unfortunately not all employees, but to a large number among them. This mainly a post independence development, a part of our efforts to establish a Socialistic pattern of Society with reduced inequalities and to wipe tears from every eye. While provident fund is a means of savings for old age, Gratuity and Pension is a retrial benefit earned by the employee for rendering service. In the older days, it was a practice to offer a gift in cash or kind to a retiring employee who has served his master well as a token of the master's gratitude and to provide for the employees old age needs.

HRD Policies and Procedures in India

India is continuously trying for industrialization for the industrial development on modern lines, the material and physical resources of the country are considered to be satisfactory, from the point of view of human resources with a population of 109 crores. India marks next only to China in population. Consequently, there is the question of finding suitable sources of gainful employment for the rapidly increasing population. A Very small proportion of the total population constitutes the working force engaged in the organized sector of the industries. This with regards to the progress of industrialization the problem of human resources is not at all a problem of number but rather it is a question of quality, type of training and improving the skill of manpower required for industries, Hence, the need of importance of training facilities in India is unquestionable.

In India, a worker training is comparatively a new idea. Only after the world war-II, it came into light that there is a need for structured training for workers. But real progress in this direction was made after independence only. During 1961, India passed the Apprentice Training Act and more than 500 Industrial Institutes were established. For apprenticeship training 300 centers were established. Some places have special training centers. Chennai has advanced training institute, Kolkata has the Central Staff Training and Research Institute, and Bangalore has the Foreman Training Institute. Up to 31st December 1962, the directorate general of employment and training, government of India established training centers under craftsman training scheme. With this scheme, the National Apprenticeship Training scheme was extended to other industrial houses also. During 1976, under apprentice ship scheme, child-training scheme were developed and now this has been extended to many networks.

As regard private and public sector, the private and public sector have not introduced any formal training programme for their new employees aimed at interning and education. These programmes educate new employees in connection with the company policies, its products, and management etc. their personnel department at times with the help of the supervisors staff conducts these programmes generally. But on the other hand , the public sector under takings use their internal training facilities for training their non-supervisory employees. In these undertaking employees are also encouraged to avail of the external training facilities. Some times they s ›onsor their candidature and meet the costs also. Some public sector organizations have started their well organized training programmes for example banks, insurance and railways etc. now, many well established private sector concern are also conducting in company programmes based on their workers needs. So we can say that Indian is marching ahead steadily in this direction.

Training is a very important component of Human Resource Development. It is perhaps the most cost effective progress of sharpening and developing skills. Knowledge and bringing attitudes changes and overall improving competencies among the man power for increasing their effectiveness in the present job as well as preparing them for their future jobs. Meaningful training also results in changed behaviour in the individual. Training is also and important motivating factor as it enhances confidence among the employees, which enable them to face the challenges of the job.

As indicated by a study on orientation and training and development practice in certain private as well as public undertakings in India as regards employee training, all the organizations in the public sector under the study provided for training managers ands institutors for designing and conducting appropriate in company and external training programmes as per the needs of the employees. The organizations and the characteristics of the industry concerned. The internal training facilities, in journal, were provided for developing the rank and file or non-supervisory employees but in the case of certain companies like Steel and air Lines Undertaking, the employees were encouraged top take advantage of facilities as well. The organizations in the private sector considered the proqrammes for employees of great importance as well as advantage with to develop their capabilities or skills, knowledge and attitudes systematically. The role of personnel executive / training specialists has been very important in such programmes for which the training needs of the employees in t of in company facilities were assessed on the basis of supervisory recommendations, analysis of job performance analysis of job requirements and employees suggestions. A number of companies also use external training facilities such as those provided by training institutes productivity councils etc.

Various organisation both in the public as well as private sector provided in company and also external facilities for the development of the their managerial personnel. For example the Indian Oil Corporation Ltd, provided training centers both at its head office as well as its branches. While functional training courses are conducted at branch training centers. The center at the head office, established since march 1966, organizes advanced courses in areas like principles and practice of personnel administration, management, productivity etc. the state trading corporation has provided for a two years management programme for young recruits from universities to up grade the managerial skills of the corporations staff at various levels.

Similarly in the private sector L&T Ltd, Mumbai has been provided with the facilities of various in-company development programmes including human relations laboratory, production planning and control programmes, and effective communication programme. TISCO provides for various management development programmers / courses for its junior level management personnel as well as supervisors. External professional institutions usually conduct specific programmes as per needs of higher management personnel.

As regards training and education in India, there was greater awareness of the problem since the publication of the report of the Royal Commission on Labour in India (1931) and some other reports that followed subsequently. The training and employment organisation committee appointment by the government of India wrote: "In the absence of a unified conception of the object of training, standards of training, methods of conducting examinations and issuing certificates vary from state to state and some time from institute to institute with in the states. An unfortunate outcome of the chaotic condition in the fields of crafts men's training has been that most training institutes have succeeded in swelling for ranks of partly trained workers rather than in producing crafts men who would be value of Industry. This not only has the problem of shortage of skilled workers not been but a fresh problem has been created". Under the crafts men training scheme recognized in 1954, in order to put greater emphasis on individual in the age group of 15-25, in certain engineering trade and non-engineering trades at 456 industrial training institutes has spread in various parts of the country. The training wings of the 'DGE&T' has introduced aptitude tests to be applied for selecting crafts men trainees in engineering trades. Such tests are applied in selecting suitable candidates as apprentices in various industries in different regions of the country. Since April 1, 1969, the financial control over the crafts men- training scheme has been transferred to respective state Governments/Union territories administration. Other training schemes currently in India are as follows:

National Apprenticeship Training Scheme

The apprentices Act, 1961 makes it obligatory for employers in specified industries to engage Apprentices whose training consists of basic training followed by on-the- job or shop-floor training according to standards prescribed by the Government in consultation with central Apprenticeship council.

Craft instructions training

Since a regular supply if man power/ personnel in various industries requires an adequate number of training instructors equipped with capabilities of imparting necessary skills and knowledge. The central training institute at Bombay, Calcutta, Hyderabad, Kanpur, Ludhiana, Madras, and New Delhi tram craft instructors required by the ITI's and apprenticeship training establishments.

Supervisors/Foreman Training

An institute to train foreman was established in Bangalore in 1971 with assistance from the Government of Germany. This institute conducts training programme for existing and potential shop foreman and supervisors in theoretical and managerial skills for operatives from industry in advanced technical skills.

Training Scheme for Industrial Workers

Under this scheme industrial workers, irrespective for their age, but possessing to years, workshop experience in a particular trade and sponsor by their employees are eligible for admission this course.

Advanced Training

The advanced training institute was set up Madras in 1971, with assistance from united nations development p[programme (UNDP), conducts advanced training courses for highly skilled craftsman industry in specialized areas of tool design, tool and die making and heat treatment.

Training in Industrial Relations & Personnel Administration

The Indian Institute of Lobour studies, set up at New Delhi in 1964, imparts in service training to managerial personnel in various organizations in the areas of industrial relations, techniques of enforcement of labour laws and personnel management. The scope of this institute is being enlarged substantially in addition to the setting up of a national labour institute and regional labour institute for the DurDOse of extending facilities regarding training and research.

Today the world is advancing towards globalization of markets and homogenization of products and services and it is rapidly changing unless the organizations are able to change their attitudes and approaches there is a real danger that a country of India's sign and potential will become peripheral in the content of workers economy. So that each and every organization needs to have well trained and experienced people to perform the activities that have to be done. The effective functioning of any organization requires that employees learn to perform their hobs at a satisfactory level of proficiency. Organization needs well-trained and experienced people to perform the activities that have to be done. If the current as potential job occupant can meet this requirement, training is not important. But when this is not the case, it is necessary to raise the skills levels and increase the versatility and adaptability of employees.

Employee training is distinct from management development or executive development. While the former refers to training given to employees in the areas of operations, technical and allied areas, the latter refers to developing an employee in the areas of principles and techniques of management, administration, organization and allied areas. Training is a systematic programme of the organization, which aims at increasing the aptitudes, skills and abilities of the workers to perform specific jobs. By training, the employees will acquire new manipulative skills, technical knowledge, problem solving ability or attitudes. Every Organization needs to have well trained and experienced people to perform the activities that have to be done. Inadequate job performance of decline in productivity or changes resulting out of job redesigning or a technical break through which require some type of training and development efforts.

Organization and individual should develop and progress simultaneously for their survival and attainment of mutual goals. So, every modern management has to develop the organization through human resources development. Employee training is the most important sub-system of human resources development. After an employee is selected, placed and introduced in an organization he/she must be provided with training facilities in order to adjust him to the job. Training is the act of increasing the knowledge and skill of an employee for doing a particular job. Training is a short-term educational process and utilizing a systematic and organized procedure by which employees learn technical knowledge and skills for a definite purpose. Employee training is distinct from management development or executive development. While the former refers to training given to employees in the areas of operations, technical and allied areas, the latter refers to developing an employee in the areas of principles and techniques of management, administration, organization and allied areas.

Strategic HRD Practices and Facilitators

Strategic HRD Practices is a holistic framework encompassing developmental fundamentals and initiatives. For any activity to be successful certain fundamental conditions have to exist before they can yield desired results. Strategic HRD practices fundamentals are those components of HRD, which have to be strong enough to ensure a congenial atmosphere in an organization for implementation of Strategic HRD initiatives. Compensation, Working conditions, Family Welfare and HRD Unit/function are some of the Strategic HRD fundamentals, while Employee Training, Performance Appraisal, Job Enrichment, Career Planning, Communication, Involvement and Empowerment are the dimensions of Strategic HRD Initiatives.

A number of factors are believed to play a vital role in facilitating the strategic HRD practices in the organizations. They include the concerns of top management, trade unions, frontline officers, individual workers, industrial relations scenario, trainability, employment externalization, downsizing etc., In other words top management, trade unions, frontline officers and individual workers devoid of any apprehension about the developmental issues might play a facilitator role, where as the apprehension of these players inhibit the Strategic HRD practices. Further, organizations find it difficult to get the commitment of unions and employees when they opt for downsizing manpower or contingent employment practices in organizations.

Conclusion

HRD is mainly concerned with providing learning experiences for the people associated with an organization through a behaviors approach adopting various processes. The term HRD, in a broader sense, means those learning experiences, which are organized for a specific time and designed to bring about the possibility of behavioral change. HRD from the organizational point of view is a process in which the employees of an organization are helped / motivated to acquire and develop technical, managerial and behavioral knowledge, skills and abilities and mould the values, beliefs and attitudes necessary to perform present and future roles by realizing the highest human potential with a view to contribute positively to the organizational, group, individual and social goals.

HRD plays a significant and crucial role in market economics under dynamic environments. HRD to be effective should essentially have a strong base of human resources planning. Recruitment and selection based on effective HRD requirements. Right man should be placed at a right time and right place / job. The success of the organization depends upon the quality and potentiality of its human resources. Thus, HRD plays a significant role in any organization to achieve the organizational goals and objectives.

31

PUBLIC SPENDING FOR HUMAN DEVELOPMENT IN ANDHRA PRADESH

M.D. Bavaiah, K. Thulasi Naik** & J. Narasimha Rao****

Introduction

The importance of public spending on social sectors in the process of human development is well recognised. This paper examines the trends and pattern of public spending on Social Sectors that are important for human development in Andhra Pradesh. This paper is mainly based on data from the Annual Budgets and Finance Accounts of the Government of Andhra Pradesh. It uses data from budget documents of Andhra Pradesh for detailed analysis of expenditure under different heads. It also uses information from the Annual Financial Statement and Budget in Brief published by the Finance Department, Government of Andhra Pradesh as well as data released by the Directorate of Economics and Statistics, Government of Andhra Pradesh.

Overall Pattern of Public Expenditure on Human Development

The extent of public expenditure on human development has been measured in the earlier studies in two ways. First, based on UNDP's Human Development Report 1991, studies

---

* Professor, **Associate Professor, Department of Economics and Applied Economics, S.K.University, Anantapur, A.P.

*** Associate Professor, Department of Economics, Osmania University, Hyderabad, A.P.

have used four ratios to indicate the priority assigned by States to expenditure on human development. These are:

(i) **Public Expenditure Ratio (PER)**, defined as the total budgetary expenditures as a proportion of Gross State Domestic Product;

(ii) **Social Allocation Ratio (SAR)**, defined as the share of budgetary expenditure on the social sector in total budgetary expenditure;

(iii) **Social Priority Ratio (SPR)**, defined as the proportion of social sector expenditure that is spent on human priority areas; and

(iv) **Human Expenditure Ratio (HER)**, which is a product of the first three ratios and measures the budgetary expenditures in human priority areas as a proportion of Gross State Domestic Product (GSDP).

The Human Development Report, 1991 provides norms for these ratios, the fulfillment of which is expected to lead to higher levels of Human Development. The norms are based upon the experience of a number of developing countries with respect to Human Development. According to the Report, the Human Expenditure Ratio (HER) may need to be around 5 per cent if a Country or State wishes to do well in Human Development. This may be achieved in an efficient manner by keeping the Public Expenditure Ratio (PER) moderate (around 25 per cent), allocate much of this to the Social Sectors (more than 40 per cent) and focus on the Social priority areas (giving them more than 50 per cent). The fulfillment of these ratios is expected to lead to higher levels of Human Development.

In addition to these ratios, studies have also used trends in per capita expenditure on social and human priority sectors to measure public spending for human development. It is important to examine trends in per capita expenditure along with the UNDP ratios as the UNDP ratios measure the human development expenditure in relation to income and do not indicate the absolute level of expenditure on human development in the State.

This paper analyses trends in both the UNDP ratios and the per capita expenditures. The first step towards such an analysis is to define what constitutes social sector and the human priority areas. In this paper, social sector is defined to comprise expenditure on broad budgetary heads called Social Services and Rural Development.

Social Services include following sub-heads:

(i) Education, sports, art and culture;

(ii) Medical and public health;

(iii) Family welfare;

(iv) Water supply and sanitation;

(v) Housing;

(vi) Urban development;

(vii) Welfare of Scheduled Castes, Scheduled Tribes and Other Backward Castes;

(viii) Labour and Labour Welfare;

(ix) Social security and welfare;

(x) Nutrition;

(xi) Relief on account of natural calamities;

(xii) Other social services.

Within the social sector, social priority areas are defined to comprise elementary education, health and family welfare (excluding medical education, training and research), nutrition, water supply and sanitation and rural development. These are sectors that are particularly important for human development.

UNDP's Human Development Report 1991 suggests that PER should be around 25 per cent, SAR around 40 per cent and SPR around 50 per cent, so that HER of a State turns out to be around 5 per cent. Table-1 shows that PER in Andhra Pradesh has been lower than the suggested norm of 25 percent in each of the years between 1990-91 and 2007-08. The calculation of

SAR for Andhra Pradesh is not strictly comparable with the norms suggested by UNDP as Expenditure on Rural Development is included within the social sector Expenditure than those defined by UNDP. The ratio is therefore inflated up. However, even with the inflated SAR, the ratio in Andhra Pradesh stood at marginally less than the suggested norm of 40 per cent in 2000s. Social Priority Ratio in Andhra Pradesh, which is also inflated, was slightly above the norm of 50 per cent. However, even with inflated SARs and HPRs, the HERs are lower than the suggested norm of 5 per cent in Andhra Pradesh, primarily due to a low PER.

The overall public expenditure in Andhra Pradesh as a share of GSDP, as reflected in PER estimates presented in Table -1, stagnated between 15 and 16 per cent during the decade of 1990s. This could be partly due to the implementation of structural adjustment programme in the state during 1990s. Since 2000-01, however, there was a sign of increase in this ratio. It increased to 17 percent in 2000-01 and it stagnated around 17 per cent up to 2004-05, but increased continuously there after and reached 22 per cent in 2007-08.

On the social sector, Andhra Pradesh State has spent around 44.11 percent of its total spending in 1990-91. However, the share of expenditure on Social Sectors has declined continuously up to 35.63 percent in 1994-95, but then it increased to 47.27 in 1997-98, making it as "U" turn. It started declining from 1998-99 onwards and reached the minimum at 32.89 percent in 2005-06, but again it started increasing in the last two years. The shares were lower in the 2000s as compared to 1990s. The Social Allocation Ratio indicates that it is higher than the norm suggested by UNDP in 1990s, but it failed to maintain that level in 2000s.

Table -1 shows that the Social Priority Ratio is higher than 50 Per cent (the norm suggested by UNDP) in all the years of the study period, except 1991-92. Therefore, it is inferred that the government of Andhra Pradesh has been spending more than enough money on Social priorities sectors.

Table -1: UNDP Indicators of Expenditure on Human Development in Andhra Pradesh

(Per cent)

Year	*Public Expenditure Ratio*	*Social Allocation Ratio*	*Social Priority Ratio*	*Human Expenditure Ratio*
1990-91	16.04	44.11	52.40	3.71
1991-92	15.19	43.15	49.74	3.26
1992-93	16.26	43.79	66.11	4.71
1993-94	15.63	39.75	52.29	3.25
1994-95	16.01	35.63	50.30	2.87
1995-96	15.77	40.65	60.36	3.87
1996-97	15.56	41.45	57.31	3.70
1997-98	15.75	41.81	56.35	3.71
1998-99	15.40	47.27	55.30	4.03
1999-2000	15.48	42.90	53.95	3.58
2000-01	17.78	35.83	52.24	3.33
2001-02	17.70	35.59	51.19	3.23
2002-03	17.75	35.06	51.56	3.21
2003-04	17.85	36.54	50.60	3.30
2004-05	17.45	35.07	53.49	3.27
2005-06	18.04	32.89	53.74	3.19
2006-07	19.07	35.02	60.84	4.06
2007-08	22.00	35.20	50.45	3.91

Source: Estimated on the basis of data from Finance Accounts of Andhra Pradesh.

PER = Public Expenditure/GSDP

SAR = Expenditure in the Social Sector/Total budgetary expenditure

SPR = Expenditure in Human Priority Areas/Expenditure in the Social sector Expenditureunder different heads has been estimated as the sum of revenue expenditure andcapital expenditure (including loans and advances net of repayments)

However, the last column of table indicates that the Government of Andhra Pradesh has not been able to maintain the international norm of 5 percent Human Expenditure Ratio. It is mostly fluctuated between 3 and 4 percent. Therefore, it is inferred that there is need for allocating more funds for Social Sectors in Andhra Pradesh.

Table-2: Per Capita Real Expenditures on Human Development in Andhra Pradesh

(Rupees)

Year	*Per Capita Public Expenditure*	*Per Capita Social Sector Expenditure*	*Per Capita Social Priority Expenditure*
1990-91	1762	777	407
1991-92	1731	747	372
1992-93	1802	789	522
1993-94	1890	751	393
1994-95	2015	718	361
1995-96	2069	841	508
1996-97	2152	892	511
1997-98	2095	876	494
1998-99	2293	1084	599
1999-2000	2401	1030	556
2000-01	2950	1057	552
2001-02	3054	1087	556
2002-03	3106	1089	561
2003-04	3385	1237	626
2004-05	3459	1213	649
2005-06	3828	1259	676
2006-07	4358	1526	928
2007-08	5501	1936	977

Source: Estimated based on data from Finance Accounts of Andhra Pradesh.

Note: Expenditure under different heads has been estimated as the sum of revenueexpenditure and capital expenditure (including loans and advances net of repayments)

It may be noted that although the public expenditure as a share of GSDP is lower than the UNDP norm of 25 percent between 1990-91 and 2007-08, there was a reallocation of public expenditure towards the Social Priority Sectors over this period. As a result, the Social Priority Ratio of the State has been higher than the UNDP norm of 50 percent over this period indicating a greater emphasis in public spending on social priority sectors.

Table-2 shows the trends in real per capita public expenditure on social sectors and social priority areas in Andhra Pradesh. The Table shows that there was a significant increase in real per capita expenditure on social and social priority sectors over this period. The per capita social sector expenditure increased from Rs. 777 in 1990-91 to Rs. 1936 in 2007-08. The expenditure on social priority sector increased from Rs. 407 per capita in 1990-91 to Rs. 977 per capita in 2007 08.

The trends in Per Capita Real Public Expenditure, Per Capita Real Social Sector Expenditure, and Per Capita Real Expenditure on Human Priority Sectors presented in Table-2, show that there has been a steady increase in all types of expenditures over the period of analysis. However, the trends show that the compound growth rate of Public Expenditure (6.39 percent) is higher than the compound growth rate of Expenditure on Social Sectors (4.84 percent) and Social Priority Sectors (4.62 percent) during the period of study.

Before starting the impact assessment of Social Sector Expenditure in Andhra Pradesh, it is always better to look at the real per capita expenditures on the Social Sectors by the Government Andhra Pradesh during the period of study. This is estimated by using the following formula.

$$RPCPESS = \frac{RPESS}{Population}$$

Where RPESS= Real Public Expenditure on Social Sectors and

RPCPESS= Real Per Capita Public Expenditure on Social Sectors.

The nominal values of Public Expenditure on Social Sectors are converted into real values of Public Expenditure on Social Sectors by using the GSDP deflator, which is given below.

$$RPESS = \frac{GDSP \quad (Base)}{GSDP \quad (Current)} \times PESS$$

Where RPESS = Real Public Expenditure on Social Sectors; GSDP (Base) = Gross State Domestic Product at base year (1999-2000) prices; GSDP (Current) = Gross State Domestic Product at current year prices; and PESS= Public Expenditure on Social Sectors.

Table 3

Estimation of Real Per Capita Public Expenditure on Social Sectors (RPCPESS) in Andhra Pradesh

(Rs. Crores)

Year	*GSDP at Base Year (1999-2000) Prices*	*GSDP at Current Year Prices (Rs. Crores)*	*GSDP Deflator*	*PESS (Rs. Cores)*	*RPESS (Rs. Lakhs)*	*Population (Lakhs)*	*RPCPESS (Rupees)*	*Real Per Capita Income (Rupees)*
1	2	3	4	5	6	7	8	9
1990-91	81666	37194	2.1957	263179	577855	743.43	777	11221
1991-92	85973	45225	1.9010	296457	563566	754.50	747	11581
1992-93	85159	49157	1.7324	350013	606358	768.08	789	11267
1993-94	94018	60033	1.5661	372975	584118	777.83	751	12222
1994-95	98988	71410	1.3862	407493	564[illegible]63	787.23	718	12667
1995-96	104640	82674	1.2657	529891	670680	797.01	841	13214
1996-97	111118	93333	1.1906	601958	716664	803.69	892	13907
1997-98	109197	99214	1.1006	653540	719300	821.31	876	13340
1998-99	122491	119021	1.0292	866358	891616	822.88	1084	14874
1999-2000	129403	129403	1.0000	859272	859272	834.48	1030	15507
2000-01	139680	145090	0.9627	924133	889675	841.44	1057	16622
2001-02	145543	157150	0.9261	990035	916912	843.53	1087	17260

(contd.)

Table 3 *(contd.)*

1	2	3	4	5	6	7	8	9
2002-03	150281	168143	0.8938	1046568	935390	859.28	1089	17486
2003-04	164213	190880	0.8603	1245425	1071432	866.02	1237	18961
2004-05	175641	210449	0.8346	1287780	1074783	885.91	1213	19871
2005-06	190957	236034	0.8090	1400469	1133012	900.00	1259	21334
2006-07	207904	269173	0.7724	1797910	1388671	909.92	1526	22835
2007-08	229461	311752	0.7360	2413983	1776781	917.73	1936	24969

Source: 1. Directorate of Economics and Statistics, Hyderabad: Estimates of GSDP of A.P., 2008

2. Government of Andhra Pradesh: Budget Documents for various years

The details of the estimation of Real Per Capita Public Expenditure on Social Sectors (RPCPESS) are shown in Table-3. Per capita real expenditure on the social sector has increased over time except during the first half of the 1990s. It increased from Rs. 777 in 1990-91 to Rs.1936 in 2007-08, but it was stagnant in the first half of the 1990s and thereafter per capita expenditure has been increased continuously. This increase in per capita terms may be partially attributed to the lower growth rate of population during 1991-2008. Table -3 also gives the data for Real Per Capita Income (RPCI).

Impact Assessment

The present study uses the regression analysis to estimate the impact coefficients, which explains the influence of a unit of expenditure on aggregate Social Sectors, education and health on the standard of living and on the indicators of education development and health development as indicated below.

Impact of Social Sectors Expenditure

The indicator for the standard of living is per capita real state domestic product or Real Per Capita Income.

The equation used for the estimation of the impact of Expenditure on Social Sectors (ESS) on Per Capita Real State Domestic Product (PCRSDP) is as follows:

$$PCRSDP = \alpha + \beta (ESS)$$

and

$$PCRSDP = \alpha + \beta (RPCESS)$$

Where the symbol α in the equation represents the constant term and the symbol β in the equation represents the impact coefficient of Expenditure on Social Services (ESS) and Real Per Capita Expenditure on Social Services (RPCESS). The data for the variables used in the impact analysis of Expenditure on Social Services on the standard of living (Real Per Capita Income) are given in the Table-3. The study considered Real Per Capita Income as proxy variable for Standard of Living and it is taken as Dependent Variable in all the three Models of Impact Assessment. Real Per Capita Public Expenditure on Social Sectors (RPCPESS) is the Independent Variable in Model - I, Public Expenditure on Social Sectors (PESS) is the Independent Variable in Model - II and Real Public Expenditure on Social Sectors (RPESS) is the Independent Variable in Model - III. The SPSS (Software Package for Social Sciences) Print outs of all the three Models are given below.

Model - I: Impact of Real Per Capita Public Expenditure on Social Sectors (RPCPE) on Real Per Capita Income (RPCI)

Dependent Variable: Real Per Capita Income

	Unstandardised Coefficients		Standardized Coefficients	t	Sig.
	B	Std. Error	Beta		
Constant	2683.200	1083.325		2.477	0.025
Real Per Capita Public Expenditure on Social Sectors	12.737	0.991	0.955	12.855	0.000

Model – II: Impact of Public Expenditure on Social Sectors (PESS)

on Real Per Capita Income (RPCI)

Dependent Variable: Real Per Capita Income

	Unstandardised Coefficients		*Standardized Coefficients*	*t*	*Sig.*
	B	Std. Error	Beta		
Constant	9581.631	379.599		25.241	0.000
Public Expenditure on Social Sectors	0.007154	0.000	0.981	20.017	0.000

Model – III: Impact of Real Public Expenditure on Social Sectors (RPESS)

on Real Per Capita Income (RPCI)

Dependent Variable: Real Per Capita Income

	Unstandardized Coefficients		Standardized Coefficients	t	Sig.
	B	Std. Error	Beta		
(Constant)	4978.217	778.553		6.394	0.000
Real Public Expenditure on Social Sectors	0.01252	0.001	0.967	15.097	0.000

An analysis on the above SPSS Print Outs shows that a one Rupee increase in Real Per Capita Public Expenditure leads to Rs.12.737 increase in Real Per Capita Income, a one Rupee increase Public Expenditure on Social Sectors leads to Rs.0.007 increase in Real Per Capita Income and a one Rupee increase Real Public Expenditure on Social Sectors leads to Rs.0.0125 increase in Real Per Capita Income. It is therefore clear that there is a positive relationship between Expenditure on Social sectors and Per Capita Income. Hence, Expenditure on Social sectors certainly influences the standard of living in Andhra Pradesh.

Impact of Education Expenditure on Education Indicators

Education is an important of social sector. It plays catalytic role in socioeconomic development. It is essential for the economic modernization of the societies and the potential instrument for bringing about social transformation and for making democracy a success. It is an integral part, an inescapable and an essential part of the development process itself. Education plays an important role in the physical, intellectual, scientific, moral, and spiritual development of an individual.

The indicators of education development are the number teachers employed, the number of schools established and the number of students enrolled. The data for the variables used in the impact analysis of Expenditure on Primary Education on the Indicators of Primary Education are given in the Table-4.

The Table shows that the expenditure on primary education increased from Rs.420 crores in 1990-91 to Rs.2407 crores in 2005-06. Number of primary schools increased from 48731 in 1990-91 to 62159 in 2005-06. The number of students enrolled in primary schools increased from 5826 thousands in 1990-91 to 9112 thousands in 1999-2000, but then declined to 5398 thousand in 2005-06. The number of teachers employed in primary schools increased from 110857 in 1990-91 to 166790 in 2005-06.

The equations used for the estimation of the impact of Education Expenditure (EE) on education indicators - Teachers (T), Schools (S) and Students Enrolled (SE) are as follows:

$$\textit{Teachers} = \alpha_T + \beta_T (EE)$$

$$\textit{Schools} = \alpha_S + \beta_S (EE)$$

$$\textit{Students} = \alpha_{SE} + \beta_{SE} (EE)$$

Where the symbol in the equations represents the constant term and the symbol in the equations represents the impact coefficient of Education Expenditure (EE).

Table -4: Expenditure on Primary Education and development indicators of primary education in Andhra Pradesh

Years	*Expenditure on primary education (Rs.in crore)*	*Number of primary schools*	*Number of students enrolled (in '000s)*	*Number of teachers appointed*
1990-91	420	48731	5826	110857
1991-92	451	49057	6021	113124
1992-93	516	50201	6084	114460
1993-94	596	49318	5328	106114
1994-95	675	49153	5413	107445
1995-96	652	49125	5484	109440
1996-97	758	48899	5635	106974
1997-98	858	49919	8370	121446
1998-99	933	51836	8798	136363
1999-00	1200	55398	9112	136853
2000-01	1420	58249	5231	127313
2001-02	1659	63362	6351	173731
2002-03	1729	63642	6255	173765
2003-04	2010	63897	5967	172601
2004-05	2139	61680	5524	166935
2005-06	2407	62159	5398	166790

Source: 1. Government of Andhra Pradesh: Explanatory Memoranda on the Budgets.
2. Government of Andhra Pradesh: Economic surveys of Andhra Pradesh.
3. Directorate of economics, Andhra Pradesh, Statistical Abstracts.

The study considered Number of Schools, Number of Students Enrolled and Number of Teachers Appointed as proxy variables for Education Indicators and they are taken as Dependent Variables respectively in Model - I, Model - II and Model - III of Impact Assessment. Public Expenditure on Primary Education (PEPE) is the Independent Variable in all the three Models. The SPSS (Software Package for Social Sciences) Print outs of all the three Models are given below.

Model - I: Impact of Public Expenditure on Primary Education (PEPE)

on the Number of Primary Schools

Dependent Variable: Number of primary schools

	Unstandardised Coefficients	*Standardized Coefficients*	*t*	*Sig.*	
Model		*B*	*Std. Error*	*Beta*	
1 (Constant)	44213.787	1143.202		38.675	.000
Expenditure on primary education	9.076	.869	.941	10.440	.000

Model - II: Impact of Public Expenditure on Primary Education (PEPE)

on the Number of Students Enrolled

Dependent Variable: Number of Students Enrolled

	Unstandardised Coefficients		*Standardized Coefficients*	*t*	*Sig.*
Model	*B*	*Std. Error*	*Beta*		
1 (Constant)	6509.763	678.710		9.591	.000
Expenditure on primary education	-.182	.516	-.094	-.353	.729

Model - III: Impact of Public Expenditure on Primary Education (PEPE)

on the Number of Teachers Appointed

Dependent Variable: Number of Teachers Appointed

	UnstandardisedStandardized Coefficients		*Coefficients*	*t*	*Sig.*
Model	*B*	*Std. Error*	*Beta*		
1 (Constant)	90062.077	5846.527		15.404	.000
Expenditure on primary education	38.171	4.446	.917	8.586	.000

An analysis on the above SPSS Print Outs shows that a one Crore Rupees increase in Public Expenditure on Primary Education leads to the increase of 9 Primary Schools, a one Crore Rupees increase Public Expenditure on Primary Education leads to reduction of 182 Students Enrolled and a one Crore Rupees increase in Public Expenditure on Primary Education leads to the increase of 38 Teachers Employed. It is therefore clear that there is a positive relationship between Expenditure on Primary Education and the Number of Schools and the Number of Teachers appointed, but negative relationship in the case of Students enrolled. Hence, Expenditure on Education certainly influences the growth of Schools and Teachers, but not Students in Andhra Pradesh.

Expenditure on Medical and Public Health Services

The broad objective of the medical and public health services in India is to bring about progressive improvement in the health of the people at large. While expenditure on medical services is to cure people who are victims of a disease, expenditure on public health is preventive and reduces the incidence and spread of diseases.

Impact of Health Expenditure

The indicators of health development are the number of hospitals and dispensaries, number of hospital beds and number of doctors.

The details relating to expenditure on primary health are three indicators of health services - number of hospitals and dispensaries, number of hospital beds and number of doctors- have been presented in Table -5.

The table shows that the expenditure on primary health increased from Rs. 163 crores in 1990-91 to Rs. 751 crores in 2005-06. Table-5 shows that the Number of Hospitals (including Dispensaries) increased from 2008 in 1990-91 to 3320 in 2005-06. The number of Beds in Hospitals increased from 31007 in 1990-91 to 35734 in 2005-06. The number of Doctors employed in Hospitals increased from 6672 in 1990-91 to 8848 in 2005-06.

Table -5: Expenditure on Primary Health and development indicators of primary health in Andhra Pradesh

Years	*Expenditure on primary health (Rs.in crore)*	*Number of hospitals*	*Number of beds in hospitals*	*No. of doctors appointed*
1990-91	163	2008	31007	6672
1991-92	188	2951	32858	6876
1992-93	212	2998	32217	8291
1993-94	252	3067	30322	8381
1994-95	268	3409	33795	8803
1995-96	290	3433	34395	8822
1996-97	359	3435	29340	8488
1997-98	373	3332	33750	9300
1998-99	403	3263	34236	9335
1999-00	467	3230	35852	10557
2000-01	531	3251	36506	11218
2001-02	560	3206	36476	10460
2002-03	563	3157	34968	9610
2003-04	726	3197	35569	9647
2004-05	747	3310	36168	7415
2005-06	751	3320	35734	8848

Source: 1. Government of Andhra Pradesh: Explanatory Memoranda on the Budgets.
2. Government of Andhra Pradesh: Economic surveys of Andhra Pradesh.
3. Directorate of Economics, Andhra Pradesh, Statistical Abstracts.
4. Reserve Bank of India, Reviews on State Finances.

The equations used for the estimation of the impact of Health Expenditure (HE) on Health indicators - Hospital and Dispensaries (HD), Hospital Beds (HB) and Doctors (D) are as follows:

Where the symbol in the equations represents the constant term and the symbol in the equations represents the impact coefficient of Health Expenditure (HE). The results of the Impact Analysis are produced in three Models in the form of SPSS Print Outs as shown below.

Model – I: Impact of Public Expenditure on Primary Health (PEPH)

on the Number of Hospitals

Dependent Variable: Number of Hospitals

Model		Unstandardized Coefficients		Standardized Coefficients	t	Sig.
		B	Std. Error	Beta		
1	(Constant)	2856.507	193.113		14.792	.000
	Expenditure on primary health	.710	.411	.419	1.728	.106

Model – II: Impact of Public Expenditure on Primary Health (PEPH)

on the Number of Beds

Dependent Variable: Number of Beds

Model		Unstandardized Coefficients		Standardized Coefficients	t	Sig.
		B	Std. Error	Beta		
1	(Constant)	30448.085	968.636		31.434	.000
	Expenditure on primary health	8.175	2.060	.728	3.968	.001

Model - III: Impact of Public Expenditure on Primary Health (PEPH)

on the Number of Doctors Appointed

Dependent Variable: Number of Doctors

Model		*Unstandardized Coefficients B*	*Std. Error*	*Standardized Coefficients Beta*	*t*	*Sig.*
1	(Constant)	7738.914	715.203		10.821	.000
	Expenditure on primary health	2.758	1.521	.436	1.813	.091

An analysis on the above SPSS Printouts shows that a one crore rupees increase in Public Expenditure on Primary Health leads to the increase of 0.71 Hospitals, a one crore rupees increase Public Expenditure on Primary Health leads to the establishment of 8 beds and a one crore rupees increase in Public Expenditure on Primary Health leads to the increase of three Doctors appointed. It is therefore clear that there is a positive relationship between Expenditure on Primary Health and the Number of Hospitals, Number of Beds and the Number of Doctors appointed. Hence, Expenditure on Health certainly influences the growth of Hospitals and Beds and Doctors in Andhra Pradesh.

Suggestions

Based on the above research findings, the study suggests the following suitable measures to increase the social sectors expenditure in order to improve the levels of knowledge, longevity and standards of living of the people that improve Human Development in Andhra Pradesh.

1. There is necessity to substantially raise the allocations to Social Priority Sectors in order to raise the present low level of Human Priority Ratio to the level of UNDP norm of 5 percent.

2. There is an urgent need for stepping up Expenditure on Social Sectors, particularly on Rural Health Services and

Rural Water Supply Programmes, because the present levels of expenditure on these services are very low and they are very effective in improving the health conditions of people.

3. There is an urgent need for rationalizing the expenditure on Primary Education, because it is generating more number of schools and more number of teachers but failed to improve the enrolment of students.

4. There is an obvious need for better utilization of allocated funds, because it is a well known fact that the effectiveness of many of the social sector programmes is poor.

5. There is a need for allocation of funds for rural development programmes with the inclusion of rural society in the process of implementation in order to reduce the wastage.

6. There is a need for allocating more funds for nutrition interventions in order to reduce malnutrition conditions in the state.

7. There is a need for simultaneous increase of expenditure on education, health and nutrition programmes to avoid the tendency of accelerating expenditures in one sector at the expense of the other.

8. While allocating funds for sub-sectors within the social sectors, proper care should be taken to allocate sufficient funds for priority sectors.

9. Finally, there is a need for adequate follow-up and continuous monitoring of schemes and programmes initiated in the social sectors. For this purpose, effective inclusion of local public participation in the implementation of social sector schemes is very much required.

32

HUMAN RESOURCES DEVELOPMENT: EMERGING ISSUES AND CONCERNS IN EDUCATION OF THE WEAKER SECTIONS

M.V.S.S. Prakasa Rao & P. Ch. Lakshminarayana***

India is rich in human resources. This has been amply demonstrated by what Indians' have achieved in all the fields of human endeavour, including science and technology. What's needed now is a long term policy for the development of human resources through education, training, health care, empowerment of women and creation of a congenial socioeconomic institutional (including legal), and political environment for the fullest possible utilisation of the vast, untapped reservoirs of human power and ingenuity. Human resources are inexhaustible and renewable hence, the only resources, which can sustain development forever, our axiom in the twenty-first century, should be human beings are both the end and the means of development.

Human Resources Development

Development is a complex process, which is affected by the economic and non-economic factors. The importance of non - economic factors in the development was duly recognized by **John Stuart Mill** of the classical school of thought that "non -

---

* Teaching Associate, Dept. of Education, Andhra University, Visakhapatnam, A.P.

** Professor, Dept. of Education, Andhra University, Visakhapatnam, A.P.

economics factors, like beliefs habits of thought, customs and institutions play an important role in the economic development, and attributed the backwardness of under developed countries to the despotic and anti-progressive character of their customs, institutions, and beliefs".

Human Resources Development is both the improvement of standard of living and a process of hierarchy. Development is defined as a widely participatory process of social change in the society, intended to bring both social and material advancement (including grater equality, freedom and other valued qualities) for the majority of the people through their gaining grater control over their environment.

Development of the poor is emerging as the main target of all-rural, urban, and tribal development efforts. Development is seen as a process of change to be set in motion and guided towards the objective of eradicating hunger, disease, injustice, exploitation and related ills that afflict vast sections of the world's population.

Sustainable development is the internationally accepted goal for the 21-st century. It has become something of a modern buzzword, whose meaning becomes more in precise the more it is repeated. It is clear that the meaning of sustainable development has different perception, but there is a broad agreement about what will be need to achieve it. The first and foremost thing is the elimination of poverty. It is accepted by all concerned that illiteracy breeds poverty. Thus literacy is and important component for the sustainable development. Therefore, innovations are essential for the development, growth of literacy for the countries like India.

Transfer of technology would bring about development. It was not recognized that development must take place from within and not brought in by out side. It demands the active and conscious participation of all the people for whom a programme or project is conceived. 'Participation of the people' has become a catchword. However, its results have not achieved the desired standard. There are several bottlenecks on the way even though participatory development has achieved a lot. There are cases of success, but we need a cautious move to reap the benefits in its real sense.

Literacy and Human Development

Literacy is considered as one of the indicators of human development. It facilitates effective execution of social, religious, and economic responsibilities. Literacy is envisaged as an effective instrument of realisation of important objectives of macro policy, focusing mainly on socioeconomic changes. It is therefore, multi-facted identity of literacy and its decisive role in the socio-economic transformation makes it imperative to analyse the literacy and growth of the nation. Education sharpens the eye of knowledge, develops awareness, and makes mind logical.

Education is its real sense is the purist of truth. It is an endless journey through knowledge and enlightment. Such a journey opens up new visits of development of humanism. According to A.P.J.Abdul Kalam. "Education is the most important element for growth and prosperity of a nation. India is in the process of transforming itself into developed nation by 2020. Yet we have 350 million people who need literacy and many more that have to acquire employable skills to suit the emerging modern India and the globe. Children who belonging to weaker sections of our society are undernourished, and only a small percentage of them manage to complete eight years of satisfactory education. It is essential that we enlighten and create widespread awareness of education among all sections of society particularly in rural areas and among urban poor."

Without proper education the scope and extent of the processes of socioeconomic changes cannot be understood by a common man and he cannot take part in the process of development. Hence, this paper deals with the importance of improving the literacy levels in India and discuss the need of mass education in the human development.

Weaker Sections

Weaker sections of the society need to be brought more into the development process. Finance Minister in his speech proposed to increase the equity support, as may be required for the National Minorities Development and Finance Corporation. A certain percentage of new schools that will be opened under the Sarva Shiksha Abhiyan as well as the Kasturba Balika Vidylaya Scheme will be located in districts or blocks having a substantial minority population of new Anganwadi centres will be located in blocks or villages, which have a substantial concentration of minorities. The Ministry of Social Justice, Empowerment, and Ministry of Human Resource Development should implement a number of schemes for pre examination coaching of candidates belonging to the weaker sections.

Scheduled Castes

Scheduled castes constitute the most deprived and oppressed section of Indian society. Historically, they have experienced extreme forms of exploitation, degradation, and inhuman treatment. For centuries, they were subjected to barbaric treatment of untouchability and were forced to live in abject misery and poverty. It was only during the freedom movement that a serious human concern was display by our national leaders to improve their socio-economic conditions. The constitution of free - India ended all sorts of discriminations based on religion, caste, creed, or race. The slavish practice of untouchability was also abolished.

The erstwhile untouchable and members of lower castes were raised to the status of free and equal citizens of the land. Besides that, they were also conferred with the constitutional status of "Scheduled Castes. " Various safeguards were provided in the constitution for protection and upliftment of these castes. Since then the 'development of Scheduled castes 'has remained on the agenda of Indian state and society. Scheduled castes are a constitutional concept. The term 'scheduled castes' was coined and used by the British Government for legal and administrative purpose. The constitution of India further standardizes and adopted them.In April 1936, the British Government issued an order specifying certain castes, races and tribes—communities earlier known as depressed classes—as scheduled castes. This was applicable to the then provinces of Assam, Bengal, Bihar, Bombay Central Provinces and Bidar, Madras, Orissa, Punjab and United Provinces. These castes, races and tribes were socially and economically depressed; they were listed in the 'Schedule' so as to ascertain their accurate numbers. The purpose was also to provide special benefits to them through legislative and executive means.

Depressed classes, according to the 1931 census report, were identifies on the basis of the following criteria; denial of services of Brahmins, Barbers, Water-carriers, Tailors and son; denial of the use Hindu temples and public conveniences such a roads, ferries, wells or schools. In addition to these was the criterion of 'pollution by contact' by virtue of which these castes or races were labeled as untouchables.

The Constitution of India does not define the term 'schedule castes'. It is essentially a juridical category. Article 341 of Indian Constitution, empowers the President to notify by an order "the castes races or tribes or parts of or groups within castes, races or tribes which shall for the purposes of the constitution be deemed to be 'Scheduled Castes with respect to individual states and union territories.

Socio-economic Conditions

Socio-economic conditions of scheduled castes, social status and the educational situation of scheduled castes is the lowest and their economic condition is extremely poor. Some preliminary aspects related to agricultural labourers, cultivators etc. which are the main economic pursuits of scheduled castes.

Social Status

Scheduled castes constitute about 15.5 percent of the country's population. According to 1981 census; there were 106 million scheduled castes in India. Although they are dispersed all over the country, their concentration in certain parts is more than other parts. Their population various from state to state. In term of absolute numbers, four states — Uttar Pradesh, West Bengal, Bihar, and Tamil Nadu have more than half the scheduled castes population of the country.

Scheduled castes are the most oppressed and exploited section of our society. In the hierarchy of caste system, their social status is very low. No doubt after independence, they have been granted equal rights as free citizens of India, but in practice, they still face various kinds of discriminations and deprivations. Social interactions with other castes, particularly in rural areas, is extremely limited. The occurrence of inter-caste dining and marriage, access to temples or wells and participation in social ceremonies alongside other castes is still negligible.

Scheduled castes form the weakest stratum of society. Their social position is so fragile that they easily become targets of oppression and maltreatment. This aspect is particularly evident and visibly reflected in the incidence of crimes and atrocities committed on them.

There are three outstanding reasons for commission of atrocities on Scheduled Castes. There are disputes over Government allotted surplus land to scheduled castes; tensions related to non – payment or underpayment of minimum wages; increasing awareness of right and privileges among scheduled castes and the attendant intolerance by other sections of society.

Towards an Educational Policy for Weaker Sections

The theoretical and empirical analysis of educational status of weaker sections has brought out that the status is very low even at the end of 20th Century. That is likely to continue even in the 21st Century. It is pointed out that, the educational distance in terms of the coefficient of equality among the weaker sections and others is too wide that it will take around 22 to 90 years (or even more in certain extreme cases) for the weaker sections to reach complete equality with the forward sections of society in education. It may be pointed out here that if the present rates of growth of education continues, it will take from now (1986-87) around 24 years for the Scheduled Castes to reach perfect equality in Upper Primary Education. In the case of secondary education, the time is estimated to be around 24.5 years and it takes 26.5 years in higher education in the professional stream and 22 years in respect of general education.

Scheduled tribes, however, need 22 years to reach the

mainstream in primary education. To achieve equality at Upper Primary Education, the constitutional limit of universalisation of elementary education, this group astonishingly requires 273 years. The corresponding figure for secondary education is 26.5 years, 90 years for professional higher education and 44 years for general education. Women and other backward classes, of course, may require a little lesser time than Scheduled Castes and Tribes. These rough estimates are made based on the pace of development of advanced groups and weaker sections. If the advanced groups outwit the weaker sections in future in their current race, the time required to get perfect equality in education may take some more years than what is projected here.

The present low levels of literacy, enrol-ment, retention, and high rates of dropouts among the weaker sections are largely related to their low socioeconomic status. The nutri-tional status of some of the school going children of the weaker sections is so low that it adversely affects their intellectual develop-ment and impairs future educational development even if all support programmes are provided to them. This calls for a large-scale land reforms and asset creation with sufficient supply of water resources to strengthen the economic base of the parents of the weaker sections' children so that it would induce them to send their children to school. If once a minimum economic standard of the family is reached, the State need not concentrate on the support programmes like subsidy, mid-day meal etc., to increase enrolment, as the parents it is assumed, will be automatically motivated to send their children to schools. However, the problem is, does it happen in the near future? If it does not happen what is the course of action? There are two possibilities here. One, allowing the historical conditions to ripen so that education be used only for conscientisa-tion of the oppressed for liberation. Two, without waiting for the so-called historical forces to take their own course as destined (?) there can be reformatory measures within the given structure so that the vulnerable sections will not be subjected to further oppression. If the second course of action is to take place within the given socio-economic and political structure 2, certain issues are to be examined before a strategy is worked out. The following are some of the important issues in t his regard.

Content and Devices of Education

It is repeatedly reported by the educationists that the content of our education is irrelevant and inappropriate to our situation and the colonial hangover is persisting in our curriculum. Further, the content of education of the socially disadvantaged, who are alienated' from the mainstream formal education for ages cannot be the same as that of the mainstream learners. A situation has arisen today that the socially disadvantaged groups are trained in the elite oriented subjects while their traditional occupations of their parents have not been diversified (particularly in the rural areas) in spite of industrialisation. This poses a problem whether the same content of mainstream learners is relevant to the socially disadvantaged groups without diversifying their traditional occupations.

Backward Classes

This concept of 'Backward Classes' has, however, not been clearly and unambiguously defined either in the Constitution or in the literature that dealt with this aspect. This led to a conflict in the interpretation of the meaning and content of the term. Therefore, it is necessary to examine briefly the genesis and development of the concept here, in order to make use of it in analysing the educational status of the Backward Classes in India.

In India on a systematic basis that triggered a national debate on this important issue in the country. This does not mean that there were no studies on backward classes prior to 1953, but they were all spasmodic in nature. It was only after Independence that the Central Government tried to define 'Other Backward Classes' with an intention to make certain concessions for their advancement, and appointed the Kaka Kalelkar Commission. But, the Central Government did not accept the recommendations of the Commission and informed the State Government t hat they were free to draw their respective lists of backward classes. As a result, we have today around 18 States and union territories which have notified lists of 'other backward classes' and have been following measures to ameliorate their backwardness. But, these concessions have been challenged by high caste Hindus in the courts as a part of their legal battle.

In order to understand the dimension of the problem, it is necessary to examine some sample of States where the other backward classes lists are drawn and the method of their approach in drawing the lists, the social and constitutional litigation involved and so on.

Constitutional Provisions

These classes have been referred to in the Constitution as 'Backward Classes' in Articles 15(4), 16(4), 338(3) and 340(1). It is under the directive principles of , the constitution (article 46) that the constitution enjoins upon the State governments "to promote with special care the educational and economic interests of the weaker sections of the people, and, in particular of the scheduled castes and schedu-led tribes and shall protect them from social injustice and all forms of exploitation". The Constitution underlines that the weaker sections can be categorized into (1) Scheduled Castes, (2) Scheduled Tribes, and (3) Other Backward Classes. Article 340(1) specifically relates to the other backward classes who are socially and educationally backward. But it is not very clear from the Constitution how to measure the social and educational backwardness of a group of people or class or community. It was the Kaka Kalelkar Commission again which attempted to apply a criteria to measure the social and educational backwardness of people.

The Commission had used 11 indicators, namely; (a) place of habitation of the person in a community, (b) ownership of land, (c) profession, (d) difficulty in establishing contacts with advanced castes, (e) social stigma, (f) taboos of intermarriage, dining, etc., (g) preven-tion of the groups to take the advantage of certain amenities of society, (h) percentage of literacy, (i) lack of leadership in community, (j) inability to pick up training for business, industry, etc., and (k) poor conception of sanitation, primitive way of work, etc. However, the Commission had ultimately given importance to caste in deciding the social and educational backwardness of a group and has listed 2,399 castes as socially and educationally backward in the country.

They have defined the backward castes as those who have, "ideas of ceremonial purity, restrictions on inter-caste marriages, taboos on food and drink, social segregation, feelings of caste loyalty and superiority have all contributed to the backwardness of a large number of communities in Indian Society". The criterion of caste as the sole measure of backwardness has been challenged in the courts and in many cases the courts upheld the view that caste cannot be taken as a mea-sure of backwardness. However, individual States have appointed their own Commissions to draw up lists of backward classes. We have given here four-case studies of such States.

The Mandal Commission

Following the popular demand for reservations for backward classes in Bihar, Uttar Pradesh and in most of the States in the Hindi-belt and the counter agitations, the Morarji Desai Government had constituted the second Backward Classes Commission in December 1978 under the Chairmanship of Bindhyeswar Prasad Mandal. This Commission is popularly known as the Mandal Commission had submitted its report in 1980 and the same was placed before the Houses of Parliament in April 1982. The recommendations of the Commission, and the methodology followed in drawing the lists of other backward classes appear to be more comprehensive than the previous commission and also the individual State commissions of backward classes. The criteria adopted by the Commission to identify the social and educational backwardness include 11 indicators: Social 4, educational 3 and economic 4. As we are interested in education backwardness of the other backward classes, the details of the three educational indicators selected by the Mandal Commission are given below.

1. Castes/classes where the number of children in the age group of 5-15 years who never attended school is at least 25 per cent above the State average.

2. Castes/classes where the rates of student dropout in the age group of 5-15 years is at least 25 per cent above the State average; and

3. Castes/classes amongst whom the proportion of matriculates is at least 25 per cent below the State average.

The Commission has taken 25 per cent as the minimum threshold to identify groups as backward since the 50 per cent divergence suggested by the Supreme Court in Balaji's case is found to be beyond arithmetical reason-ing. For instance, the Commission stated that, 'now, 80 per cent of the population of Bihar (1971 Census) is illiterate.

The Commission has also identified the non-Hindu backward communities by following the criteria that:

(a) All untouchables converted to any non-Hindu religion, and

(b) Such occupational communities which are known by the name of their traditional hereditary occupation as whose Hindu counter parts have been included in the list of O.B.C.'s (Examples: Dhobi, Teli, Dheemar, Nah Gujar, Kumbar, Lohar, Darji, Badhai, etc.). After this exercise, the Commission has also estimated the total population of the other backward classes on the basis of the population projections (based on 1931 Census data). The Commission has come out with an estimated population 10 of 52 per cent of total population in India as backward. This is further subdivided into the following categories.

Education and Socio-economic Backwardness

The educational backwardness of people that need to be identified and the same should be used as a criterion in determining the back-wardness of other backward classes. We have already referred to the role played by the cognitive and affective domains of knowledge in the formation of concepts that are very important in t he educational advancement of a person. It is well established by studies that the so called backward castes (classes) are alienated from the main stream literate learning for ages which constitute an important impediment for their educational development.

Further, the family and social environment, educated parents, language and all other factors that are conducive for educational upliftment of the backward castes are so poor that educations in the family in about a generation do not bring any perceptible change in the education of the present or immediate future generations. Economic status of the family has nothing to do with education though it may help to continue education if an opportunity is provided. But, it is of no use if educational opportunities are denied. Further economic status does not help to overcome the educational handicaps that have been imposed on castes for generations. Equality of opportunity in education cannot be established 'overnight. This has to be pursued till the conditions of family, language, etc. are equated among the competing groups. This requires protective discrimination. Moreover, education has a close relationship with the economic status of a person as the positions of power and jobs in a modern society are necessarily linked with the educational attainment of a person.

Strategy for the Development of Education of the Weaker Sections

After examining the various issues that are involved in the formulation of an educational policy for weaker sections, it is possible to develop a strategy. A strategy for the development of education for the socially disadvantaged groups is however, an exercise in understanding the socio-cultural and economic background of the groups and the correlation between these factors, and education. The strategy must however, take into consideration the issues that are identified in the previous sec-tions as limitations of a universal strategy. The following are some important policies, which can be taken into consideration for devising a scientific strategy.

1. At the stage of the formulation of the plan for human resources development, there is a need for the preparation of special sub-plan for the human resource development of the Scheduled Castes and Tribes, handicapped and other backward classes,

and it should be linked with the overall plan.

2. Most of the children in the age group 6-14 in the rural areas are used as child labour by the parents due to poor economic conditions with a view to supplement their family income with the child's earnings. The problem can be solved if the parents are paid a compensation to the extent of the earnings foregone by the children while they are in school.

3. The children of the Scheduled Castes and Tribes have hardly any preparation for school at home. Therefore, pre-primary schools should be started within the vicinity of the Scheduled Castes and Tribes habitat.

4. There are certain unclean occupations like scavenging, tanning etc., which go against the preconditions of enrolment of children in schools. These unclean occupations should be abolished and the children belonging to these families should be adopted by the State to provide all possible assistance till they attain the age of 18.

5. More and sufficient hostel facilities with sufficient scope for remedial classes at home should be provided to all those children who demand such facilities.

6. The present land reform measures and rural development programmes can be gear EJ to a constructive programme like the one experimented in Kibaha centre in Tancinia which had paid rich dividends. The Kibz- is centre is an attempt of simultaneous and coordinated attack on ignorance, disease and poverty. The centre has five sections namely, (1) primary and secondary Education where students engage in agricultural productive activities and mass literacy, (2) a health training centre where emphasis is laid on curative and preventive medicines, (3) a farmer's training centre intended for both young and adults, (4) a rural development unit, and (5) a library unit for the neo-literates. If these centres are combined in a capsule form by pooling all types of resources meant for the welfare of the weaker sections, it would prove to be a comprehensive measure as the problem of literacy is interrelated with many other f actors.

7. The present strategy of enrolment mobilisation on the basis of the individual as a unit is to be replaced by group enrolment mobilisation so that the socially disadvantaged children move in a group and develop confidence.

8. The so-called high quality institutions like the English medium convents and public schools should be subjected to a mandate of enrolling at least 30 per cent of the children from weaker sections. A similar amount of students from these institutions should also be transferred to municipal schools so that the educated parents of these children will be vigilant about the schooling facilities even in these schools. (The development of pressure groups of this type through such measures would affect the educational policy of the Government).

9. At present, it some State Governments are providing old age pensions to the old and destitute women. The scheme can be diversified and productively used for the development of pre-school education of weaker sections children by providing some training to these beneficiaries in Balwadi and Anganwadi system and posting them as guardians in the villages or habitats of the weaker sections when the parents are out for work.

10. In the process of land reforms in India, some of the weaker sections are given small pieces of surplus land. Sometimes the piece of land is so small and is subject to litigations that it will not bring any perceptible change in the household. Instead, the surplus land that is meant for distribution among, the weaker sections can be given as a grant to a school or institution so that the income from the land be utilised for the educational upliftment of the children of weaker sections in the school.

Weaker Sections: Issues and Concerns in Education

The basic principle of the UPA is "to provide for full equality of opportunity, particularly in education and employment for scheduled casts, scheduled tribes, OBCs, and religious minorities. Besides the National Common Minimum Programme (NCMP) of the UPA government contains the following provisions aimed at welfare and empowerment of these communities.

1. UPA Government will take immediate steps to reverse the trend of comminalisation of education that has set in the past five-years.
2. Steps will be taken to remove the communalization of the school syllabus that has taken place in the past five-years. A review committee of experts will be set up for this purpose.
3. The UPA will ensure that nobody is denied professional education because he or she is poor.
4. All reservation quotas, including those relating to promotions are fulfilled in a time bound manner.
5. To modify all reservations, a Reservation Act will be enacted.
6. The UPA Government is very sensitive to the issue of affirmative action, including reservations, in the private sector.

Special Provisions

Pursuant to the National Policy on Education 1986 and the Programme of Action (POA) 1992, the following special provisions for SCs and STs have been incorporated in the existing schemes of the Departments of Elementary Education and Literacy and Secondary and Higher Education. Relaxed norms for opening of primary / middle schools.

Abolition of tuition fee in all states in government schools at least up to the upper primary level. Incentives like free textbook, uniforms, stationery, school bags etc., for these students. The Constitutional (86th amendment Bill, notified on December 13, 2002, provides for free and compulsory elementary education as a fundamental right for all children in the age group 6-14 years. SSA is a historic stride towards achieving the long cherished goal of Universalition of Elementary Education (UEE) through a time integrated approach, in partnership with states SSA, which promises to change the face of elementary education sector of the country. It aims to provide useful and quality elementary education to all children in the 6 to 14 age group by 2010. The main features of the programme are: Focus on girls. especially belonging to SC/ST communities and minority groups. Back to school camps for out of schoolgirls, special coaching/remedial classes for girls and a congenial learning environment. Supply of free textbooks for girls. Teacher's sensitization programmes to promote equitable learning opportunities. special focus for innovative projects related to girl's education Recruitment of female teachers at least 50% in primary schools.

REFERENCES

Ambedkar, B.R.(1970): *Who are the Sudras*? Thackar and Co. Ltd., Bombay.

Blaug, M.B, (1976) *An Introduction to the Economics of Education,* Penguin,

Chalam, K.S. (1978): "Attitudes of Villagers towards Education: A case Study of a village in Andhra Pradesh, August.

Chalam, K.S. (1987): Human Resource Development for Weaker Sections in Rural Areas: Some Issues for Discussion" paper submitted at the UGC National Seminar on HRD and Rural Development, held at P.G. Department of Economics, The Hindu College, Machilipatnam. Feb.

Chalam K.S. *Education and Weaker Section* Inter- India Publications, New Delhi, 1988.

Government of India, First Backward Classes Commission, Chairman, Kakasahab Kelelkar, 1953.

Government of Andhra Pradesh, *Report of the Backward Classes Commission,* Hyderabad. 1970.

Government of India, *Report of the Backward Classes Commission*, 1980, Second Part, p. 157,

Government of India, *Mandal Commission*, vol.I & II, p. 52.

Mandal Commission, *op. cit,* vol. III to VII, p. 230.

Roy Choudhury, T. and Habib Irban (Ed.)1969): *The Cambridge Economics History of India,* Orient Longman, 1984.

Shrma, R.C. and Sapra C.L. (1969): *Wastage and Stagnation in Primary and Middle schools in India,* NCERT, New Delhi, 1969.

Yojana, a monthly journal volume No:49, September 2005.

Yojana, a monthly journal volume No: 47 May 2003.

INDEX

A

Afghanistan, 138

Agrarian zones, 183

American Economic
  Association, 79

Andhra Pradesh, 183
  cost differential in secondary
    education of Rayalaseema
      region of, 86
  health expenditure and shifts
    in human development in,
      323-329
  HDR 2007 on, 169
  Human Development Report,
    74-78
    brief note on, 75
    important features of, 76
  inter-sectoral allocations of
    education expenditure
      in, 66-173
  public spending for human
    development in, 342-360
  social indicators in,77
  uniqueness of, 77

Anganwadi worker,
  other activities of, 215
  role of for child
    development, 211
  referral services by, 215
  status of, 209

ASEAN, 21

Asian Development Bank, 218

B

Backward classes, 368
  constitutional provisions, 369

Balaji's case, 371

Bangladesh, 130, 137

BCT, 269, 270, 271

Bhutan, 138

Bihar, 371

BIMARU states, 121

Biwako Millennium Framework,
  192

Brazil, 27

C

Calcutta University
  Commission, 107, 108

Carbon dioxide,
  evolution, 4, 191

CDPO, 209

CEE & VT, 254

CESS, 75

Child development,
  role of Anganwadi workers
    for, 207-216

Children,
  and disabilities, 194

China, 21, 22, 26, 69, 130, 137,
  239

Climate change, 181-191
  and human development, 185

impact of, 187
strategies and mitigation of, 188
Constitution of India, 365
Continuing education, 260
for HRD, 258-266
objectives of, 260
types of programmes, 262
CWSN, 228

D

Disability, 226
DRDA, 280

E

East India Company, 54, 106
Economic analysis,
role of, 12
Economic development,
and HRD, 83
Economic growth,
and human development, 119
education as revenue of, 79
Education, 31, 33, 318
and economic analysis, 11-20
and economic growth , 84
and socio-economic backwardness, 371
as growth industry, 80
economic characteristics of, 82
economics of, 80
perception of economists on, 81
Education services,
export of, 27
Educational institutions,
growth of, 56
Employment Assurance Scheme, 121
Entrepreneurship development, 149
European Union, 21

F

Female enrolment, 57
Food Security Programme, 304
drawbacks of, 305

G

GATS, 29
Gender inequality, 55
Gender justice, 1126
Gurukula Education, 193

H

Health,
definition of, 219
dimensions of, 219
major trends in India, 224
meaning of, 218
Health and health care system, 317
Health education,
components of, 222
definition of, 221
importance of, 222
objectives of, 221
Health status, 122
Higher Education, 25, 33, 106
development of in India, 53-65
economics of, 31-52
emergence of India in global economies of, 21-30
internationalizing, 29
trends in growth of (1950-51-2005-06), 105
Human Development Report (1993), 86
Human Development, 75, 145
and literacy, 363

basis for participatory, 309
in India, 182
major issues in financing, 276
need of knowledge
management services for, 298-298
overall pattern of public
expenditure on, 342
practices in university
system, 154-167
threat of climate change to,
181-191

Human health,
and extreme weather, 184

Human Resource Development
(HRD), 143, 259, 361
and globalization, 178-180
and quality of life, 192-198
facilitators at national level,
148
implications in India, 179
need for at national level,
144
of Indian women, 239-257
perspective, 332
prerequisites of national, 147
role of ministry of, 147
role of UNDP in, 145
significance of, 331

Human Resource Development,
83

Human resource planning,
benefits of, 201
definitions of, 200
factors affecting, 202
importance of, 199-206
need of, 199
process of, 205

I

ICDS, 141, 208, 209

IGNOU, 252, 253

IMR, 122, 124

India, 21, 29, 37
economic growth and human
development in, 118-129
growth, poverty and HRD in,
315-323
healthcare providers in, 234
health education and health
care in, 217-238
HRD policies and procedures
in, 334
human development, 171
human resource development
in, 143-167, 330-341
inter-state variations of HDI
in, 168-177
priorities in, 23
trends in growth of higher
education in,105-117
trends in human
development spending in,
274-291

Indian Education Commission,
54

Indian women,
and HRD, 239-257
empowerment, 244
economic, 247
national policy for, 246
social, 248
special focus on, 240

Information management, 296

International Commission on
Education, 105

International Year of Disabled
Persons, 193

IPCC, 191

IRDP, 268, 308
drawbacks of, 303

ITG, 25

J

Jawahar Rozgar Yojana, 121

JLG, 311

K

Kaka Kalelkar Commission, 369

Kerala, 173

Knowledge management, 292
- and information management, 295
- and types of knowledge, 293
- concept and definitions of, 294
- principles of,295
- services in society, 296

Kothari Commission, 108, 109

Kyoto Protocol, 191

L

Latin America, 140

Life expectancy, 225
- female, 225
- male, 225

Literacy and enrolment, 126

M

Malnutrition, 220

Mandal Commission, 370, 371

Manpower planning,
- ingredients of, 204
- rationale of, 204

Maternal health, 223

Medical and public health services,
- expenditure on, 350

Medical tourism, 234

Millennium Development Goals, 121, 131, 223
- achievements of, 140
- eight goals, 131
- Indian scenario, 130-142

N

National Apprenticeship Training Scheme, 387

National Clean Development Mechanism Authority, 189

National Policy on Education(1986), 26, 109

National Population Policy, 249

NCMP, 274

NHDR (2001), 171, 173

NIRD, 308

NORAD, 253

NREGA, 308

O

Orissa, 720, 121, 122

P

Philippines, 87

Planning Commission, 171

PoA, 375

Poverty, 121, 136, 315

Primary education,
- assessment of, 101
- financial resources and cost effective analysis in, 97-104

Q

QLID, 197

QLIPs, 264

Quality manpower, 27

Quran, 54

R

Ramamurti Committee Report, 109

Regional disparities, 128

Rural and human development, 297
- elements of, 201

Rural Development Programmes, 302
missing link in, 308

S

Sarva Shiksha Abhiyan, 364
Scheduled Castes, 364
socio-economic conditions, 365
social status, 365
SEWA, 245
SEZ, 23
SHGs, 252, 255
Social mobilization, 310
Social Security Programmes, 305
South Korea, 87
Sri Lanka, 87
States (Indian)
trends in human development, 280
STEP, 253
Supplementary nutrition, 212

T

Teachers,
growth in no. of, 114
Thrift Cooperative, 312
TISCO, 336
Trickle down effect, 299
TRYSEM, 308

U

UEE, 375
UGC, 107
UN Charter of Human Rights, 196
UN Development Programme, 140
UN Economic and Social Commission for Asia and Pacific, 227
UN General Assembly, 227
UNDP, 74, 145, 170, 171, 173, 181, 239, 315
United States, 21, 26, 36, 111
University Education Commission, 54
UP, 120, 121, 122

V

Vietnam, 137
Voluntary organizations, HRD in, 267, 273
Voluntary sector organizations, 252

W

WADI, 311
Wage Employment Programme, drawbacks of, 303
Water shortage,
and diseases, 183
Weaker sections, 262
educational policy for, 366
issues and concerns, 374
WEP, 252
Women,
development indicators, 131
empowering through professional studies, 65
faculty-wise enrolment of, 62
statewise enrolment of in India, 60-62
Wood's Education Dispatch (1854), 107
World Bank, 121, 218
World War I, 244
World War II, 21

❑❑❑